The Great Gospel Deception

Other books by David Servant

Christ's Incredible Cross

Forgive Me for Waiting so Long to Tell You This

God's Tests

Modern Myths About Satan and Spiritual Warfare

Your Best Year Yet

The Disciple-Making Minister

The
GREAT
GOSPEL
DECEPTION

Exposing the False Promise
of Heaven Without Holiness

DAVID A. SERVANT

ETHNOS PRESS
Pittsburgh, Pennsylvania

The Great Gospel Deception
Exposing the False Promise of Heaven Without Holiness
First Printing: April 1999
Second Printing: March 2008

All Scripture quotations in this book, except those noted otherwise, are from the New American Standard Bible, © 1960, 1962, 1963, 1971, 1972, 1973, 1975, and 1977 by The Lockman Foundation, and are used by permission.

Printed in the United States of America
International Standard Book Number: 0-9629-6257-0

To the King of Kings
and Lord of Lords.
May the Lamb who was slain
receive the reward of His suffering!

Acknowledgements

Some of the most wonderful people I know have helped me on this endeavor. My sincere thanks goes to Herb and Laverne Kirkwood, Jane and Toni Ivanhoe, Val Huber, and Jerome Aul for their helpful suggestions and editing work. And what book project would be complete without the artistic talents and philosophical insight of Tony Condello? The humble service of these fine folks is clear evidence of the Christ who lives in them.

Contents

Introduction

It was, with little doubt, the most devious deception of the past century, a devilish scheme perpetrated upon trainloads of trusting men, women and children. It happened on the outskirts of a Polish town named Oswieçim during the Second World War. There, under the direction of Adolf Hitler, a slave labor camp was established for people he considered subhuman. It was only after the war's end that the world would learn all the shocking facts of that place, known today by its German name, *Auschwitz*.

Auschwitz was much more than a labor camp. The primary industry there was murder. At least one million people who walked through the wrought-iron gates of Auschwitz never made it out alive. The large majority of them didn't have a clue that they and their families would be dead within hours of their arrival.

Gathered from all over Nazi-occupied Europe, Jewish families were transported to Auschwitz in crowded freight and cattle cars. Upon arrival, all newcomers were immediately separated into two groups. To one side went the minority—only those men who appeared to be able to withstand heavy labor. To the other side went everyone else. They were the men of small frame, the women, the sick, frail, and elderly, as well as babies and children who wept as they were separated from their strong fathers.

The larger of the two groups was then herded to another place in the camp where their eyes fell upon a puzzling scene. Before them was a small orchestra of young women, neatly dressed, playing an upbeat, joyful tune. Each girl was concentrating intensely—almost too intensely—on the pages of music before her, seemingly oblivious to the hundreds of people who were now their audience.

An apologetic announcement was made: There had been an infestation of lice in the camp, and everyone must be disinfected in a communal shower before being admitted to the living quarters. Instructed to disrobe, each Jewish family neatly folded its clothes and placed them on a table with their other personal belongings. They were assured that their embarrassment would be over in just a few minutes, once they were sprayed with a harmless disinfectant.

As many as two thousand people at a time were paraded, naked, through the doors of a large, low building that was built into a hillside. Above the door a sign, bordered neatly with flowers, said "BATHS." Once the last person was inside, the doors were slid shut and locked securely.

The orchestra stopped playing.

Through vents from above, Nazi workers dropped a small quantity of Zyklon B crystals, a poison manufactured for killing rodents. Inside, deadly vapors of hydrocyanic gas began to waft from the ceilings.

The clusters of Jewish families quickly realized something was very wrong. People began coughing, then choking convulsively and vomiting. Shouting and screaming in terror, the panicked crowd instinctively surged toward the sealed doors they had entered. The victims pushed, clawed, and climbed over each other, hoping desperately to escape their sure fate. Many quickly met their death, crushed on the concrete floor by the onrush. For the more aggressive, the hellish battle raged on a while longer.

After twenty-three minutes, all struggle ceased and the room was silent. The doors slid open, and workers dressed in gas masks and rubber boots entered to begin their gruesome task of disentangling the piles of contorted bodies and transporting them to nearby incinerators.

Finally, the room was efficiently washed of the filth of vomit, urine and fecal matter—the final bodily functions of hundreds of victims—lest the next trainload of Jewish families become suspicious of what really happened in the bathhouse. There was a tight schedule to keep—another train was scheduled to arrive soon—filled with more trusting people to deceive, murder and incinerate.

The wholesale slaughter of so many people is, to us, a heinous crime of the highest degree, and the deceptive means by which the Nazis lured their victims into the gas chambers only makes their sin more abhorrent to moral minds. Yet the deceit and horror of Auschwitz pales in comparison to a future scene about which the Bible tells us. Then the degree of the deception will be much greater; the fate of the condemned will be much worse; and then their numbers will be much higher.

Unlike Auschwitz, where Jewish families, knowing the hatred of their captors, approached the doors of the gas chambers with some apprehension, these future crowds will be filled with peace as they approach their doom. They had been singing songs of celebration for years in anticipation of the joys they suppose soon await them, but they will be fully *self*-deceived. And unlike those in Auschwitz, whose horrible sufferings ended after twenty-three minutes, these will suffer much longer. The pungent smoke of Auschwitz's incinerators ultimately ceased rising into the dark sky. The smoke from hell, however, shall rise forever (see Rev. 14:11).

Picture the scene as Jesus foretold it:

> Many will say to Me on that day, '"Lord, Lord, did we not prophesy in Your name, and in Your name cast out demons, and in Your name perform many miracles?" And then I will declare to them, "I never knew you; depart from Me, you who practice lawlessness" (Matt. 7:22-23).

Jesus obviously revealed only the climax of a much longer story, but from this short segment, we can deduce other tragic details.

First, we can safely assume that the arguing we just read of the "many" who stand before Jesus is their *final* defense. They obviously had *already* been denied entrance into the heavenly kingdom. Now, with hearts beating wildly and minds spinning, they make their last desperate attempt to convince the Lord of His error.

To debate with God! How outrageous! What could drive a person to be so insane as to hope he might win such a dispute? Only pure desperation. Like a drowning man who grasps at anything, these panicked people pathetically hope to change the decree of the unchanging One.

And what was going through their minds when they heard His decree for the first time? He was their Savior, or so they thought. They loved Him, they thought. They had been looking forward to this day for a long time, expecting to hear Him say, "Well done, good and faithful slave...enter into the joy of your master" (Matt. 25:21).

They had served Him in ministry, experiencing the flow of His power, or so they thought. They had been on the cutting edge of Christianity, prophesying, casting out demons, and performing acts that they considered to be miraculous. Is it not safe to assume they had studied parts of the Bible, attended church, perhaps even attended special seminars on spiritual warfare?

Now, marveling at His glory and filled with joyful anticipation, they listen intently as He is about to speak. Every word will be more precious than gold. Time stands still. Eternity has begun.

His voice breaks the silence: "You are denied entrance into My kingdom."

Did He really say what I think I just heard Him say? Surely not. It couldn't be. This is my Lord and Savior. "Lord, I must be so excited that my hearing has gone bad. Could You repeat what You just said?"

Again He speaks. "You are denied entrance into My kingdom."

What? No! No! No! This can't be happening. "Lord, I'm a Christian! I'm Your own! I belong to the family of God! I accepted You as my Savior! I've gone to church for years. Lord, You must be mistaken! Somehow there's been a misunderstanding! I believed in You! You're supposed to let me in!"

"You were deceived because you ignored much of what I said, as well as what I said through Paul, Peter, James, John and Jude. I repeatedly forewarned you of this. I said, 'Not everyone who says to Me, "Lord, Lord," will enter the kingdom of heaven; but he who *does the will of My Father* who is in heaven' (Matt. 7:21, emphasis added). You did not do the will of My Father while you were on the earth, proving that you did not truly believe in Me. Sin was your practice."

"Lord, Lord, did we not prophesy in Your name, and in Your name cast out demons, and in Your name perform many miracles?"

"Your prophecy was not inspired by My Holy Spirit, but from your own mind. Much of what you prophesied contradicted My Word. The demons you thought you cast out of your fellow false Christians didn't exist. You were trying to deal with their sin by blaming it on a demon, when what they needed was repentance, faith and the new birth. The miracles you thought you performed were a sham. You accumulated teachers who told you what you wanted to hear. They proclaimed a false grace, misleading you into thinking you could get into heaven without holiness. You thought you were saved, but you weren't. I never knew you; depart from Me, you who practice lawlessness."

Will such a scene as I've just described actually occur? There is no doubt that it will, although I've obviously added some details to what has been foretold in Matthew 7:21-23. Nevertheless, standing before Jesus one day will be many people who have called Him Lord, who have been involved in "ministry," and who expect to enter heaven. Yet, shockingly, they will be denied entrance.

I'm sure you'll agree that it would be better to discover sooner rather than later if we're currently self-deceived. Now there is time to change; then it will be too late.

"But I'm certain I'm not deceived!" you say. *Do you realize that is what every deceived person would claim?* Deceived people don't realize they're deceived—otherwise they would no longer be deceived. Better to say, "I *may* be deceived, and if I am, I want to know it."

Let us then consider what Scripture says, and as we do, examine ourselves to see if we are truly "in the faith" (2 Cor. 13:5). And please, take your time as you read. What could be more important?

ONE

The Unrighteous
Shall Not Inherit

Test yourselves to see if you are in the faith; examine yourselves!
Or do you not recognize this about yourselves, that Jesus Christ is
in you—unless indeed you fail the test? (2 Cor. 13:5).

In the above-quoted verse of Scripture, we find a succinct definition of what a Christian is: He is a person in whom Christ lives. This, as other scriptures reveal, is not a physical but a spiritual indwelling.

If Christ lives within a person, Christ changes him. Obviously, according to Paul, it is possible—and advisable—to determine if Christ actually does live inside of us by means of self-examination. Each of us who professes to be a follower of Christ should heed Paul's admonition to the Corinthians, by examining ourselves to see if we are "in the faith."

Quite obviously, Paul also believed that it was very possible for church members to be self-deceived, thinking they believed when they really didn't. And what error could be greater? What presumption could have more serious consequences? If an unsaved person knows he's unsaved, at least there's a chance he'll acknowledge his state, repent, and turn to Christ. But the self-deceived person is blind to his need. He's smiling on the road to hell. Worse yet, he considers the peace and joy he feels to be evidence of his salvation, not realizing that they are only the fruit of his self-deception. In his case, unfortunately, ignorance *is* bliss, but only temporarily.

Transforming Grace

Ignorance was indeed the problem in the Corinthian church. Like so many in the church today, their understanding of the gospel was deficient. In their thinking, anyone who made a verbal confession of Christ was a true Christian, regardless of how he lived his life. Case in point: One of their members in good standing was living in sexual immorality with his stepmother. Nothing was being done to correct the matter.

Paul, however, needed no further facts before rendering judgment. He instructed them to excommunicate the man immediately, describing him as wicked: "Remove the wicked man from among yourselves" (1 Cor. 5:13).

Paul then offered the Corinthian Christians some important insight into the gospel: The grace that forgives also transforms. Thus, people who have *not* been transformed are *not* forgiven. They will not inherit God's kingdom. They are all those who are unrighteous in their behavior, and Paul even went so far as to list several examples of the kinds of people God considers unrighteous. Notice he included fornicators in his list:

> Do you not know that the unrighteous shall not inherit the kingdom of God? Do not be deceived; neither fornicators, nor idolaters, nor adulterers, nor effeminate, nor homosexuals, nor thieves, nor the covetous, nor drunkards, nor revilers, nor swindlers, shall inherit the kingdom of God (1 Cor. 6:9-10).

Some of Paul's modern readers have been puzzled over this particular passage. Why didn't he instruct the Corinthian church to follow the three steps of church discipline given by Christ, that is, to first confront the wayward brother privately, then by means of a small group, and finally by the entire church, before excommunicating him?[1]

---

1 Some have suggested that the Corinthians had completed the first and second steps of proper church discipline, and that Paul was instructing them to take the final step. This is proven to be an incorrect interpretation, however, by Paul's words in 5:2, which describe how the Corinthians were treating the wicked man: "And you have become arrogant, and have not mourned instead, in order that the one who had done this deed might be removed from your midst." Rather than mourning over and confronting the sin of their fellow church member, they were proud of their toleration.

The simple answer is that Christ's instructions apply only to dealing with a true Christian believer who has sinned. The immoral man at Corinth, however, had proven beyond all doubt that he was not a true believer in Jesus. He was a phony. His lifestyle betrayed his true character. He was living in fornication. Such persons, along with idolaters, the effeminate, homosexuals, thieves, the covetous, drunkards, revilers and swindlers, Paul categorically stated will not inherit God's kingdom. They demonstrate by their lifestyles that they do not possess saving faith in Christ; they are not regenerated by the Holy Spirit. Christ does not live in them; thus they don't belong to Him (see Rom. 8:9).

The Corinthians should have known better. Paul had previously written to them on this very subject, but they had apparently misunderstood him:

> I wrote you in my letter not to associate with immoral people; I did not at all mean with the immoral people of this world, or with the covetous and swindlers, or with idolaters; for then you would have to go out of the world. But actually, I wrote to you not to associate with any *so-called brother* if he should be an immoral person, or covetous, or an idolater, or a reviler, or a drunkard, or a swindler—not even to eat with such a one[2] (1 Cor. 5:9-11, emphasis added).

The immoral Corinthian church member was, according to Paul, not a true brother, but only a *so-called* brother. And failing to understand the inseparable correlation between belief and behavior, the church to which he belonged failed to discern that his confession of faith was bogus.[3]

Spiritual Babes or Phony Believers?

Realizing the far-reaching effects of such lack of discernment by the church, Paul had good reason to question, not only the salvation

---

2 If we are not supposed to eat with so-called brothers who are immoral, covetous, and so on, then we must have the right to judge those who are within the church in such matters. This Paul endorses; see 1 Cor. 5:12.

3 Many modern commentators make the same mistake as the Corinthians, maintaining that the immoral man was a true Christian, thus completely missing Paul's point in this passage. Yet there are at least five indications that Paul considered the immoral Corinthian man to be unsaved: (1) Paul called him a "so-called brother" (5:11); (2) Paul called him a "wicked man" (5:13); (3) Paul did not follow Christ's instructions for disciplining a brother who had sinned, indicating that he didn't believe the man was a brother; (4) Paul turned the immoral man over to Satan "that his spirit may be saved in the day of the Lord Jesus" (5:5), indicating that, if the man continued in his present state, his spirit would not be saved. However, by excommunicating him, there would be hope that he would repent and be saved once he recognized that the church didn't accept his testimony of faith; and (5) Paul clearly stated that fornicators and adulterers would not inherit God's kingdom (6:9-10). It is crystal clear.

of one immoral Corinthian church member, but the salvation of others within the same church. There was strife, factions and jealousy (see 1 Cor. 1:10-12; 3:1-4). For those who have just been born again, these can be indications of spiritual babyhood, due primarily to lack of knowledge of God's will. Until now, the Corinthians had only been fed the milk of God's Word (see 1 Cor. 3:2). So Paul informed them how their selfishness displeased God, expecting that they, now enlightened to the truth, would repent.

Persisting in these same sins after enlightenment, however, is a different story. In his letter to the Galatians, Paul included jealousy and strife in a list quite similar to his Corinthian catalog, sins which, if practiced, are evidence that a person, like the practicing adulterer or fornicator, will not inherit God's kingdom:

> Now the deeds of the flesh are evident, which are: immorality, impurity, sensuality, idolatry, sorcery, *enmities, strife, jealousy, outbursts of anger, disputes, dissensions, factions, envying,* drunkenness, carousing, and things like these, of which I forewarn you just as I have forewarned you that *those who practice such things shall not inherit the kingdom of God* (Gal. 5:19-21, emphasis added).

Clearly, what may mark one person as a babe in Christ can mark another person as unsaved. The difference between the two is time and knowledge. God expects that His true children will obey Him once they know what He expects. Those who profess to be His children yet persist in the practice of lawlessness even after enlightenment are deceived. People who have been truly born again yearn to be holy; they "hunger and thirst for righteousness" (Matt. 5:6). God is at work within them to complete the good work He began in their lives (see Phil. 1:6; 2:13). Thus, if our faith is not resulting in our sanctification (increasing holiness), let us not think our faith is resulting in our justification (being declared guiltless before God) either. There is no such thing as justification that is not followed by sanctification. For this reason Scripture says, "Pursue...the sanctification *without which no one will see the Lord*" (Heb. 12:14, emphasis added). Heaven is not for the unholy.

Is this Not Salvation by Works?

When Paul warns us that those who practice unrighteousness will not inherit God's kingdom, is he not contradicting his own teaching that salvation is purely by God's grace, received through faith? Is salvation earned by not practicing certain sins?

No, as we will clearly discover as we study more closely what Paul taught, those who truly receive by faith God's gracious gift of salvation are transformed by His Holy Spirit. Because of His wonderful work in their lives, they become holy and continue to grow holier. They are born again, and the power of sin is broken over their lives. Christ lives in them. They become new creations. No longer are their lives characterized by the practice of sin. Certainly, true believers sometimes still do sin, but they no longer *practice* it. As the apostle John wrote:

> If we say that we have no sin, we are deceiving ourselves, and the truth is not in us. If we confess our sins, He is faithful and righteous to forgive us our sins and to cleanse us from all unrighteousness....No one who is born of God *practices sin*, because His seed abides in him; and he cannot sin, because he is born of God (1 John 1:8-9; 3:9, emphasis added).

The salvation that comes through Jesus Christ not only provides forgiveness *of* sin, it provides deliverance *from* sin. A growing holiness is the result of receiving the free gift of salvation. Note carefully the words that follow Paul's most well-known affirmation of the freeness of salvation:

> For by grace you have been saved through faith; and that not of yourselves, it is the gift of God; not as a result of works, that no one should boast. *For we are His workmanship, created in Christ Jesus for good works, which God prepared beforehand, that we should walk in them* (Eph. 2:8-10, emphasis added).

Salvation is not a result of our good works; good works, however, are a result of our salvation.

God's Purpose in Salvation

God's purpose in saving us was not just to give us a legal stamp of forgiveness that nullifies our list of sins. His purpose was to make us holy, obedient people, conformed to the image of Christ. He gives not only an imputed legal righteousness, but re-creates us to experience a real and practical righteousness. One cannot be received exclusive of the other. In fact, the apostle John tells us who has truly received imputed legal righteousness: those who practice a lifestyle of *practical* righteousness:

> Little children, let no one deceive you; *the one who practices righteousness is righteous,* just as He is righteous; the one who practices sin is of the devil; for the devil has sinned from the beginning. The Son of God appeared for this purpose, that He might destroy the works of the devil (1 John 3:7-8, emphasis added).

Sin is the work of the devil. The salvation Jesus offers destroys Satan's works in our lives.

James on Works

Of course, before we can receive the salvation that forgives and delivers us from sin, we must realize our need for it. Tragically, many church members consider themselves Christians simply because they've prayed a "sinner's prayer" or acknowledged certain theological facts. They think they possess a salvation that has provided forgiveness, but that provides very little, if any, transformation in their lives. Yet it doesn't bother them because they know that salvation is by grace and not works. In their minds, works are unimportant and optional.

Yet the Bible states that it is impossible to have a saving faith that doesn't produce works. The apostle James wrote that a faith void of works is useless, dead, and cannot save:

> What use is it, my brethren, if a man says he has faith, but he has no works? *Can that faith save him?*....Even so faith, if it has no works, is dead, being by itself....But are you willing to recognize, you foolish fellow, that faith without works is useless? (James 2:14, 17, 20, emphasis added).

Thus, the true test of our faith is our behavior. And that is why Paul warns us, admonishing us to examine our lives to determine if our faith and salvation are bogus. Again, our works don't earn us salvation; our works prove that we possess true saving faith and the indwelling Holy Spirit.

Let us, then, heed Paul's admonition to examine ourselves using his own God-given tests. Determining where we stand is the first step. If we discover that we fail the test of experiencing true salvation, then there is hope that we can and will receive it.

An Initial Self-Exam

Consider these three scriptures (two of which we've already examined), in which Paul lists specific sinful practices that characterize those who will not inherit God's kingdom:

> Do you not know that the unrighteous shall not inherit the kingdom of God? Do not be deceived; neither *fornicators*, nor *idolaters*, nor *adulterers*, nor *effeminate*, nor *homosexuals*, nor *thieves*, nor the *covetous*, nor *drunkards*, nor *revilers*, nor *swindlers*, shall inherit the kingdom of God (1 Cor. 6:9-10, emphasis added).

> Now the deeds of the flesh are evident, which are: *immorality, impurity, sensuality, idolatry, sorcery, enmities, strife, jealousy, outbursts of anger, disputes, dissensions, factions, envying, drunkenness, carousing, and things like these,* of which I forewarn you just as I have forewarned you that those who practice such things shall not inherit the kingdom of God (Gal. 5:19-21, emphasis added).

> For this you know with certainty, that no *immoral* or *impure* person or *covetous* man, who is an idolater, has an inheritance in the kingdom of Christ and God. Let no one deceive you with empty words, for because of these things the wrath of God comes upon the sons of disobedience (Eph. 5:5-6, emphasis added).

From these three passages of Scripture, we can compile a list of sins, which, if practiced, are sure evidence that a person has not been regenerated. They can be classed in five categories, the first being sexual sins: fornication, adultery, immorality, impurity, sensuality, effeminacy, and homosexuality. The second are sins of larceny: greed/coveting, thievery, and swindling. The third are sins of intemperance: drunkenness, carousing and reviling. The fourth are sins of hatred: enmity, strife, jealousy, outbursts of anger, disputes, dissensions, factions and envying. The fifth are sins of false religion: idolatry and sorcery.

Notice, however, that Paul's lists are by no means exhaustive. He states in general that *all* unrighteous people will not inherit God's kingdom (see 1 Cor. 6:9). At the end of his list of sins in Galatians 5, Paul adds, "and things like these" (Gal. 5:21). We also note that neither murderers nor liars are mentioned in any of Paul's lists, but this doesn't exempt them. John wrote, "No murderer has eternal life abiding in him" (1 John 3:15), and, "All liars, their part will be in the lake that burns with fire and brimstone" (Rev. 21:8).

Although it is certainly possible for a born-again person to reluctantly and temporarily stumble into one or more of these various sins, no true believer will *practice* these sins. His life is characterized by righteousness, not unrighteousness, because he has submitted to the Lord from his heart, and his spirit has been re-created by the Holy Spirit.

An Objection Answered

It has been proposed by some recent authors that when Paul warned practicing sinners that they would "not inherit the kingdom of God," he was not speaking of eternal salvation. "Not inheriting the kingdom of God" is interpreted as being either (1) the forfeiture of certain earthly blessings or (2) the loss of certain heavenly "bonuses," perks that more holy Christians will automatically enjoy.

Those who want us to believe that Paul was referring only to earthly blessings point out that Paul was speaking about the "kingdom of God," and not the "kingdom of heaven." Thus, they conclude that he was not talking about getting into heaven, but about walking in the full blessing of God's kingdom now on earth.

A study of the phrase, "the kingdom of God," however, as it was used by Jesus, reveals that it is synonymous with the phrase "kingdom of heaven." Only Matthew quotes Jesus as using the phrase "kingdom of heaven," probably in deference to his Jewish readership, whereas Mark and Luke quote Jesus using the phrase "kingdom of God" in parallel passages (compare, for example, Matthew 13:11 with Mark 4:11 and Luke 8:10). The kingdom of God is the same as the kingdom of heaven.

Some who subscribe to the theory that Paul was referring only to heavenly bonuses point out that he didn't warn about not *entering* God's kingdom, but rather, warned about not *inheriting* it, claiming there is a difference between the two. Unholy Christians will *enter* God's kingdom, but not *inherit* it! They'll supposedly miss out on some heavenly rewards.

Is this the true meaning of what Paul wanted to convey? Or did he mean that practicing sinners will not *enter* heaven?

Quite obviously, for a number of good reasons, Paul was speaking of ultimate salvation and entering heaven.

First, because that is the most natural interpretation of his words. Why would Paul's warnings to practicing sinners be so solemn if those sinners were only in danger of missing out on some heavenly bonuses? And if forfeiting heavenly bonuses was the danger Paul had in mind, why didn't he express his meaning more clearly? Like the innocent little boy who, after hearing his pastor explain "what Paul really meant" in a certain scripture passage, I also ask, "If Paul didn't mean what he said, why didn't he just say what he meant?"

Second, Paul pronounced God's eternal condemnation upon homosexuals in his letter to the Romans (see Rom. 1:26-2:5). Are we then to think that his Corinthian warning to homosexuals that they will not inherit God's kingdom is only a warning that they will miss out on some heavenly rewards on their certain journey to heaven?

Third, the apostle John wrote that immoral people and idolaters "will be in the lake that burns with fire and brimstone, which is the second death" (Rev. 21:8). Are we then to think that Paul's Corinthian warning to immoral people and idolaters is only a warning that they will miss out on some heavenly rewards on their certain journey to heaven?

Fourth, Paul used the phrase "inherit the kingdom of God" twice while writing to the Corinthians, once in his warning to practicing sinners and once in the fifteenth chapter. In the context of the second usage, Paul was unmistakably writing about the time when we will enter into heaven:

> Now I say this, brethren, that flesh and blood cannot *inherit the kingdom of God*; nor does the perishable inherit the imperishable (1 Cor. 15:50, emphasis added).

Paul was clearly communicating that our perishable, flesh and blood bodies cannot enter heaven. No doubt he borrowed the expression under consideration from Jesus Himself:

> Then the King will say to those on His right, "Come, you who are blessed of My Father, *inherit the kingdom* prepared for you from the foundation of the world" (Matt. 25:34, emphasis added).

Was "the King" speaking about receiving earthly blessings or heavenly perks, or was He speaking of getting into heaven? The answer is quite obvious. The King will say to the other group assembled before Him, "Depart from Me, accursed ones, into the eternal fire" (Matt. 25:41).

For these and other reasons, we can rest assured that when Paul warned practicing sinners about not inheriting God's kingdom, he was talking about entering heaven. His choice of words, using *inherit* as opposed to *enter*, only serves to emphasize that heaven is a gift of God's grace, inherited, and not earned.

A Second Objection

One popular author claims that the initial text I've used for this chapter, 2 Corinthians 13:5, where Paul admonished the Corinthians to test themselves to see if they are in the faith, was written to encourage the Corinthians to "recognize the salvation they clearly possess." That is, they should have been "checking themselves not for *information* but for *confirmation*." Supposedly Paul was "very confident of their salvation" and certainly didn't intend for them to question their possessing it.

Is this true? Clearly the answer is *no*. Let us consider Paul's words in their immediate context. First, let's consider the preceding verses:

> For I am afraid that perhaps when I come *I may find you to be not what I wish* and may be found by you to be not what you wish; *that perhaps there may be strife, jealousy, angry tempers, disputes, slanders, gossip, arrogance, disturbances*; I am afraid that when I come again my God may humiliate me before you, and *I may mourn over many of those who have sinned in the past and not repented of the impurity, immorality and sensuality which they have practiced* (2 Cor. 12:20-21, emphasis added).

Clearly, Paul was concerned that when he visited the Corinthians again, he would be disappointed by their behavior. He cites numerous sins of which he had previously mentioned in his letters to them, and he states his specific fear of finding them guilty and unrepentant of practicing *impurity, immorality and sensuality*. Paul listed *those very same three sins* in Galatians 5:19, stating that those who practice them will not inherit God's kingdom. Additionally, Paul had written in his first letter to the Corinthians that neither fornicators, adulterers, effeminate nor homosexuals would inherit God's kingdom (see 1 Cor. 6:9-10).

Beyond this, Paul also expressed his fear of finding strife, jealousy, angry tempers and disputes when he came to Corinth, four other sins which he listed in Galatians 5:20, stating that those who practice such things will not inherit God's kingdom. Are we to conclude that Paul was "confident of their salvation," as one very popular author wants us to believe, when he has made it so clear that people who act like some of the Corinthians were acting are obviously not saved?

Read carefully as Paul continues:

> This is the third time I am coming to you. Every fact is to be confirmed by the testimony of two or three witnesses.

I have previously said when present the second time, and though now absent I say in advance to *those who have sinned* in the past and to all the rest as well, that if I come again, *I will not spare anyone* (2 Cor. 13:1-2, emphasis added).

What kind of facts was Paul speaking of that were to be confirmed by the testimony of two or three witnesses? Paul could only have been speaking of the facts of the sins committed by professing Corinthian believers. The context as well as the phrasing points to this (see the verse before and after 13:1, as well as Deut. 19:15).

Paul then threatens those "who have sinned in the past and to all the rest as well" that if he returns, he "will not spare anyone." In what way will he not spare them? Will he tell them that they are doing wrong? No, he's already clearly told them that. Paul can only be threatening that he will do what he ordered the Corinthians to do to a false believer in the church who was living in immorality: He will excommunicate them also as false believers, as proven by their continued practice of grievous sin and lack of repentance. Otherwise his bark has no bite.

Paul continues:

Since you are seeking for proof of the Christ who speaks in me, and who is not weak toward you, but mighty in you. For indeed He was crucified because of weakness, yet He lives because of the power of God. For we also are weak in Him, yet we shall live with Him because of the power of God directed toward you. *Test yourselves to see if you are in the faith; examine yourselves!* Or do you not recognize this about yourselves, that Jesus Christ is in you—*unless indeed you fail the test?* But I trust that you will realize that we ourselves do not fail the test (2 Cor. 13:3-6, emphasis added).

Paul wrote, "Test yourselves to see *if* you are in the faith." Notice the word *if.* That indicates the possibility that they were not "in the faith." Paul did not say, "Test yourselves and you will see that you are in the faith, because I'm very confident of your salvation."

Notice he also wrote that they should recognize that Jesus was in them, "*unless indeed you fail the test.*" Is this not a clear indication that Paul believed the sure possibility existed that some of them might fail the test? Certainly. This becomes even more clear in 13:6 when he contrasts himself and Timothy (see 2 Cor. 1:1) with them: "But I trust that you will realize that we ourselves do not fail the test."

The Corinthians might fail the test, but he and Timothy would not. It was obvious that Jesus lived in Paul and Timothy, but it was not so obvious that Jesus lived in all the Corinthians who professed to believe in Him.

The Conclusion?

The biblical evidence is overwhelming: The new birth changes the behavior of sinners, sometimes radically in the case of gross sinners. Why is it then that the behavior of so many people who claim to be born again is not much different from those who don't claim to be born again? For example, pollster George Barna has noted,

> A recent study we conducted showed that born-again Christians substantially differed from non-Christians on just nine of the 66 variables on which we compared the two groups. Even more significant was the finding that Christians were virtually indistinguishable from nonbelievers on all 65 of the nonreligious variables we examined—matters of core values, defining attitudes and central behavior tendencies.[4]

Barna's polls also revealed that, while 87% of non-Christians said they had watched a PG-13 or R-rated movie in the past three months, 76% of born-again Christians had done the same. Amazingly, *non-*Christians were more likely than born-again Christians to have given to a nonprofit organization in the past year, and were also more likely to have given money to a homeless or poor person.[5]

There can be only one conclusion: Many people who think they are born again are not. They think they are going to heaven but aren't.

How do you measure up? If you've just realized that you have been self-deceived, you should fall on your knees before God, repent of all known sins, and cry out to God to change you by His Holy Spirit. Truly receive Jesus as your Savior from God's wrath and sin, trusting in Him alone. Make Him your Lord and Master. He will begin a transforming work in you and deliver you from sin's power!

4 *Igniting a Moral and Spiritual Revolution: Social Scientist Analyzes the Data*, by George Barna, in *the Promise Keeper*, Vol. 2, No. 1, January/February 1999, p. 1.

5 See *The Second Coming of the Church* (Word: Dallas, 1998), by George Barna, p. 6.

TWO

The Immoral "Christian"

By day he works in a downtown office. He's a hard worker and has received steady promotions. Everyone likes him. He's trustworthy and pleasant to be around. A model father of three children, no one would ever suspect his dark secret.

By night he stalks through suburban neighborhoods, crouching along fences and behind trees. He looks for modest homes, the kind owned by young couples, and only those that are single-story. That way the bedrooms aren't on a second floor.

It's another Friday, and tonight he's back in familiar territory. His heart beats faster as he nears a house where he "scored" last weekend. Newlyweds recently bought the attractive ranch, and he smiles as he sees a dim light shining through a window from the rear of the house. He draws closer, hoping to hear soft music, which tells him that the window is open on this hot summer night. Yes! It's faint jazz. This could be another score. Closer he creeps until he's against the house, where he tiptoes silently to the window. His mind is filled with images of what he's seen before.

A man such as I've just described is known by the familiar term, "Peeping Tom." His activity is considered criminal, and rightfully so. Most of us agree that such people ought to be in jail. He's a pervert, and he's certainly not the kind of person we expect to see in heaven. Certainly no Christian would ever practice such behavior.

With this, the Bible agrees:

For this you know with certainty, that no *immoral* or *impure* person...has an inheritance in the kingdom of Christ and God. Let no one deceive you with empty words, for because of these things the wrath of God comes upon the sons of disobedience (Eph. 5:5-6, emphasis added).

Are peeping Toms moral or immoral? Pure or impure? The answer is obvious. And according to Scripture, they have no inheritance in the kingdom of Christ and God. Truly born-again people are not peeping Toms.

A Second Scene:

By day he works in a downtown office. He's a hard worker and has received steady promotions. Everyone likes him. He's trustworthy, pleasant to be around, and a model father of three children. He attends an evangelical church every Sunday morning and even teaches a Sunday School class twice a month. Elected a deacon last year, he's close to the pastor and well-respected among the congregation. His car antenna has a white ribbon tied to it in protest against pornography. It is well with his soul.

After working hard all week, he likes to relax on Friday evenings. So on the way home from work he stops at the neighborhood video store. There's a new release that he's heard about and he hopes there will be a copy still available to rent. There is. It features several of his favorite actors and actresses. It's rated R, and he knows full well that it will contain explicit sexual scenes and lots of profanity.

For a moment, his conscience speaks as he views the provocative photo on the slipcover. But his defense is already planned: When he discusses the movie with fellow believers in church, he will bemoan all the sex and vulgar language:

"Isn't it a shame that movie-makers think all that filth is necessary?"

"Yes! Yes! What a shame!"

Once the kids are in bed, he slides the video into his VCR and sits down on the couch with his wife. She would never suspect how much he is looking forward to seeing the tanned and trim female bodies in various degrees of undress that are about to be paraded before him. He overheard some of the unsaved guys at the office talk about how the bedroom scenes are awesome. It's another Friday night.

A Comparison of the Two Men

What is the difference between the first man and the second?

The peeping Tom watched *live* sex in bedrooms. The other watched *filmed* sex in bedrooms. The peeping Tom could only see limitedly through a partially opened window. The other man had a close up and very intimate view. The peeping Tom watched two people who possessed a lifetime commitment express their love for one another. They would have been horrified to know they had company. The second man watched two *unmarried* people who were *paid large sums of money* to undress and engage in sex in front of a potential audience of millions, making them some of the highest-paid prostitutes in the world. In fact, a portion of his money went to them. *In essence, he paid prostitutes to have filmed sex so he could be entertained.*

Of course, the first man was a peeping Tom on the road to hell. The second man was a follower of Christ, on his way to heaven.

Or was he? Didn't we just read that no immoral or impure person will inherit God's kingdom? *Which man was more immoral?*

Two other points worth noting about the second man, the supposed follower of Christ: By renting a sexually-explicit video, he has financially supported the pornography industry, casting his vote that more of such movies be produced.[1] His dollars will thus provide others the opportunity to watch more of the same filth; thus he has promoted sin in the lives of others. This the peeping Tom did not do.

Second, the movie the "Christian" paid to view was filled with profanity. God's name was frequently used as a swear word. Doesn't it seem strange that one who prays every Sunday in church that God's name will be hallowed would use his money to be entertained by people who repeatedly blaspheme God's name?

Why Hypocrites Act Holy

If the second man in our scenario was more immoral than the unsaved peeping Tom, why is it that so many professing Christians act just like that second man, regularly fueling their lust, viewing graphic immorality as a means of entertainment? The answer is that they are not truly saved.

If you agree that the second man was equally or more immoral than the first, and you believe that immoral people will not inherit God's kingdom (as the Bible states), then you must agree with my

---

1 I realize that in more recent years, many would object to my labeling sexually-explicit R-rated movies as *pornographic*. Pornographic movies, in the minds of many, are only those that carry an X rating. But how would God define the word *pornography*, derived from the Greek word, *pornia*, most often translated "immorality" in the New Testament, and the word *graphic*, a visual display? Pornography is any visual display of immorality. Webster's Dictionary defines pornography as, "The presentation of sexually explicit behavior, as in a photograph, intended to arouse sexual excitement." Are we to think that God considers the acting in and viewing of sexually-explicit R-rated movies as not being *immoral*?

conclusion. But why are so many people deceived in this matter?

It's safe to assume that the average professing Christian who regularly views explicit sex scenes in movies would never stalk suburban neighborhoods to peek through bedroom windows. In fact, he would consider the peeping Tom to be abhorrent. And why? Is it because he loves God? Is it because of his holiness or inward purity? No, those *couldn't* be the reasons—or he would be equally abhorred with the thought of personally viewing filmed sex between unmarried people.

His inconsistency betrays what really motivates him not to stalk suburban neighborhoods at night: *pure selfishness*. If he were caught being a peeping Tom he might suffer negative consequences. His reputation might be ruined. He would be disgraced before his church. He could even end up in jail.

However, he's found a way to regularly do, with no risk, just what the peeping Tom does. His "holiness" is patterned not after God's standards, but the world's. It has become quite acceptable to watch sexually-explicit movies in our culture, and so he has nothing to worry about. His reputation won't be ruined. He won't lose his wife or job. He won't go to jail. If he were a *true* follower of Christ, however, he would have taken seriously Jesus' very solemn warnings about the dire consequences of lust:

> You have heard that it was said, "You shall not commit adultery"; but I say to you, that everyone who looks on a woman to lust for her has committed adultery with her already in his heart. And if your right eye makes you stumble, tear it out, and throw it from you; for it is better *for you that one of the parts of your body perish, than for your whole body to be thrown into hell*. And if your right hand makes you stumble, cut it off, and throw it from you; for *it is better for you that one of the parts of your body perish, than for your whole body to go into hell* (Matt. 5:27-30, emphasis added).

Whether he realizes it or not, the second man does have something to worry about that is much worse than losing his reputation or job: His lustful behavior will send him to hell forever. Yet he ignores or explains away what Christ clearly taught, trusting in a grace that forgives but doesn't transform him, *a grace that doesn't exist.*

When Virtue is Vice

Yet there is still more to say about the second man. His practice of immorality coupled with a life that outwardly appears righteous makes him a hypocrite. A hypocrite isn't a person who's a mixture of good and evil—a hypocrite is completely evil. The reason he tied a white ribbon to his car antenna is not because he's opposed to pornography. That's obvious, because he regularly spends his money to view graphic immorality and financially supports the pornography industry, thus supporting the exploitation of women and the corruption of children. The reason he tied a white ribbon on his antenna is because he wants to *appear* righteous. His public life is an act. His motivation is not obedience to God or compassion for those harmed by pornography—his motivation is pure selfishness—he wants others to think more highly of him. All of his "good deeds" are tainted by this same fact. He's a hypocrite, opposed to "hard porn" but supporting "soft porn."

Our character is revealed, not by what we do on Sunday mornings, but what we do all week. It is revealed more by "little" things and by what we do when alone. Take the sin of stealing, listed in the Ten Commandments and mentioned as a sin that, if practiced, is a sure sign that a person is going to hell (see 1 Cor. 6:10).

Very few professing Christians rob banks at gunpoint. Yet many regularly cheat on their income tax, effectively stealing from every American citizen. Some pay their employees "under the table" (or accept such payments as employees) to avoid paying taxes, again, stealing from every American. Many habitually steal small items from their employers. If they are given more change than they are entitled at the grocery store, they keep it. They illegally download music that they don't pay for. They use pirated software on their computers. They *are* thieves. Thus the obvious reason they don't rob banks is not because they are basically unselfish or love God—their small thefts prove otherwise. The reason they don't rob banks is because they're afraid they might get caught. The "goodness" that they *do* display is really just another indication of their selfishness. If they could rob a bank with as little risk to their reputation and future freedom as they can cheat on their income tax, they would. But the same selfishness that motivates them to steal small things that no one will know about also motivates them to be "good" in big things. *Our true character is revealed when we are tempted to do wrong with little risk of adverse consequences.*

God's Hidden Camera

Imagine that you are an employer who has a favorite employee.

That employee arrives early each day, leaves late, works hard, and is well liked by your other employees.

However, one day you have hidden cameras installed in your business, and to your horror, you witness your star employee conceal a company-owned item under his jacket, take it outside, and, after looking left and right, place it in his car trunk. Do you think to yourself, *Ah, well, he's still a great employee. He just has a small flaw. I'll overlook it?*

No, suddenly your entire opinion of your star employee changes. Now, all of his previous good points are seen in a different light. Now you begin to wonder *why* he comes in early and leaves late. Is it so he can steal from the company when fewer people are around? Is it to make you think more highly of him so you won't be suspicious of him when certain items are discovered missing? Now that you know his true character, all his good works are exposed as evil. That's how God sees every hypocrite. That's how God views the second man in the previous story. His inconsistency reveals his true character. He's not a Christian with a minor flaw. He's a hypocrite who is entirely corrupt. His good deeds don't offset his one minor flaw; rather, they are a damning revelation of just how evil and selfish he is.

One who has been truly born again is indwelt by God's Spirit and is progressively made holy as he cooperates with the Spirit. He will not lead a double life. Certainly he may stumble at times and sin. But that is not his consistent behavior. His life is primarily characterized by obedience to the God whom he loves all the time. As the apostle John wrote: "No one who is born of God practices sin, because His seed abides in him; and he cannot sin, because he is born of God" (1 John 3:9). The new birth is the beginning of a new life of holiness. And as the true Christian learns more of God's will, he is transformed more and more to be like Jesus (see Rom. 12:2).

Contrariwise, the one who has experienced only a counterfeit conversion does many things at home and abroad that he would never do at church or in the company of other Christians. His moral principles are patterned not after what God says but by what the world says, and the world's standards are on an ever-downward spiral. That is why the counterfeit Christian habitually does what would have appalled even non-Christians just a few decades ago. Case in point: Today, multitudes of professing Christians don't even flinch at the worst obscenity, profanity, violence and perversion portrayed in motion pictures—what would have shocked non-Christians in the not-to-distant past. Some nationally-recognized

Christian leaders even recommend such films, as long as they contain some "redeeming" moral theme, such as courage, honor, or self-sacrifice!

True Christians are motivated to be holy because they've been regenerated by the Holy Spirit and because they love God. *On the other hand, what motivates counterfeit Christians to be as moral as they are is their own self-interest, the same thing that motivates non-Christians to be as moral as they are.*

Unholy Motives

Why do non-Christians restrain themselves from committing certain sins? It is because they fear adverse consequences. This principle has been proven repeatedly throughout human history during times when the usual moral restraints, such as governmental law or public opinion, have been removed. When brutality becomes acceptable, brutality prevails. The piles of human skulls in Cambodian killing fields and crumbling incinerators of Nazi concentration camps stand as mute testimony to the true nature of unregenerate human nature. What happens when murder is legalized, when the law of the State or public opinion says it's OK to exterminate Jews or rip the unborn to pieces in their mothers' wombs? No one has to speculate on the answer to that question.

How many professing Christians are motivated, in their limited morality and holiness, not by love for God and regeneration by the Holy Spirit, but by ever-changing public sentiment, the continually-revised law of the land, or peer-pressure of their fellow church members? Only God knows for certain. But through honest self-examination, each one of us can determine what truly motivates us. If every professing Christian would do that, many would be shocked to discover that all their goodness is really wickedness, motivated by nothing higher than self-interest.

Is it really possible to do good things, yet be motivated by pure selfishness? Absolutely. As I've already pointed out, most of the "virtuous" deeds done by non-Christians spring from selfish motivations. Consider the words of Paul in this regard:

> If I give all my possessions to feed the poor, and if I deliver my body to be burned, but do not have love, it profits me nothing (1 Cor. 13:3).

Jesus, Exposer of Hypocrites

Most modern, professing Christians are opposed to pornography. But vocalizing disapproval of that evil is not the litmus test of authentic Christian conversion. If a person is motivated by love for God and fellow man in his opposition to this evil, his *actions, thoughts and words* will be consistent in that regard; he will practice in his own life an opposition to these sins and those sins which are closely related. Again, if the second man in the previous example had truly been opposed to pornography based upon his concern for the victims of pornography or love of God's law, he wouldn't be regularly watching sexually-explicit videos. His attitude toward all immorality would be consistent.

Jesus exposed similar hypocrisy among religious people of His day, revealing a timeless principle applicable to everyone who thinks he's on the way to heaven. Let's consider again His words that are found in a sermon about salvation, commonly known as the Sermon on the Mount. See if you can find the significance in His teaching for modern professing Christians who are vocally opposed to pornography, but who indulge in other forms of sexual immorality:

> You have heard that it was said, "You shall not commit adultery"; but I say to you, that everyone who looks on a woman to lust for her has committed adultery with her already in his heart. And if your right eye makes you stumble, tear it out, and throw it from you; for it is better for you that one of the parts of your body perish, than for your whole body to be thrown into hell. And if your right hand makes you stumble, cut it off, and throw it from you; for it is better for you that one of the parts of your body perish, than for your whole body to go into hell (Matt. 5:27-30).

First, note that Jesus is warning certain people about hell. Contextually, they are people who are not *physically* committing adultery. They are, however, *mentally* committing adultery, and Jesus said that unless they repent, they are heading for hell.

The Letter and Spirit of the Law

Was Jesus adding extra requirements to the Seventh Commandment? No, He was closing a loophole that existed only in people's minds and revealed the full implication of what God meant from the time He first gave the Ten Commandments. Contained within the commandment that forbade adultery was also a prohibition against lust. Obviously, if having a sexual relationship with your neighbor's wife is a sin, then mentally undressing your neighbor's wife is also a sin. Any honest, thinking person would have to admit that.[2] But Christ's audience was like so many today—they keep the letter of the Law but ignore the spirit of it. *They are vocally opposed to specific sins of which they aren't guilty, yet practice the same sins in other forms.* God's will for our sexual purity far exceeds just abstinence from adultery, fornication and homosexuality. He expects that we be sexually pure in our minds, as Jesus made so clear, as well as in our mouths. For example, Paul wrote,

> But do not let immorality or any impurity or greed even be named among you, as is proper among saints; and there must be no filthiness and silly talk, or coarse jesting, which are not fitting, but rather giving of thanks (Eph. 5:3-4).

The *New Living Translation* clarifies the sins of filthiness, silly talk and coarse jesting as "obscene stories, foolish talk and coarse jokes." Obscene stories and coarse jokes are obviously speech that convey sexually-immoral ideas in a positive or humorous way, and "foolish talk" may well describe the sexually-perverted conversations of people whom the Bible characterizes as fools. Paul's point is that no follower of Christ should be involved in sexual immorality, any impurity, or anything even related to those sins, impure conversation included. What do you suppose Paul would say to Christians who entertain themselves by viewing today's sexually-suggestive television sitcoms? What would he have to say about most PG-13 and even many PG movies being produced today?

Modern False Teaching

Sadly, some (so-called) Bible teachers use the above-quoted verse from Ephesians to counteract the "guilt-inducing" and "unbalanced" teaching that is being broadcast by teachers such as myself. Their logic goes like this: "It's obviously possible for true Christians to commit sins of immorality and impurity, otherwise Paul wouldn't have addressed the issue."

I'm not saying that it is impossible for a Christian to commit adultery or fornication. Of course it is possible, because Christians are still free moral agents. A true Christian could fall into immorality. Paul's purpose, however, in writing the above-quoted words was not to assure people who were committing sins of immorality and impurity that they were truly saved in spite of their lifestyles. Rather,

---

2 Not to mention the fact that the tenth commandment forbids coveting one's neighbor's wife. Most men don't covet their neighbor's wife because of her personality.

he was writing to warn Christians to steer as far away as possible from any shadow of such sins, because they are sins that characterize hell-bound people. As Paul went on to say in the next two verses,

> For this you know with certainty, that no immoral or impure person or covetous man, who is an idolater, has an inheritance in the kingdom of Christ and God. Let no one deceive you with empty words, for because of these things the wrath of God comes upon the sons of disobedience (Eph. 5:5-6).

Yes, a Christian could yield to the temptation of immorality. But those who do so with any regularity mark themselves as being immoral and impure, and thus expose themselves as being counterfeit Christians. Because of the addictive nature of sin, particularly of sexual lust, the wise follower of Christ will avoid and resist any thought, word or deed related to sexual immorality. A very young Christian, perhaps, may not know God's standards of sexual purity, but as soon as he reads Ephesians 5:3-5, his excuse of ignorance is no longer valid. That is precisely why Paul wrote what he did.

Other Cloudy Questions

To further cloud the issue and make meaningless the clear warnings of Scripture, some people ask, "What constitutes the *practice* of a sin? If I committed adultery once this year and once three years ago, does that make me a practicing adulterer who is thus proved to be a phony Christian? Or did I just stumble twice?"

The first question to ask is, "Did you repent and ask God's forgiveness after you sinned?" There is a vast difference between the person who does and the person who does not. If a true Christian yielded to temptation and committed adultery, he would feel extremely guilty and should cry out for God's forgiveness. If he does, God will forgive him.

Was his salvation in jeopardy before he asked for God's forgiveness? What if he had not asked for God's forgiveness and repeated his sinful act? How many times must he commit adultery before he is considered to be "practicing" adultery? The answers to these questions have been hotly debated. I don't pretend to have the sure answer.[3] But any person who wants to know how many times he can commit adultery without repenting and still go to heaven should question

---

3 Later, we will consider what Scripture teaches regarding the possibility of a believer forfeiting his salvation.

his salvation. Those who have been truly born again desire to be holy—body, soul and spirit. They are striving to be *completely* pure, in thought, word and deed.

Others object, again, in an attempt to make the clear warnings of Scripture meaningless, by saying, "I want to be free from the practice of immorality, but I can't. I love the Lord, and I truly and sincerely want to be free, but I'm not." They are hoping that the determining factor is not what they *do* but what they say they *desire*.

They are, in an indirect way, saying that sin's grip on them is more powerful than God, and that His salvation provides forgiveness but not transformation. The New Testament repeatedly affirms, however, that believers in Christ have been set free from sin's power (see Rom. 6:6-7, 17-18, 22). Scripture also testifies of the complete deliverance from certain grievous sins and the dramatic behavioral differences experienced by true believers (see 1 Cor. 6:11; 2 Cor. 5:17; Tit. 2:11-14; 1 John 3:7-10).

Moreover, God has promised us that He will not allow us to be tempted beyond what we are able to resist, and will always provide a way of escape (see 1 Cor. 10:13). In light of such clear and abundant truth, one's excuse that he wants to stop sinning but can't rings hollow. I've often found that those who claim they want freedom from sexual immorality or impurity are unwilling to remove from their lives what causes them to repeatedly stumble, whether it be discarding their TV, canceling a magazine subscription, avoiding certain places of business, breaking off wrong relationships, or disconnecting from the internet. Paul wrote that we should "make no provision for the flesh in regard to its lusts" (Rom. 13:14), and Jesus said that we should cut off what often causes us to stumble. Those who refuse to obey Jesus' clear command reveal that He is really not their Lord at all. They have no intention of obeying Him.

Sin loses its grip when we repent, because that is when God forgives and delivers us. But repentance involves a turning away from all known sin. It is an attitude of our heart and an act of our will. People who truly repent demonstrate their repentance by their actions (see Luke 3:8; Acts 26:20).

If you're convinced that you are a born-again person who can't break free of the practice of immorality or some other sin, perhaps a simple question will help you understand your self-deception: Would you stop your sinful practice if someone offered you ten million dollars to stop? If you *would*, that proves you *could*; and if you *could*, you *can*; and if you *can*, you *should!* The problem is not that you can't stop, but that you won't stop. *Why would you do for money what you will not do for love of Christ?*

Of course, there is no way to avoid all temptation, and no Christian should think he's abnormal because he's tempted, struggles against sin, or has a healthy sex drive. As has been so well said: "You can't keep the birds from flying over your head, but you can keep them from making a nest in your hair." It is when we yield to what we know is wrong that we should be concerned.

Every Christian should strive for perfect sexual purity, in body, mouth and mind. Adultery, fornication, homosexuality, pornography of any degree (including advertisements and short bedroom scenes in "good" movies), "dirty" jokes, immoral fantasies, and reading about or listening to something sexually immoral for the purpose of entertainment are all wrong in God's eyes. If we claim that we are continually stumbling but don't remove the stumbling block as Jesus commanded, we are fooling ourselves.

THREE

The Greedy "Christian"

Standing on your right is an elderly Korean woman, the wrinkles of many hard years etched across her face. To your left stands a short, young Russian man. His worn clothing and calloused hands make you suspect he was a farmer or factory worker.

Like everyone else in the sea of people around you, those two silently stare at the raised platform off in the distance. From your vantage, hundreds of yards away, it appears to be at least forty feet high. It shines with a brilliance unlike anything you've ever seen, as if it were made from gold, encased in one huge diamond. A solitary piece of furniture sits on the front of the platform, what is obviously a king's throne. The hushed multitudes gaze with wonderment. Obviously something awesome is about to happen on the surreal stage.

Daring to pull your eyes away for just a moment, you survey the crowd around you. There are more people than you've ever seen, stretching for what must be miles in every direction. In fact, you realize that no ground is visible in any direction; even the horizon is made up of far-away people bordered by a golden sky that stretches like a dome above them.

Studying those nearby, you note that they are a kaleidoscope of every kind of people—white, red, brown and black. Some are wearing business suits; others various kinds of ethnic dress; a few others wear only loincloths. The only similarity they share is that all are silent, and all stand transfixed, staring at the shining stage and its golden throne.

His Appearance

Suddenly, a sound breaks the silence. Coming from the platform is heard a deep, resonating chord, powerful and majestic, unlike anything you've ever heard. Its crescendo is like a mixture of a thousand symphonies coupled with the roar of Niagara.

A glistening rainbow arches over the stage, and then a Being appears, seated on the throne. His form is barely discernible, for His brilliance is like the sun. His presence is felt by all, and as they shield their eyes from His glory, one collective thought seizes their minds: *He is pure*—purer than the freshest spring water or crystal snowflakes. *He is Holy.* Nothing is hidden from His sight. Hearts race.

The brilliant Being lifts up His arms, hands clasped together, and then pulls them apart, sweeping His arms to each side. Instantly you feel an invisible power lifting you upward, until you find yourself floating, along with many others, above the heads of a few who remain in their places. Together, you are pulled by an irresistible force to the right, while you observe that the few below you are pulled to the left, and once the two groups are separated, the invisible force sets you down again on your feet. Neither the Korean woman nor Russian man are with you now.

The great Being speaks to the mass on His left. His voice is not audible, but deep within, you hear His unmistakable utterance. Obviously, from looking at the shock on the faces of those around you, everyone else is hearing the same words in his or her own language:

> Depart from Me, accursed ones, into the eternal fire which has been prepared for the devil and his angels; for I was hungry, and you gave Me nothing to eat; I was thirsty, and you gave Me nothing to drink; I was a stranger, and you did not invite Me in; naked, and you did not clothe Me; sick, and in prison, and you did not visit Me (Matt. 25:41-43).

In unbelieving horror, the once-silent crowd collectively responds with a cacophony of questions: "Lord, when did we see You hungry, or thirsty, or a stranger, or naked, or sick, or in prison, and did not take care of You?" (Matt. 25:44). "Surely You've never been in those conditions! You're the Lord! We see You now, shining like the sun; if we had seen You before, we would have known it! What in the world do You mean that we had seen You before, starving, thirsty, homeless, naked, sick or in prison?"

He answers: "Those who believed in Me on earth became one with Me. They became members of My body and I came to live in them. I placed My love in them. Thus it is obvious who truly believed in Me. Those who did, loved My brethren. Those who didn't love My brethren didn't believe in Me or love Me. And those who did love My brethren *demonstrated* their love. They cared about their brethren who were suffering, and they did what they could to relieve their pain, even if it cost them money or time. They denied themselves, truly following Me. They didn't do those kind deeds to earn salvation—they did it because they were transformed by My grace.

"I even warned you of this very judgment, and My warning is recorded in Matthew, chapter 25. You didn't heed My warning, and now it's too late. Truly I say to you, to the extent that you did not do it to one of the least of these My brethren, you did not do it to Me. Depart from Me into the everlasting fire."

The Condemnation

His words are final. There is no sense arguing. It seems impossible, but you are condemned. As a new gravity begins to pull you downward, images race through your mind. Together, they constitute your former idea of what Christianity is all about:

Church services. Hundreds of them.

Church dinners.

Church picnics.

Church choir practices.

Church committee meetings.

Sermons and more sermons. *What did the pastor say about the judgment of Matthew 25?* Now you see him standing in the pulpit: "This judgment of the sheep and goats is not a judgment that Christians will face, but is considered by many Bible scholars to be a final judgment of unbelievers."

How foolish! Why didn't we notice that there were believers at the Matthew 25 judgment scene? Why didn't we notice that the crowd at this judgment consisted of "all the nations"?

Another scene flashes into your mind: Listening to a radio preacher in your car while driving to work: "This judgment of Matthew 25 is not one Christians need fear. Most likely, it is a judgment of various nations after the Tribulation Period. Those nations that extended kindness to the nation of Israel will be permitted to enter the Millennium. They are represented by the sheep. Those that were unkind to Israel during the Tribulation, the goats, will be sent to hell."

As your descent accelerates, more images enter your mind, things that consumed *all* your time, energy and money on the earth, so that you had *no* time, energy or money to assist suffering Christians. Now you see all those things in a brand new light:

Watching TV and paying the cable bills.

Hobbies.

Taking care of pets.

Vacations.

Christmas time. Loads of new toys.

Sports.

Church services.

New electronic gadgets.

Eating out.

Buying the latest fashions.

Surfing the internet.

Seconds later, you stand before the gates of hell. One final thought springs into your spinning mind before the horror of your eternal nightmare overtakes every cell of your brain: *Didn't the money that I gave to the church count for something?* Your conscience, now free from being suppressed by all the former lies, speaks clearly: *The church you attended gave no money to help destitute and suffering believers. The small amount of money that you gave to your church helped pay for the mortgage, so you could have a building in which to enjoy church services. Your money also helped pay the utility bills, so you could be warm in winter and cool in summer during your church services. Your money also helped pay for the Sunday School curriculum so your children could have fun classes. Your money also helped pay for the pastor's and staff salaries, whose time was spent completely on activities related to keeping the congregation happy. Your money thus benefited you, and it was not given out of love for God, but love for yourself. And, in fact, you gave less than your fair share compared to other church members, effectively sponging off them. Additionally, what little you did give required no sacrifice on your part.* Demonic laughter echoes from the smoke-filled canyons beyond Hell's gates.

In the past year, how many hungry Christians have you fed? How many thirsty believers have you supplied with drinking water? How many homeless children of God have you provided with shelter? How many naked Christians have you furnished with clothing? How many sick or imprisoned followers of Christ have you visited? *If you were to die at this moment and stand in the judgment Jesus described in Matthew 25, would you be among the sheep or goats?* These can be sobering questions for those whose lives more closely resemble that of the goats.

The Truth about the Sheep and Goats Judgment

Are Jesus' words of warning in Matthew 25:31-46 applicable to us?

Or did He describe a judgment from which Christians are exempt?

We can begin to answer that question by noting that there will indeed be saved individuals, Christian believers, who are a part of that future judgment. No one can intelligently dispute that the sheep, those on Jesus' right, are not saved people and Christian believers. They "inherit the kingdom prepared for [them] from the foundation of the world" (Matt. 25:34). They are called "the righteous" who receive "eternal life" (Matt. 25:46).

The theory that the separation of the sheep and goats is not a separation of individuals, but of nations, based on how they treat Israel during the Tribulation, is also exposed as being absurd by considering these same facts. Moreover, are we to believe that after two chapters of warnings from Jesus' lips that address the responsibility of individuals, His words now suddenly apply only to geo-political nations? And is He warning us in order that we will make sure we're living in one of the "sheep" countries if we're alive on the earth during the Tribulation? And are we to believe that the country we're living in, regardless of our personal actions or opinions about Israel during the Tribulation, is what determines if we will receive eternal life or eternal damnation?

Also against this idea of geo-political nations being separated rather than individuals is the fact that the word *nations* (25:32) is not a reference to geo-political nations of the world, of which there are presently about two hundred. The Greek word, *ethne*, refers to ethnic groups, distinct from each other by such things as their language, culture, geographical location and such, and of which there are at least ten thousand in the world today. Jesus said that "*all* the nations will be gathered before Him" (Matt. 25:32, emphasis added), indicating that there is no ethnic group that will not be found at this judgment. Are we to think that He is going to separate ethnic groups from each other, into sheep and goat categories, based on how they treated Israel during the Tribulation? Will He take all the Koreans from among the scores of nations in which they reside, and allow them entrance into the Millennium if, for instance, the majority of them were kind toward Israel during the Tribulation? The theory becomes more absurd the more it is considered.

A Second Poor Theory

Is it possible that the believers mentioned in the Matthew 25 judgment are a special group of Christians, such as those who will be saved during the Tribulation? Perhaps, but such an idea is not even intimated by Jesus. Are you willing to rest your eternal salvation on something Jesus didn't say?

Even if we suppose that only a certain group of tribulational Christians will be part of the Matthew 25 judgment, is there any good reason to believe that they will be judged by a different or higher criteria than all others who will ultimately "inherit the kingdom prepared for [them] from the foundation of the world" (Matt. 25:34)? No, there isn't, especially when so many other scriptures convey the same concept in other words. For example, in John's first epistle we find an echo of Matthew 25:31-46:

> We know that we have passed out of death into life, because we love the brethren. He who does not love abides in death....We know love by this, that He laid down His life for us; and we ought to lay down our lives for the brethren. But whoever has the world's goods, and beholds his brother in need and closes his heart against him, how does the love of God abide in him? Little children, let us not love with word or with tongue, but in deed and truth. We shall know by this that we are of the truth, and shall assure our heart before Him (1 John 3:14, 16-19).

John couldn't have made it clearer that true Christians, those who have passed from being spiritually dead to being spiritually alive, naturally love their fellow Christians. And the love of which John writes is not a mere sentimental feeling, but a true love expressed by action, specifically in providing essential material needs. John wrote that when we express our love for the brethren in such ways, it assures us that we are "of the truth" (1 John 3:19). If we have the means to help a fellow believer whom we know is facing critical, essential needs, but don't help him, God's love does not abide in us, and we will have no assurance that we have passed from death to life.

James and John the Baptist Agree

Another echo of Matthew 25:31-46 is found in James' epistle. He also equated love of the brethren, expressed through providing pressing material needs, as a sign of authentic faith and salvation:

> What use is it, my brethren, if a man says he has faith, but he has no works? Can that faith save him? If a brother or sister is without clothing and in need of daily food, and one of you says to them, "Go in peace, be warmed and be filled," and yet you do not give them what is necessary for their

body, what use is that? Even so faith, if it has no works, is dead, being by itself (Jas. 2:14-17).

According to James, faith void of works cannot save us. And specifically what kind of works did he then mention to illustrate his point? The works of providing food and clothing for poor brethren.

Yet another echo of Matthew 25:31-46 is heard in the preaching of John the Baptist. No one can intelligently argue that John was not preaching a message of repentance that led to forgiveness of sins, referred to by Luke as being "the gospel" (see Luke 3:3, 18). John warned his audiences that unless they repented and brought forth fruit, hell was their destiny (see Matt. 3:7-12; Luke 3:7-17). Thus, John's message should certainly be considered one about salvation.

When questioned by the convicted multitudes on what they should specifically do to demonstrate their repentance, John responded, "Let the man who has two tunics share with him who has none; and let him who has food do likewise" (Luke 3:11). John was obviously calling people to repent of their selfishness, selfishness manifested by their ignoring the desperate needs of their naked, starving neighbors. If they had responded by saying, "We have faith in the Messiah whom you say is coming soon, but we will *not* have compassion on the poor among us," do you suppose that John would have assured them of their salvation?

Jesus' Consistent Message

Additional echoes of Matthew 25:31-46 are found in Jesus' other teachings. The rich young ruler (whose story is found in three of the four Gospels) came to Jesus seeking eternal life (see Matt. 19:16). Jesus told him to keep the commandments and listed six in particular, which the rich young ruler subsequently claimed to have kept from his youth. Jesus then told him, "One thing you still lack; sell all that you possess, and distribute it to the poor, and you shall have treasure in heaven; and come, follow Me" (Luke 18:22). And this, the rich young man would not do.

Was Jesus actually telling him that in order to get into heaven, he had to sell his possessions and give the money to the poor? As difficult as it is for many to admit it, the answer is *yes*. Jesus' very next words, as the rich man sadly walked away, were, "How hard it is for those who are wealthy to *enter the kingdom of God!* For it is easier for a camel to go through the eye of a needle, than for a rich man to *enter the kingdom of God*" (Luke 18:24-25, emphasis added). Jesus was talking about getting into heaven (see also Matt. 19:23).

Obviously Jesus' words have application, not just to one rich man who lived 2,000 years ago, but to any and all wealthy people who want eternal life but who refuse to repent of greed and selfishness as it relates to the poor. Jesus said, "How hard it is *for those who are wealthy* to enter the kingdom of God!" (Luke 18:24). It wouldn't be "hard" for them if they weren't required to give up any of their possessions. But because they refuse to love their neighbor as themselves by sharing their material wealth, thus refusing to repent and submit to God, they can't be saved. Is this not a very loud echo of Matthew 25:31-46? The rich young ruler will be among the goats.

It should be noted that Jesus certainly does not want anyone to believe that he can earn eternal life by giving away all his material wealth. Eternal life is received by believing in, and thus following Jesus. That was what the rich young ruler lacked. His wealth is what stood in the way of his following Jesus. His money was his master, as was evidenced by his actions, and so Jesus could not be his master. As Jesus said, "No one can serve two masters; for either he will hate the one and love the other, or he will hold to one and despise the other. You cannot serve God and mammon" (Matt. 6:24).

More Echoes

What is the obvious message of Jesus' story of the rich man and Lazarus? A wealthy, uncompassionate man who ignores the pathetic plight of an impoverished man at his doorstep, dies and goes to hell (see Luke 16:19-31). Another goat.

How about Jesus' parable of the rich man found in Luke 12:16-21? Jesus prefaced it with the solemn warning, "Beware, and be on your guard against every form of greed; for not even when one has an abundance does his life consist of his possessions" (Luke 12:15). Then He told the parable:

> The land of a certain rich man was very productive. And he began reasoning to himself, saying, "What shall I do, since I have no place to store my crops?" And he said, "This is what I will do: I will tear down my barns and build larger ones, and there I will store all my grain and my goods. And I will say to my soul, 'Soul, you have many goods laid up for many years to come; take your ease, eat, drink and be merry.'" But God said to him, "You fool! This very night your soul is required of you; and now who will own what you have prepared?" So is the man who lays up treasure for himself, and is not rich toward God.

Although Jesus didn't say the man went to hell, it doesn't seem reasonable to conclude that this selfish rich man went to heaven. God called him a *fool*, because at his death, he was materially rich but spiritually poor. Jesus wasn't condemning the man's prosperity; in fact, God was at least partially responsible for the man's prosperity— He sent favorable weather that resulted in a bumper crop. Jesus was, however, condemning what the man *did* with his prosperity. Instead of considering what God would have him do with his abundance, he only thought of himself, retired early, and planned to live the rest of his life in ease. The very night he made his selfish decision, he died. Will he be a sheep or goat at the Matthew 25 judgment?

Jesus pronounced that salvation had come to Zaccheus' house after Zaccheus declared he would give half his possessions to the poor and pay back those he had defrauded fourfold (see Luke 19:8-9). How would Jesus have responded if Zaccheus had said, "Lord, I accept You as my Lord and Savior, but I will continue to defraud people and ignore the plight of the poor"?

Jesus, of course, lived what He preached. Perfectly obedient to the Law, He must have given to the poor all His life. Scripture informs us that He gave to the poor during His ministry (see John 12:6; 13:29). When Christ comes to live within a believer, is He the same Christ who gives to the poor? Of course He is. Jesus Himself said, "Truly, truly, I say to you, he who believes in Me, the works that I do shall he do also" (John 14:12).

The First Christians Care for the Poor

Matthew 25:31-46 echoes through the book of Acts, where we discover that taking care of the poor was a regular feature of New Testament life. Apparently those first believers took seriously Jesus' command to His followers, "Sell your possessions and give to charity; make yourselves purses which do not wear out, an unfailing treasure in heaven, where no thief comes near, nor moth destroys" (Luke 12:33):

> And all those who had believed were together, and had all things in common; and they began selling their property and possessions, and were sharing them with all, as anyone might have need. And the congregation of those who believed were of one heart and soul; and not one of them claimed that anything belonging to him was his own; but all things were common property to them....and abundant grace was upon them all. For there was not a needy person among

them, for all who were owners of land or houses would sell them and bring the proceeds of the sales, and lay them at the apostles' feet; and they would be distributed to each, as any had need (Acts 2:44-45; 4:32-35).

Notice Luke's mentioning in the above passages that God's grace was behind all the sharing in the first church. The same grace that forgave those early Christians also transformed them.

Scripture is clear that the early church fed and provided for the pressing needs of poor widows (see Acts 6:1; 1 Tim. 5:3-10). Was it because they were trying to earn their salvation? No, it was because they had repented of greed and had been regenerated by the Holy Spirit.

Paul, the greatest apostle to have ever lived, entrusted by God to take the gospel to the Gentiles, human author of a large majority of New Testament epistles, considered ministering to the material needs of the poor an essential part of his ministry. Among the churches he founded, Paul raised large sums of money for poor Christians (see Acts 11:27-30; 24:17; Rom. 15:25-28; 1 Cor. 16:1-4; 2 Cor. 8-9; Gal. 2:10). At least seventeen years after his conversion, Paul journeyed to Jerusalem to submit the gospel he'd received to the scrutiny of Peter, James and John. None of them could find anything wrong with the message he'd been preaching, and as Paul recounted the occasion in his Galatian letter, he remembered, "They only asked us to remember the poor—the very thing I also was eager to do" (Gal. 2:10). In the minds of Peter, James, John and Paul, showing compassion to the poor was second only to the proclamation of the gospel.

Paul's Teaching Against Greed

Paul also warned against greed using the strongest terms. He equated it to idolatry (see Eph. 5:3-5 and Col. 3:5), and emphatically declared that greedy people would not enter God's kingdom:

> But do not let immorality or any impurity or greed even be named among you, as is proper among saints....For this you know with certainty, that no immoral or impure person or *covetous* [greedy][1] *man, who is an idolater, has an inheritance in the kingdom of Christ and God.* Let no one deceive you with empty words, for because of these things the wrath of God comes upon the sons of disobedience (Eph. 5:3, 5-6, emphasis added; see also 1 Cor. 5:11; 6:9-11).

1 The word *covetous* here is the same Greek word translated *greed* just two verses before.

What is greed? It is a selfish desire for possessions and wealth. It is possible to have an unselfish desire for material wealth when one's ultimate motive is to share what one acquires. In fact, one can't materially bless others unless he is first blessed himself. However, when a person lives to acquire and accumulate material possessions for personal pleasure—when that pursuit becomes his highest priority—he is guilty of greed.

The Selfish Acquiring of Money

Greed is an attitude of the heart, but one that cannot remain hidden. It always manifests itself by what people do to acquire money and material things and by what they do with their money and material things once they are acquired. Let's first consider the acquiring side of greed. When the acquiring of material things is one's chief aim in life, rich or poor, that person is sinning. Jesus warned even poor believers against this sin, people who were tempted to worry about basic necessities:

> No one can serve two masters; for either he will hate the one and love the other, or he will hold to one and despise the other. You cannot serve God and mammon. For this reason I say to you, do not be anxious for your life, as to what you shall eat, or what you shall drink; nor for your body, as to what you shall put on. Is not life more than food, and the body than clothing? Look at the birds of the air, that they do not sow, neither do they reap, nor gather into barns, and yet your heavenly Father feeds them. Are you not worth much more than they? And which of you by being anxious can add a single cubit to his life's span? And why are you anxious about clothing? Observe how the lilies of the field grow; they do not toil nor do they spin, yet I say to you that even Solomon in all his glory did not clothe himself like one of these. But if God so arrays the grass of the field, which is alive today and tomorrow is thrown into the furnace, will He not much more do so for you, O men of little faith? Do not be anxious then, saying, "What shall we eat?" or "What shall we drink?" or "With what shall we clothe ourselves?" For all these things the Gentiles eagerly seek; for your heavenly Father knows that you need all these things. But seek first His kingdom and His righteousness; and all these things shall be added to you (Matt. 6:24-33).

Notice that Jesus began this portion of His Sermon on the Mount by warning about the impossibility of serving God and money. He equated greed with making money our god, that is, allowing money to direct our lives rather than God. Jesus warned His audience against making the pursuit of even basic necessities their consuming desire. *How much truer are His words when applied to the pursuit of non-essential material things?* The primary pursuit of Christ's true followers should be "His kingdom and His righteousness" (Matt. 6:33). Of course, Christians can and must have other pursuits. Jesus didn't say, "seek only," but "seek first."

Hard work in itself is not an outward manifestation of greed, but it can be. When a person works long hours in order to attain a certain standard of living, and his devotion to Christ is negatively affected, he has made money his god. The ancient proverb admonishes those who fall into this category: "Do not weary yourself to gain wealth, cease from your consideration of it. When you set your eyes on it, it is gone. For wealth certainly makes itself wings, like an eagle that flies toward the heavens" (Prov. 23:4-5).

Making money dishonestly or unethically is always wrong and is another manifestation of greed. The Word of God states, "He who increases his wealth by interest and usury, gathers it for him who is gracious to the poor" (Prov. 28:8).[2]

Scripture commends the one who increases his wealth by honest means and who gives away a portion of his earnings (see Prov. 13:11; 22:9). Likewise, Scripture condemns slothfulness and laziness for several reasons, one being that the person who has no earnings subsequently has nothing to share with those who are needy (see Eph. 4:28). When the goal of making money is to have money to share, making money is virtuous.

The Selfish Use of Money

Now let's consider how greed is manifested once money has been acquired. In this regard, greed is the selfish *use* of money. What is it that could make it morally wrong to spend all the money that you've legitimately earned on yourself? Does it have something to do with the fact that others, including many of God's own children, who work just as hard if not harder (or who are unable to work), struggle just to survive, lacking basic necessities such as sufficient food? Is it

---

2 It seems reasonable to think that the kind of interest earnings condemned here are those that were forbidden under the Law: charging interest to impoverished fellow Israelites who were forced to borrow money just to survive. See Ex. 22:25-27; Deut. 23:19-20. Thus, lending money at interest as venture capital, or profiting from dividends and capital gains through ethical investment is not wrong. God promised to bless Israel so much that they would be able to lend to many nations if they obeyed Him (see Deut. 15:6), so obviously God is not opposed to all lending. *Usury*, also condemned, is the practice of charging extremely high interest rates from people who have no alternative but to borrow, thus selfishly taking advantage of them.

morally right that one person lives in luxury while others fall asleep hungry each night through no fault of their own?

There are, of course, a myriad of excuses for doing nothing to assist desperately poor believers and non-believers, but well-fed Christians will find no solace from the Bible. Although no one can rightfully set up arbitrary rules concerning how much should be given and how much should be kept, the consensus of Scripture is clear: Christians who are able to give to the poor are expected by God to give, especially to impoverished fellow believers (see Gal. 6:10). Professing Christians who demonstrate no such concern are very likely counterfeit Christians, and this obviously includes many among modern Christendom who have bought into the modern lie of a customized Christianity of selfish convenience.

According to a Gallup pole, only 25% of evangelical Christians tithe. Forty percent claim that God is the most important thing in their lives, yet those who make between $50-75,000 per year give an average of 1.5 percent of their incomes to charity, including religious charity. Meanwhile, they spend an average of 12% of their incomes on leisure pursuits.[3]

Greed is not only expressed by what we do with our money, but also by what we do with our time. If all our time is spent on selfish pursuits or pleasures, we are being greedy. The time God has given to us on this earth is a sacred trust. We should spend as much of our time as we can in serving. All of us, not just pastors, can obey Jesus' command to visit fellow believers who are sick or imprisoned.

Greed's Justifications

Like every sin, greed has its excuses. One is that because we pay taxes, a portion of which is used to help impoverished people, we are relieved of any individual responsibility to help them.

I suppose it is good that our government feels some responsibility to help the poor. However, much of what the government gives to the poor is actually in opposition to God's will. According to God's Word, poor people who are able to work but who refuse to do so should not be supported: "If anyone will not work, neither let him eat" (2 Thes. 3:10). Moreover, poor people who are poor because of their practice of sin should first demonstrate some repentance before they are assisted. Governments should not offer monetary incentives to encourage people's laziness, irresponsibility or immoral behav-

---

3 These statistics are cited by Charles Colson and Ellen Santilli Vaughn on page 31 of their book, *The Body*, Word Publishing, 1992.

ior. Unlike the government, our giving should be done intelligently, with the ultimate purpose of furthering God's kingdom. When we help the unsaved poor, we should also share the gospel with them. This, the government does not do.

Additionally, our government does very little if anything to help impoverished Christians in other countries, and we have a responsibility to our world-wide family, not just those within the geographical boundaries of our own nation.

How Poor Are We?

Another excuse for our greed is that so many of us think we're poor ourselves; thus we think we're not expected to help the poor. But just how poor are we? 1.3 billion people in the world live on an income of less than a dollar per day. Another 2 billion live on less than two dollars a day. (I've just described more than half of the world's population.)

According to United Nations statistics, 1.45 billion people still have no access to health services; 1.33 billion do not have access to safe water; 2.25 billion do not have access to sanitation. Since you began reading this chapter, over five hundred children have died from hunger or preventable diseases. Five hundred mothers are weeping right now over a child they've lost in the past 25 minutes due to malnutrition or a preventable disease. If we remain indifferent, how are we any different than the rich man who ignored Lazarus?

In his book, *Rich Christians in an Age of Hunger*, Ron Sider quotes economist Robert Heilbroner, who "itemized the 'luxuries we would have to abandon if we were to adopt the lifestyle of our 1.3 billion neighbors who live in desperate poverty'":

> We begin by invading the house of our imaginary American family to strip it of its furniture. Everything goes: beds, chairs, tables, television set, lamps. We will leave the family with a few old blankets, a kitchen table, a wooden chair. Along with the bureaus go the clothes. Each member of the family may keep in his "wardrobe" his oldest suit or dress, a shirt or blouse. We will permit a pair of shoes for the head of the family, but none for the wife or children.
>
> We move to the kitchen. The appliances have already been taken out, so we turn to the cupboards....The box of matches may stay, a small bag of flour, some sugar, and salt. A few moldy potatoes, already in the garbage can, must be hastily rescued, for they will provide much of tonight's

meal. We will leave a handful of onions, and a dish of dried beans. All the rest we take away: the meat, the fresh vegetables, the canned goods, the crackers, the candy.

Now we have stripped the house: the bathroom has been dismantled, the running water shut off, the electric wires taken out. Next we take away the house. The family can move to the tool shed....

Communications must go next. No more newspapers, magazines, books—not that they are missed, since we must take away our family's literacy as well. Instead, in our shantytown we will allow one radio....

Now government services must go. No more postman, no more firemen. There is a school, but it is three miles away and consists of two classrooms....There are, of course, no hospitals or doctors nearby. The nearest clinic is ten miles away and is tended by a midwife. It can be reached by bicycle, provided that the family has a bicycle, which is unlikely....

Finally, money. We will allow our family a cash hoard of $5.00. This will prevent our breadwinner from experiencing the tragedy of an Iranian peasant who went blind because he could not raise the $3.94, which he mistakenly thought he needed to receive admission to a hospital where he could have been cured.[4]

What Can't We Afford?

Our excuse that we cannot afford to help our desperately poor brothers and sisters in Christ is exposed as blatant hypocrisy by what we *can* afford: monthly cable TV, cellular phones, magazine subscriptions, pet food, expensive entertainment, hobbies and vacations, new cars, dining out, the latest fashions in clothing, cigarettes, junk food, the newest electronic gadgets, as well as hoards of senseless Christmas and birthday gifts for our children. Take a look around your home or apartment and note all that you possess that *no one* possessed a century ago. People survived for thousands of years without any of these "necessities," and most of the world continues to live without them. Yet the income of many professing Christians is consumed by the acquiring of these things. All the while, the one we call our Lord cries out, "Do not lay up for yourselves treasures upon earth, where moth and rust destroy, and where thieves break in and steal. But lay up for yourselves treasures in heaven, where neither moth nor rust

---

4 Ron Sider, *Rich Christians in an Age of Hunger* (Dallas: Word, 1997), pp.1-2

destroys, and where thieves do not break in or steal; for where your treasure is, there will your heart be also" (Matt. 6:19-21).

Not only must we have what the neighbors have, we must have what they have *now*, so we purchase these depreciating items by borrowing money, resulting in a good portion of our income going toward the paying of interest. In many cases, more than one-fourth of people's income is spent on interest, and often only because of their desire for instant selfish gratification. Will God accept their excuse that they couldn't afford to do anything to relieve the sufferings of His impoverished children?

I'm certainly not advocating that one must live in squalor to be a Christian, or that it is a sin for Christians to own modern conveniences. But Scripture teaches that God wants us to share a portion of our income with the poor. God blesses us, at least in part, to enable us to be a blessing to others.

"But what good would the little I could give do in light of the world's needs?" some offer as an excuse. The translation of this excuse is, "I can't do everything, so I'll do nothing." The truth is that you can give a little and dramatically improve one person's life. By giving two dollars a day, you could double the income of one person among the 3.3 billion who live on less than two dollars a day.

"Didn't Jesus say that the world would always have poor people?" some say. "Then why should we work to eliminate what Jesus said would always exist?" Yes, Jesus did say, "For the poor you always have with you," but He went on to say, "and whenever you wish, you can do them good" (Mark 14:7). We will always have opportunity to demonstrate God's love for the poor, and Jesus obviously assumed that we would, at least occasionally, wish to do them good.

Some think that our responsibility is only to assist poor *Christians*, thus we can maintain a clear conscience as we ignore the plight of poor pagans. Although Scripture emphasizes our responsibility towards fellow believers, it certainly doesn't limit us to caring only for those within our spiritual family. For example, Proverbs 25:21 states, "If your enemy is hungry, give him food to eat; and if he is thirsty, give him water to drink."

There are a myriad of other excuses that cardboard Christians use to justify their selfishness, but none of them nullifies the clear commands of Christ and the Scriptures.

What Must We Do?

The only proper response to any of Christ's commands against which we are transgressing is to repent. Where do you start? Begin by doing a spiritual inventory. If you've lived a lifestyle characterized by greed, you aren't truly born again yet. Repent of all known sins in your life and call on the Lord in faith to be your Savior and absolute Lord and Master. Turn over everything to Him and submit yourself as His slave.

Next, take a financial inventory. Do you have an income? Then you should be giving away a portion of it. The most basic standard under the Law of Moses was to tithe, which means to give a tenth of your income, and tithing is a good starting place for every Christian who has an income. If you decide to give your entire tithe to your church, make sure your church regularly and significantly gives help to the poor. Otherwise, I wouldn't give my church a full ten percent. (Personally, neither would I attend a church that wasn't regularly giving to the poor.)

You can't afford to give a tenth of your income? Then something has to change. You must either increase your income or decrease your expenses. Usually the most feasible of those two options is to decrease expenses. Sure it will require self-denial. But that is what following Christ is all about (see Matt. 16:24).

How can you reduce your expenses? Make a list of everything on which you spent money last month. Then start scratching off that list the most non-essential expenses until those scratched-off expenses equal ten percent of your income. Until your income increases, spend no money on what has been scratched off your list. Now you can tithe.

Eliminating Debt

If you are like most Americans, you already have considerable personal debt. Now as a true follower of Christ, you should desire to get out of debt so you'll have more money to give away. Begin by eliminating high-interest debt such as credit card debt. There are four ways you can get money to pay off your debt: (1) increase your income, (2) sell non-essential items you own, (3) pull out your expense list once more and continue scratching off the most non-essential expenses, eliminating them from your budget, and (4) lower certain expenses by economizing. For example, you can turn your thermostat even lower than usual in the winter months, add more covers to your bed, and save on heating bills. If people took all four of these options seriously, they could soon eliminate their credit card debt.

If you can't control credit card spending (and if you have credit card debt, that's a good indication that you can't), then cut up your credit cards. (This is called *plastic surgery*.)

Next, work to eliminate all debt on depreciating items. You can do that by using the income you used to pay off high-interest debt. Once you've paid off what you owe on depreciating items, save and invest the income you formerly used for payments, and from then on purchase all depreciating items with cash. In other words, if you can't pay for something with cash, don't buy it. And don't buy what you don't need.

Using the same means, work to eliminate all debt on appreciating items.

Finally, chart your financial course for the remaining years of your life. Consistently smart, unselfish choices can result in enabling you to be a big blessing to the poor. There are scores of ways that most of us could live more simply, enabling us to give away more money. For example, the person who buys used cars all his life, paying cash, as opposed to purchasing new cars with credit, is enabled to give away tens or even hundreds of thousands of dollars during his life, depending on the age of the cars he buys and how long he keeps them. We can make decisions regarding housing, clothing, transportation, hobbies, pets, gifts, vacations, destructive habits, food and entertainment that can enable us to save and give away thousands of dollars.

A Word to the Wealthy

What if you are a wealthy person even by American standards, and you have excess money saved or invested, should you give it all away? *Yes.* However, sometimes the shared earnings from invested capital can be a bigger blessing than giving away the capital. For example, if you have $100,000 invested that is earning a 10% return, you could give away $10,000 every year for the rest of your life. This is a good reason for any Christian to consider investing a portion of his excess money once he is out of debt.[5] Of course, as a follower of Christ, you should not invest in anything that would be displeasing to God.

Every follower of Christ, especially those who are wealthy, should realize that God is the source of his wealth (see Deut. 8:18). Thus the blesser has the absolute right to direct what the blessee does with the blessing. True disciples of Christ have turned over all their material possessions to Christ's lordship. Jesus said, "So therefore, no one of you can be My disciple who does not give up all his own posses-

---

5 On the other hand, giving $100,000 immediately to the proper missions organizations could have a greater impact in building God's kingdom than giving $10,000 each year for the rest of your life. If giving $100,000 now results in one thousand people being saved, what those one thousand people give toward the gospel, and what their converts give to the gospel, could have a multiplied effect that would far exceed what your annual gift of $10,000 would accomplish.

sions" (Luke 14:33). Every financial decision is a spiritual decision for those who have truly submitted themselves to Jesus.

Those who are blessed abundantly should be very generous. To Timothy Paul wrote,

> Instruct those who are rich in this present world not to be conceited or to fix their hope on the uncertainty of riches, but on God, who richly supplies us with all things to enjoy. Instruct them to do good, to be rich in good works, to be generous and ready to share, storing up for themselves the treasure of a good foundation for the future, *so that they may take hold of that which is life indeed* (1 Tim. 6:17-19, emphasis added).

Clearly, Paul believed that wealthy people could only hope to "take hold of that which is life indeed" (eternal life) if they "rich in good works" and "generous and ready to share." Greedy people go to hell.

How much of *your* income should *you* give away? As much as you possibly can. I guarantee that in heaven, you will not regret any sacrifice you made on the earth.

The more you deny yourself, the more you are like Christ. Keep in mind that the amount of money given away is not nearly as significant as the amount of sacrifice expressed in the giving. We read in Mark's Gospel:

> And [Jesus] sat down opposite the treasury, and began observing how the multitude were putting money into the treasury; and many rich people were putting in large sums. And a poor widow came and put in two small copper coins, which amount to a cent. And calling His disciples to Him, He said to them, "Truly I say to you, this poor widow put in more than all the contributors to the treasury; for they all put in out of their surplus, but she, out of her poverty, put in all she owned, all she had to live on" (Mark 12:41-44).

Channels of Blessing

How can you get money into the hands of the desperately poor of this world? There are many worthy ministries the serve the poor, but do your homework, specifically investigating the salaries of those who lead them. Some ministry heads are making hundreds of thousands of dollars each year while they solicit your gifts for the poor (see CharityNavigator.org for help).

Two branches of the ministry that I oversee, *I Was Hungry* (IWasHungry.org) and *Orphan's Tear* (OrphansTear.org), exist to meet the pressing needs of very poor believers in developing nations. 100% of your contributions are sent to the beneficiaries of your kindness.

God promises to reward those who help the poor as well as discipline those who ignore them:

> He who shuts his ear to the cry of the poor will also cry himself and not be answered....He who gives to the poor will never want, but he who shuts his eyes will have many curses (Prov. 21:13; 28:27).

A True Story

In conclusion, I want to share with you a touching interview of a poor Christian man named Pablito, who lived with his family on the edge of a large public dump in Manila, Philippines. This interview was originally published in *Christian Aid's* quarterly magazine, *Christian Mission,*[6] along with the following editor's note:

> In 1985 the Association of Philippine Churches (APC) sent a young missionary couple, Nemuel and Ruth Palma, to the poorest of the poor, Manila's dump dwellers. Here hundreds of families live in rows of hovels stacked up like matchboxes, with dirty plastic sheets or pieces of flattened tin cans for roofs, and sackcloth and cardboard milkboxes for walls. An average family of seven lives in a structure no better than a pig sty, and no bigger than a full-sized bed!
>
> The terrible stench, the utter filthiness, the continual burning of garbage, the presence of dens of thieves and hoodlums, prompted one APC worker to describe it as "man's version of hell, where the worms do not die, and the fire is everlasting." It is a place where rats outnumber children by the thousands, and flies outnumber the rats by the millions.

The Interview of Pablito

Q. When did you come to know the Lord Jesus?

A. I received the Lord as my Savior through the witness of an APC worker five years ago. But my faith has been greatly strengthened through the testimony of my three little children.

At the time when I came to Christ, I was a street vendor selling smuggled cigarettes. I immediately realized that this was not consistent with my Christian faith, so I stopped

6 Christian Mission, May/June 1987, pp. 8-9. Reprinted by permission of Christian Aid.

peddling cigarettes and started selling local newspapers and magazines on the sidewalks.

But though I was selling a lot and making more profit, I did not stay long in this business either because I found out that they contained dirty pictures and pornographic stories.

Q. *How did you become a garbage scavenger?*

A. I really wanted to live the life of a true Christian. So I built a small wooden pushcart and went around Manila's public markets scavenging the garbage dumps for food leftovers, used bottles and tin cans which I sell for recycling.

Compared to cigarette and newspaper vending, it is very hard and dirty work. I am always tired after a day's work and I smell terrible. But I feel clean inside, and that is what is important to myself and my family. We want to have clean hearts and minds before the Lord.

Q. *How was your life affected when your children received Christ?*

A. My family and I have a small home at the south corner of the dump. It is only a shanty built with things I found in the dump, but it is a home full of joy because we all love the Lord. We have family devotions every evening. Our daughters are always singing songs they have learned at Bible classes. How I love to hear them sing! They are the sunshine of my life.

My daughters' enthusiasm for attending church and Sunday school, and praying, has greatly affected my wife and me. In the Palma's classes they are taught about hygiene, so my daughters want to wear clean clothes all the time.

They also urge my wife and me to wear clean clothes when we are not scavenging. As a result, our family seems to stand out here in the neighborhood. Our neighbors tease me when I wear my Sunday best by calling me "Mr. Lawyer." I just smile at this, because I know deep inside they, too, want to be clean—both inside and out.

Q. *How do you grow in the Lord?*

A. Our three little girls attend the feeding and educational program conducted by Nemuel and Ruth Palma. My wife and I attend the weekly Bible study for parents held by the Palmas at the dump.

I feel grateful to the Lord for making our lives happy despite our poverty. So much so that I find myself sharing this joy with my fellow scavengers. I hold a Bible study for my neighbors, and have started another Bible study for 12 people living on the west side of the dump.

But we need more Bibles here. Bibles are one thing that we can't get from the garbage because they are never thrown away. But they are expensive. (Note: Bibles in the Philippine language cost about $4.00 each.)

Q. *How do you make ends meet with scavenging as your means of livelihood?*

A. Scavenging does not earn much. One earns 20 to 30 pesos (around $1.50) per day. But the Lord has provided for us very well from the garbage dump. See this pair of pants I'm wearing? They look good, don't they? I got them from the dump.

Some months ago I found out that I needed reading glasses. I prayed to the Lord, and a few days later I found these! (Pablito points to a pair of glasses he is wearing, attached to his ears by a piece of string). I found them in a pile of freshly dumped garbage. And they were the exact power of lens for my eyes!

Almost everything we have and use, from my belt to my wife's hair curlers and our little daughters' shoes and toys, we found at the dump. God knows our small needs, so whatever we need is provided by Him just a stone's throw away from us.

Q. *What other important changes have happened in your life?*

A. With Jesus in our hearts, Rosita and I have learned to accept the hardships of life with a smile. We stopped using foul language, and I learned to love my neighbors and to forgive quickly.

Do you know why I do not have a pair of shoes? Yesterday was Sunday, and I planned to be in church early for prayer. I put my best clothes on and my only pair of shoes, which I had found at the dump. I wanted to really look nice for the Lord because it was only two days after my forty-eighth birthday. So I convinced myself to spend five pesos to have my shoes shined by a bootblack. The bootblack took my shoes off to shine them, and I stood nearby.

Then I noticed a small flower stand just across the street, and I thought of buying the Lord a bunch of yellow flowers. I hurriedly crossed the street and bought them, but when I returned to the bootblack's stand, he had run away with my shoes!

I almost wanted to cry! I was not surprised that I didn't get angry, though I admit I was a bit self-conscious when I walked back home in my Sunday best, barefoot, with a bouquet of yellow flowers clutched in my hand. What a time my neighbors had in teasing me! And I was late for the morning service.

But when I prayed in church that day I knew that one day I will find a new pair of shoes, and unlike the old pair, they will be a perfect match.

Missionary Nemuel Palma (at the door) visits with Pablito (with eye-glasses found at the dump), his wife Rosita, next to him, and his three daughter: Luz (8), Rebecca (6) and Ruth (4), and two neighbors.

Several months after the above interview, a correspondent from *Christian Aid* visited Pablito and found that he was no longer scavenging for a living. Rather, he was drawing water in four-gallon plastic cans from a private faucet a kilometer away, and selling the water to fellow dump-dwellers for six cents a can. He was paying the owner of the faucet about one cent per can, and was thus able to earn $1.50 on a good day. However, Pablito worked only in the mornings on four of his six weekly workdays in order to conduct Bible studies for his fellow dump-dwellers in the afternoons and evenings. Pablito admitted to the correspondent that he often gave half of his earnings to "the poor."

FOUR

The Uncommitted "Christian"

Recently released from jail, a young communist disciple wrote to his fianceé, breaking off their engagement:

> We communists have a high casualty rate. We are the ones who get shot and hung and ridiculed and fired from our jobs and in every other way made as uncomfortable as possible. A certain percentage of us get killed or imprisoned. We live in virtual poverty. We turn back to the party every penny we make above what is absolutely necessary to keep us alive. We communists do not have the time or the money for many movies, or concerts, or T-bone steaks, or decent homes, or new cars. We have been described as fanatics. We are fanatics. Our lives are dominated by one great overshadowing factor: The struggle for world communism. We communists have a philosophy of life that no amount of money can buy. We have a cause to fight for, a definite purpose in life. We subordinate our petty personal selves to the great movement of humanity; and if our personal lives seem hard or our egos appear to suffer through subordination to the party, then we are adequately compensated by the thought that each of us in his small way is contributing to something

new and true and better for mankind.

> There is one thing in which I am in dead earnest about, and that is the communist cause. It is my life, my business, my religion, my hobby, my sweetheart, my wife, and my mistress, my breath and meat. I work at it in the daytime and dream of it at night. Its hold on me grows, not lessens, as time goes on; therefore, I cannot carry on a friendship, a love affair, or even a conversation without relating it to this force that both drives and guides my life. I evaluate people, books, ideas and actions according to how they affect the communist cause, and by their attitude toward it. I've already been in jail because of my ideals, and if necessary, I'm ready to go before a firing squad.

Although deceived and misguided, this young communist disciple possessed what so many professing Christians lack: commitment. We may shake our heads in pity for his deluded belief, but at least his belief was proved to be genuine by his actions, something that cannot always be said of those who claim to be followers of Christ.

True faith always manifests itself by deeds. There is an inseparable correlation between belief and behavior. As Martin Luther wrote in the preface to his commentary on the book of Romans, "It is impossible, indeed, to separate works from faith, just as it is impossible to separate heat and light from fire."[1]

How do you know a person believes what you tell him? If he acts as if he believes you. If you tell him a deadly spider is crawling up his leg, and he smiles and continues conversing with you, you can be sure he doesn't believe you. Likewise, the person who believes in Jesus acts accordingly. His faith is evidenced by his obedience.

Although many professing Christians claim to believe that Jesus is the Son of God, it's obvious by their actions that they don't believe at all. As Paul wrote, "They profess to know God, but by their deeds they deny Him" (Titus 1:16).

Jesus, CEO

Imagine that you work for a large multi-national company. One day, as you are working at your station, a well-dressed man whom you've never seen before enters through a door on the far side of the room. He walks over to your desk and says, "Smith, I'm the CEO of

1 John Dillenberger, ed., *Martin Luther* (New York: Doubleday, 1961), p. 24.

this company. Straighten up the mess on your desk immediately!" What would you do? It all depends, of course, whether or not you believe he is who he claims to be. The CEO yields more authority than anyone else in the company. He is the one, above all others in the company, whom you wouldn't want to displease. So, if you believe he's the CEO, you'll immediately obey him. If you don't obey him, it would indicate that you don't believe he's the CEO.

The analogy is obvious. Believing in Jesus results in submitting to Jesus. We are saved through faith in Jesus, but our faith must be a submissive faith, otherwise it is not faith at all. This is why Paul twice mentions is his epistle to the Romans the "obedience of faith" (see Rom 1:5; 16:26). The entire goal of his ministry was to bring about the "obedience of faith" among all the Gentiles (see Rom. 1:5).

"Your analogy is flawed" some may argue, "because Jesus is not a CEO to be feared."

Such an objection reveals the very heart of the problem. If the CEO analogy is flawed, it is only so because Jesus is *much more* than a CEO. He is the Creator of all people, the Judge of the living and the dead; He possesses a name above every other name.

In the minds of so many professing Christians, however, Jesus is Savior but not Lord. He's a friendly neighbor, not the Head of the Church. He possesses all love but not *all* authority in heaven and on earth. He's a best buddy, not King of kings. He's a jolly good fellow, but not the One before whom every knee shall bow. He's good but He's not God. In reality, however, such a Jesus does not exist, and those who are convinced otherwise are the worst kind of idolaters— they've invented a god of their own imaginations.

The apostle James repeatedly warned against being deluded by a faith that is void of the works of obedience:

> But prove yourselves doers of the word, and not merely *hearers who delude themselves*....If anyone thinks himself to be religious, and yet does not bridle his tongue *but deceives his own heart, this man's religion is worthless*....What use is it, my brethren, if a man says he has faith, but he has no works? Can that faith save him? (James 1:22, 26; 2:14, emphasis added).

James couldn't make his point more clear. Faith without works cannot save us. What we believe is revealed by our words and deeds. Moreover, it is possible to deceive our own hearts in this matter and possess a worthless religion.

James continues:

> But someone may well say, "You have faith, and I have works; show me your faith without the works, and I will show you my faith by my works." You believe that God is one. You do well; the demons also believe, and shudder. But are you willing to recognize, you foolish fellow, that *faith without works is useless?*....You see that a man is justified by works, and not by faith alone....For just as the body without the spirit is dead, so also faith without works is dead (James 2:18-20, 24, 26, emphasis added).

James points out that even demons possess some degree of faith,[2] and their faith is manifested by actions: they shudder in fear. *Yet how many professing believers demonstrate less faith than demons, demonstrating no fear of God?* [3]

Jesus Called Non-Believers to Obedient Faith

Note also that James challenges anyone to show his faith without works (see 2:18). Works cannot be dissected from true faith. That is why true saving faith always begins with repentance. *And that is precisely why Jesus' calls to salvation were so often calls to commitment and obedience.* Jesus called people to a faith that was obedient, and to the chagrin of many who would divorce works from faith, Jesus often said *nothing at all about faith* when He called people to salvation. His true followers would show their faith by their works.

Amazingly, Jesus' calls to costly commitment are often shamelessly ignored by professing Christians. Or, if they are acknowledged, are explained away as being calls to a deeper relationship that are supposedly addressed, not to the unsaved, but to those who have already received God's saving grace. Yet, sadly, so many of these "believers" who claim that Jesus' calls to costly commitment are addressed to them rather than the unsaved *do not heed His calls as they interpret them.* In their minds, they have the option not to respond in obedience, and they never do.

---

2 Demons, of course, can't possess saving faith because salvation has not been offered to them.

3 How enlightening it is to examine what Scripture says about the fear of the Lord. For example, the psalmist wrote, "The fear of the Lord is the beginning of wisdom; a good understanding have all those who do His commandments....How blessed is the man who fears the Lord, who greatly delights in His commandments" (Ps. 111:10; 112:1). In the New Testament, we are *commanded* to fear God (see 1 Pet. 2:17), and are admonished to "cleanse ourselves from all defilement of flesh and spirit, *perfecting holiness in the fear of God*" (2 Cor. 7:1, emphasis added).

First Steps or a Deeper Walk?

Let's consider one of Jesus' invitations to salvation that is often wrongfully thought to be a call to a deeper walk by professing Christians:

> And [Jesus] summoned the multitude with His disciples, and said to them, "If anyone wishes to come after Me, let him deny himself, and take up his cross, and follow Me. For whoever wishes to save his life shall lose it; but whoever loses his life for My sake and the gospel's shall save it. For what does it profit a man to gain the whole world, and forfeit his soul? For what shall a man give in exchange for his soul? For whoever is ashamed of Me and My words in this adulterous and sinful generation, the Son of Man will also be ashamed of him when He comes in the glory of His Father with the holy angels" (Mark 8:34-38).

Is this an invitation to salvation addressed to unbelievers or an invitation to a more committed relationship addressed to believers? As we read honestly, the answer becomes obvious.

First, notice that the crowd Jesus was speaking to consisted of "the multitude" *and* His disciples (v. 34). Clearly then, the "multitude" was not His disciples. They, in fact, were "summoned" by Him to hear what He was about to say. Jesus wanted everyone, followers and seekers, to understand the truth He was about to teach. Notice also that He then began by saying, "If *anyone*...." (v. 34, emphasis added). His words apply to anyone and everyone.

As we continue reading, it becomes even more clear who Jesus was addressing. Specifically, His words were aimed at every person who desired to "come after" Him, "save his life," not "forfeit his soul," and be among those whom He will not be ashamed of when He "comes in the glory of His Father with the holy angels." All of these expressions indicate Jesus was describing people who desired to be saved. Are we to think that there is a heaven-bound person who does not want to "come after" Jesus and "save his life"? Are we to believe that there are true believers who will "forfeit their souls," are ashamed of Jesus and His words, and of whom Jesus will be ashamed when He returns? *Obviously*, Jesus was talking about eternal salvation.

Notice that each of the last four sentences in this five-sentence passage all begin with the word "For." Thus, each sentence helps to explain and expand upon the previous sentence. No sentence within this passage should be interpreted without considering how the others illuminate it. Let's consider Jesus' words sentence by sentence in that light.

<h3 style="text-align:center">Sentence #1</h3>

"If anyone wishes to come after Me, let him deny himself, and take up his cross, and follow Me" (Mark 8:34).

Again, note that Jesus' words were addressed to anyone who wished to come after Him, anyone who wanted to become His follower. *This is the only relationship Jesus initially offers.*

Many desire to be His friend without being His follower, but such an option does not exist. Jesus didn't consider anyone His friend unless they obeyed Him: "You are My friends, if you do what I command you" (John 15:14).

Many would like to be His brother without being His follower, but, again, Jesus didn't extend that option. He considered no one His brother unless they were obedient: "Whoever does the will of My Father who is in heaven, *he* is My brother" (Matt. 12:50, emphasis added).

Many wish to join Jesus in heaven without being His follower, but Jesus conveyed the impossibility of such an occurrence. Only those who obey are heaven-bound: "Not everyone who says to Me, 'Lord, Lord,' will enter the kingdom of heaven; but he who does the will of My Father who is in heaven" (Matt. 7:21).

In the sentence under consideration, Jesus informed those who wanted to follow Him that they couldn't follow Him unless they denied themselves. They must be willing to put their desires aside, making them subordinate to His will. Self-denial and submission is the essence of following Jesus.

But to what degree of self-denial does Jesus expect? Was He speaking of giving up candy for Lent? Within the first sentence, Jesus used an expression that made His meaning unmistakable: "Let him...take up his cross." It was, perhaps, not an original expression, but a common expression of His day. What does it mean?

In Jesus' day, the only people who took up crosses were those condemned to die. Of course, it was the last thing anyone would *want* to do, because it was the last thing a person *would ever* do. When a criminal took up his cross, he lifted up the beam to which he would soon be nailed to die a slow, excruciating death. It was a dreaded moment of facing up to the inevitable.

Thus, the expression, "to take up one's cross," would have been synonymous with doing that which one wouldn't want to do by natural inclination. It symbolizes a high degree of self-denial, doing what one was loathe to do. If it was a common expression of Jesus' day, one can almost imagine fathers admonishing reluctant sons, "Son, you know it's your responsibility to dig out the latrine when it's full. Now take up your cross and get to it." Or wives saying to grimacing husbands, "Honey, I know you don't want to hear this, but today our taxes are due to the Roman government, and we *do* have the money that is being demanded by that dishonest tax collector. We don't really have any choice in the matter, so why don't you take up your cross and visit the tax collector's office this morning?"[4]

Sentence #2

Jesus' second sentence makes the meaning of His first sentence even more clear: "For whoever wishes to save his life shall lose it; but whoever loses his life for My sake and the gospel's shall save it" (Mark 8:35).

Again, notice this sentence begins with "For," connecting it with the first sentence, adding clarification. Here Jesus contrasts two people, the same two people who were implied in the first sentence, that is, the one who *would* deny himself and take up his cross to follow Him and the one who *would not*. Now they are contrasted as one who would lose his life for Christ and the gospel's sake and one who would not. The one who wouldn't deny himself wishes to save his life but will lose it, while the one who would deny himself loses his life but ultimately saves it.

Clearly, Jesus was not speaking about one losing or saving his physical life. The majority of His closest followers lost their physical lives sooner than what they probably would have because they followed Him, dying as martyrs. Moreover, later sentences in this passage indicate that Jesus had eternal losses and gains in mind.[5]

The person in the first sentence who would not deny himself corresponds with person in the second sentence who wished to save his life. Thus we can safely conclude that "saving one's life" means "keeping one's own agenda for his life." This becomes even more clear when we consider the contrasted man who "loses his life for Christ and the gospel's sake." He is the one who denies himself,

4 If the expression of taking up one's cross was not a common expression, but one that Jesus coined, then at bare minimum, it still must represent a high degree of self-denial. Some commentators suggest that it represents taking the first step in a determination to live the rest of one's life on the journey to death to self. Others think Jesus meant that His followers must make a commitment of willingness to die for Him. Regardless, the remaining sentences in this passage expand on what it means to take up one's cross.

5 Also note a similar expression by Jesus recorded in John 12:25: "He who loves his life loses it; and he who hates his life in this world shall keep it to *life eternal*" (emphasis added). Clearly, Jesus was referring to eternal life, not physical life.

takes up his cross, and gives up his own agenda, now living for the purpose of furthering Christ's agenda and the spread of the gospel. He is the one who will ultimately "save his life," while the other will lose his. The person who seeks to please Christ rather than himself will ultimately find himself happy in heaven, while the one who continues to please himself will ultimately find himself miserable in hell, there losing all freedom to follow his own agenda.

Sentences #3 & 4

Now the third and fourth sentences: "For what does it profit a man to gain the whole world, and forfeit his soul? For what shall a man give in exchange for his soul?" (Mark 8:36-37). In these the person is highlighted who will not deny himself. He is the one who wishes to save his life but ultimately loses it. Now he is spoken of as one who pursues what the world has to offer and who ultimately "forfeits his soul." Jesus exposes the folly of such a person by comparing the worth of the whole world with that of one's soul. Of course, there is no comparison. A person might theoretically acquire all the world has to offer, but, if the ultimate consequence of his life is that he spends eternity in hell, he has made the gravest of errors.

From these third and fourth sentences we also gain insight into what pulls people away from denying themselves to become Christ's followers. It is their desire for self-gratification, offered by the world. Motivated by love of self, those who refuse to follow Christ seek sinful pleasures, which Christ's true followers shun out of love and obedience to Him. Those who are out to "grab all the gusto they can," pursue wealth, power and prestige, while Christ's true followers seek first His kingdom and His righteousness. Any wealth, power or prestige that is gained by them is considered a stewardship from God and is used unselfishly for His glory.

Sentence #5

Finally, we arrive at the fifth sentence in the passage under consideration. Notice again how it is joined to the others by the beginning word, *for*: "For whoever is ashamed of Me and My words in this adulterous and sinful generation, the Son of Man will also be ashamed of him when He comes in the glory of His Father with the holy angels" (Mark 8:38).

This again is the person who would not deny himself, but who wished to follow his own agenda, pursuing what the world had to offer, and who thus ultimately lost his life and forfeited his soul. Now he is characterized as one who is ashamed of Christ and His words. His shame, of course, stems from his unbelief. If he had truly believed that Jesus was God's Son, he certainly would not have been ashamed of Him or His words. But he is a member of an "adulterous and sinful generation," and Jesus will be ashamed of him when He returns. Clearly, Jesus was not describing a saved person.

The conclusion to all of this? The entire passage cannot rightfully be considered a call to a more committed life addressed to those who are already on the way to heaven. It is obviously a revealing of the way of salvation by means of comparing those who are truly saved and those who are unsaved. Not once did Jesus say anything about faith or believing, although the entire reason a person would refuse to deny himself, continuing to pursue the world's offers in sinful rebellion against Christ, is because he truly doesn't believe in Christ. The fruit of unbelief is disobedience. Jesus was not proclaiming salvation *earned* by works, but a salvation that *resulted* in works, born from a sincere faith. By His definition, there is no such thing as an "uncommitted Christian."

Baptism, Nepalese Style

The call to salvation is a call to commitment to Christ. In many nations of the world, where persecution is common, this is automatically understood by new believers. They know that by following Christ, there will be a price to pay.

Sundar Thapa, a Nepalese Christian who has planted over one hundred churches in his Buddhist nation, shared with me the eight questions he asks every new convert before his baptism. They are:

1.) Are you willing to be forced to leave your home and parents?
2.) Are you willing to lose the inheritance of your father?
3.) Are you willing to lose your job if people come to know you are a Christian?
4.) Are you willing to go to jail?
5.) Are you willing to be beaten and tortured by police?
6.) Are you willing to die for Christ's sake if necessary?
7.) Are you willing to tell others about Jesus?
8.) Are you willing to bring all of the tithe and offering into the house of the Lord?

If the new convert answers in the affirmative to all eight questions, he then must sign a statement as a record of his answers, and then, and only then, is he baptized. How many of us would be considered Christians in Nepal? More importantly, how many of us will be considered Christians when we stand before Jesus?

"Believers" Who Aren't Disciples

Perhaps the greatest example of wrongly interpreting Jesus' salvation invitations as calls to a "deeper walk" is the modern theological classification that makes a distinction between Christian believers and disciples. So many in the church are convinced that one can be a heaven-bound believer in Christ without being His disciple. The level of commitment Jesus required for one to be classed as His disciple is so high that many professing Christians must readily admit that they don't measure up. But, not to worry, because in their minds the step of discipleship is optional. Not understanding the nature of saving faith, they conclude that becoming a disciple is not synonymous with becoming a Christian, because there is a cost to become a disciple, whereas salvation is free.

But such an understanding is seriously flawed. An honest examination of the New Testament reveals that disciples are not more highly committed believers—they are the only true believers. In the early church, the modern distinction of "believers" and "disciples" did not exist. Everyone who believed in Jesus was His disciple. In fact, "the *disciples* were first called *Christians* in Antioch" (Acts 11:26, emphasis added).

To believe in Jesus was to follow Him obediently, and it still is. Salvation is indeed an unmerited gift, but one that can be received only by a living faith. The commitment that stems from such a faith is not meritorious; rather, it is validating. The grace that forgives us also transforms us.

Jesus' Requirements for Discipleship

Let's examine the requirements Jesus enumerated for one to be His disciple and, as we do, consider if Scripture teaches that all true believers are disciples.

We read in Luke 14:25 that "great multitudes were going along with" Jesus. Jesus, however, wasn't satisfied. Big crowds of fair-weather fans didn't impress Him. He wanted whole-hearted, unreserved commitment. He expected the highest allegiance and devotion. Thus He said to them,

> If anyone comes to Me, and does not hate his own father
> and mother and wife and children and brothers and sisters,
> yes, and even his own life, he cannot be My disciple (Luke
> 14:26).

No intelligent interpreter of Scripture would argue that Jesus meant that one must literally hate the most cherished persons in his life in order to be His disciple. Jesus was obviously using a figure of speech we call *hyperbole*, that is, exaggeration for effect. He could only have meant that our love for our loved ones should seem like hate when compared to our love for Him. He must be the supreme object of our affection. His disciples must love Him far more than any other person, and they must love Him even more than their own lives, being willing to die for Him.

Jesus continued: "Whoever does not carry his own cross and come after Me cannot be My disciple" (Luke 14:27).

Again, His words are obviously not to be taken literally. He doesn't expect His disciples to carry wooden crosses with them everywhere. Carrying one's own cross must be symbolic of something, and whatever that something is, who would conjecture that Jesus was speaking of something easy or pleasant? At bare minimum, committed self-denial is what He had in mind.

Notice also that this second requirement of carrying one's own cross is exactly what Jesus required of all who wanted to *follow* Him, as we learned from our earlier study in this chapter of Mark 8:34-38. In that portion of Scripture, Jesus was unmistakably laying down the requirements for salvation, offering clear evidence that the requirements for salvation and discipleship are the same.

As Jesus continued His discourse on discipleship, He then admonished His audience to count the cost before they set out to be His disciples:

> For which one of you, when he wants to build a tower, does
> not first sit down and calculate the cost, to see if he has
> enough to complete it? Otherwise, when he has laid a foun-
> dation, and is not able to finish, all who observe it begin to
> ridicule him, saying, "This man began to build and was not
> able to finish." Or what king, when he sets out to meet an-
> other king in battle, will not first sit down and take counsel
> whether he is strong enough with ten thousand men to en-
> counter the one coming against him with twenty thousand?
> Or else, while the other is still far away, he sends a delega-

tion and asks terms of peace (Luke 14:28-32).

Who can reasonably argue that there is no cost to becoming Christ's disciple in light of such words?

Jesus concluded: "So therefore, no one of you can be My disciple who does not give up all his own possessions" (Luke 14:33). In order to be Jesus' disciple, we must relinquish ownership of all our possessions to His control. We become stewards of what is now His, and our material wealth will be used for His purposes. Otherwise we are not His disciples.

Clearly, Jesus wanted to convey that becoming His disciple was a costly commitment. He must be first in our lives, and we must love Him more than our own lives, our loved ones, and any material possessions.

Another Requirement

On another occasion, Jesus explained what it meant to be His disciple. As He spoke in the Temple, John reported,

> Many came to believe in Him. Jesus therefore was saying to those Jews who had believed Him, "If you abide in My word, then you are truly disciples of Mine; and you shall know the truth, and the truth shall make you free" (John 8:30-32).

Notice that *twice* John specifically tells us that Jesus' words of 8:31-32 were addressed to people who believed in Him. To those new believers, Jesus did not say, "Eventually you will want to consider becoming committed disciples." No, He addressed them immediately as disciples. To Jesus, believing in Him was equivalent to becoming His disciple. In fact, the first thing He explained to those new believers was how to determine whether or not they truly were His disciples. Was their faith genuine? They could be sure it was if they would abide in His word.

To abide in Jesus' word meant to live in it, making it your home. It implies the desire to know and obey His word, just as He said: "You shall *know the truth*, and the truth shall *make you free*" (John 8:32, emphasis added). Specifically, Jesus was speaking about freedom from sin (see John 8:34-36). This again tells us that Jesus' true disciples, those who have truly believed in Him and are thus born again, are characterized by growing holiness.

The Baptism of Disciples

In the Great Commission, recorded in the final verses of Matthew's Gospel, Jesus used the word *disciple* in a way that leaves no doubt about His definition of the word. He said, "Go therefore and make *disciples* of all the nations, baptizing them in the name of the Father and the Son and the Holy Spirit, teaching them to observe all that I commanded you; and lo, I am with you always, even to the end of the age" (Matt. 28:19-20, emphasis added).

We first note that it is disciples that Jesus wants, and He wants these disciples to be baptized. Yet we also know that Jesus and the New Testament authors unanimously agree that everyone who believes in Jesus should be baptized as soon as possible after confessing faith in Christ. This proves once again that all *true* Christian believers are disciples. Certainly Jesus was not saying in His Great Commission that we should *not* baptize those who believe in Christ, only baptizing those who take the step of becoming committed disciples.

From reading the Great Commission, it is also clear that Jesus considered a disciple to be one who would want to learn all His commandments, with the goal of obeying them (see Matthew 28:20). Obviously learning is a process, so no disciple is instantly obedient in everything. However, every true disciple is obviously submitted to Christ, devoted to learning and doing His will, and so is every true believer since all true believers are disciples.

John's Testimony

Further proof that believers and disciples are one and the same is found in John's Gospel and his first epistle. Compare the following verses:

> A new commandment I give to you, that you love one another, even as I have loved you, that you also love one another. By this all men will know that you are My *disciples*, if you have love for one another (John 13:34-35, emphasis added).

> We know that we have passed out of death into life, because we love the brethren. He who does not love abides in death (1 John 3:14).

Unselfish love for the brethren is what characterizes Christ's true disciples, and it is also what characterizes those who have passed out of death into life, those who have been born again. The reason is simply because Christ's disciples are the only ones who have been truly born again.[6]

---

6 Note also that unselfish love, expressed by meeting pressing needs of Christ's brethren, was what characterized the saved people at the Matthew 25:31-46 judgment, considered previously in chapter 3.

Abiding Branches in the Vine

One final invitation to salvation that is often interpreted as a call to a "deeper walk" is found in John 15. Here, again, Jesus defines what it means to be His disciple:

> I am the true vine, and My Father is the vinedresser. Every branch in Me that does not bear fruit, He takes away; and every branch that bears fruit, He prunes it, that it may bear more fruit. You are already clean because of the word which I have spoken to you. Abide in Me, and I in you. As the branch cannot bear fruit of itself, unless it abides in the vine, so neither can you, unless you abide in Me. I am the vine, you are the branches; he who abides in Me, and I in him, he bears much fruit; for apart from Me you can do nothing. If anyone does not abide in Me, he is thrown away as a branch, and dries up; and they gather them, and cast them into the fire, and they are burned. If you abide in Me, and My words abide in you, ask whatever you wish, and it shall be done for you. By this is My Father glorified, that you bear much fruit, and so prove to be My *disciples* (John 15:1-8, emphasis added).

How many sermons have been preached admonishing professing Christians to "draw closer to Jesus" and abide in Him so that they can bear much fruit? But Jesus does not want us to think that abiding in Him is an option for heaven-bound believers to consider. Abiding in Him is equivalent to being saved, as Jesus made so clear: "If anyone does not abide in Me, he is thrown away as a branch, and dries up; and they gather them, and cast them into the fire, and they are burned" (John 15:6). Those who don't abide in Christ are damned.[7] Those who do abide in Christ bear fruit, proving themselves to be His disciples, just as Jesus said (see John 15:8). Again we see that truly saved people are fruit-bearing disciples.

Grapes can only grow on a branch that is attached to the vine. It is from the vine that the branch receives its flow of life and all that is necessary to produce fruit. And what a fine analogy of our relationship to Christ is pictured by the vine and branches. When we believe in Christ, we become a living, fruit-producing branch in Him. Just as the sap that flows from the vine is the source of the branch's ability to produce fruit, so it is the indwelling Holy Spirit who is the source

---

7 Note that it was not their works that are burned, as some want us to think. The branches themselves were burned.

of the believer's fruit.

And what kind of fruit is produced by the Holy Spirit? Naturally, the *Holy* Spirit produces the fruit of *holiness*. Paul's list of the fruit of the Spirit found in the fifth chapter of Galatians begins with love, which, as noted previously, is the mark of Christ's true disciples. That list continues with joy, peace, patience, kindness, goodness, faithfulness, gentleness and self-control (see Gal. 5:22). These are what the indwelling Holy Spirit produces, and these are what characterize every true believer to some degree. For example, we read that the early disciples were "continually filled with joy and with the Holy Spirit" (Acts 13:52).[8]

Of course, fruit can ripen and mature, and so it is true for the fruit of the Spirit. Young Christians often have fruit that is still green. Nevertheless, if the Spirit indwells someone (and He does every true believer; see Rom. 8:9), it is impossible for Him not to produce His fruit.

What About the Fruitless Branch in Christ?

But did not Jesus speak of the possibility of a branch "in Him" that produced no fruit? Yes, He did. His statement must be interpreted, however, within the context of His vine and branch analogy. First, note that the fruitless branch "in Him" was "taken away" (John 15:2). At bare minimum, this must mean that the branch that *was* attached is *no longer* attached. What happened to the branch after it was "taken away" is somewhat a matter of conjecture. However, once the branch was "taken away" and no longer attached, it obviously was no longer "abiding in the vine." What happens to branches that don't abide in the vine? Jesus said a few verses later, "If anyone does not abide in Me, he is thrown away as a branch, and dries up; and they gather them, and cast them into the fire, and they are burned" (John 15:6).

We, of course, must be careful in interpreting any analogy, parable or metaphor. A metaphor is defined as a comparison of two things that are basically dissimilar but which share some similarities. When I tell my wife that her eyes are like pools, I mean that they are deep, dark, blue and inviting. But that is where the similarities end. I don't mean that fish swim in them or that ducks land on them or that they freeze over in the winter.

Jesus' analogies are no different. We can mistakenly search for spiritual significance in details long after the intended similarities end. For

---

8 The first believers of Acts were also noted for their love, peace, kindness and goodness; see Acts 9:31, 36; 11:24.

example, I would not use Jesus' "vine and branches" analogy to prove that Christians bear more fruit in the summer months, as do grapevines. That is pouring unwarranted significance into the analogy.

Likewise, I wouldn't jump to the conclusion that Jesus was trying to convey that a true believer in Him might never produce fruit, *especially when we realize that the main point of His entire analogy contradicts that very idea.* The most logical conclusion is that the fruitless branch that was "in Him" represents a believer who apostatizes (cf. Luke 8:12-13). He thus becomes unfruitful and is ultimately cut off from Christ. In spite of what so many think, such a thing can happen according to Scripture (and I'll prove it in a later chapter). The only other possibility is that the fruitless branch represents a false believer, supposedly attached to Christ, but obviously dead and not drawing from His life, as evidenced by the absence of fruit. Jesus, however, did not define the branches as including those who only profess to be in Him but are actually not. Clearly, He defined the branches as being those who are in Him.

Those who do produce fruit are promised a pruning by God Himself. Perhaps Jesus was speaking about the radical pruning that occurs at the new birth once a person manifests the initial fruit of faith and repentance.[9] Or perhaps He was describing the ongoing process of sanctification that God performs in the life of every cooperative believer (see Phil. 2:13). Either way, the analogy of God as a vinedresser speaks of His cutting away from our lives what is undesirable to Him. Anything that hinders fruit from being produced by the indwelling Spirit is susceptible to His shears.

A Small Objection

Grasping at spiritual straws, a question is sometimes raised about Joseph of Arimathea, whom the Bible states was a "secret disciple" of Jesus (see John 19:38). How could he be spoken of as being a disciple if his devotion was secret? Does this not contradict all I've written about the commitment demonstrated by true disciples?

May I first say that it always troubles me when, after presenting scripture after scripture that proves a certain truth, someone will dig up one obscure verse that seemingly contradicts what I've taught. Then he proudly quotes it as if that one verse somehow invalidates all the rest that we've just considered. This objection is a case in point.

---

9 This idea is supported somewhat by the fact that Jesus told His disciples that they were already pruned because of the word He had spoken to them (see John 15:3). The word translated *clean* in this verse in the NASB is the same word translated *prune* in 15:2.

Everything I've written about the costly commitment of discipleship has been based on Scripture. I've said precisely what the Bible says. So the burden of reconciling the secret discipleship of Joseph of Arimathea with all Jesus taught about the costly commitment of true discipleship falls on all of us, not just me.

Now, to answer the objection: Joseph of Arimathea was very devoted to Jesus, by the biblical record, a "good and righteous man" (Luke 23:50). However, as a prominent member of the Sanhedrin, he kept his devotion secret for "fear of the Jews" (John 19:38). The Jews whom he feared must have been the other members of the Jewish Sanhedrin.

Obviously, Joseph of Arimathea knew there would be some negative consequences if he revealed how he really felt about Jesus. It's quite possible that what he feared was removal from the Sanhedrin, which would have resulted in losing his opportunity before them as a positive influence for Christ. We learn from Luke 23:51 that Joseph had "not consented" to the Sanhedrin's "plan and action" concerning the arrest, trial and condemnation of Jesus. And after Jesus' death, he clearly risked facing what he previously feared, as we learn that "he gathered up courage and went in before Pilate, and asked for the body of Jesus" (Mark 15:43). He then personally prepared the body of Jesus and buried it in his own tomb. Surely there was every possibility that his actions would be discovered by the Sanhedrin! Yet once Jesus had been crucified, it seemed that he no longer cared what his fellow members of the Sanhedrin thought.

Joseph's commitment to Christ was obvious, and the limited secrecy of his devotion was only temporary. Beyond all this, it is certainly possible to be a devoted disciple of Christ and yet be afraid of negative consequences that might result from that devotion. Joseph of Arimathea certainly had enough other fruit in his life to validate his commitment to Christ.

What About "Carnal" Christians?

Another objection that is often raised is the issue of so-called "carnal Christians." They are a modern classification of supposedly authentic believers who continually yield to the flesh, and whose carnal behavior makes them indistinguishable from non-Christians. Although they have "accepted Christ" (a very unbiblical phrase), they display no commitment to Him. Many of them have no regular fellowship with other believers and are involved in all kinds of sin, yet they are supposedly secure in God's grace, heaven-bound.

From where did this concept of carnal Christians originate? Its source is a commonly-held and very twisted interpretation of what Paul wrote in the third chapter of his first letter to the Corinthians:

> And I, brethren, could not speak to you as to spiritual men, but as to men of flesh, as to babes in Christ. I gave you milk to drink, not solid food; for you were not yet able to receive it. Indeed, even now you are not yet able, for you are still fleshly. For since there is jealousy and strife among you, are you not fleshly, and are you not walking like mere men? (1 Cor. 3:1-3).

The *King James Version* translates the same word that the NASB translates *fleshly*, as "carnal," thus the origin of the phrase, "carnal Christians."

The question is, was Paul defining a category of Christians who are indistinguishable from non-Christians due to their following after the fleshly nature? In contradiction to what the rest of the New Testament teaches, many say *Yes*. "Did not Paul say to these Christians," they ask, "that they were 'walking like mere men' (3:3), indicating that they were acting identically as unsaved people would?"

The answer is found by considering all Paul said about the Corinthians. As we do, we discover that the "carnal Corinthians" were certainly not indistinguishable from unsaved people, because their living faith was manifested by many outward indications of their devotion to Christ. Yes, being two-natured, as are all Christians, they faced the battle between the Spirit and flesh. Many of them, being spiritually immature, were to some degree yielding to their old nature (the flesh), not walking in love toward one another. They were arguing about who their favorite teachers were and showing inconsideration during the Lord's Supper. Some were filing lawsuits against fellow believers. They needed to grow in the fruit of love, and Paul wrote much to admonish them to that end.

The primary reason for their problem was their own ignorance of what God expected of them. Because they were babes in Christ whom Paul had only fed with the milk of God's Word rather than the meat (see 3:2), their knowledge was limited. That was why Paul wrote to them and addressed their various wrongs. Once he told them what God expected, he expected them to line up.

The Spiritual, "Carnal" Corinthians

What were some of the works of the Corinthian Christians that identified them as possessing a devoted faith? What characterized them as distinct from non-Christians? Here are some that are revealed by Scripture:

First, when Paul initially preached the gospel at Corinth, he met with great success. God Himself told him that there were many people in Corinth who would be saved (see Acts 18:10), and Paul stayed there for a year and a half. Many "were believing and being baptized" (Acts 18:8). Baptism was their first act of obedience to Christ.

Describing some of the Corinthian Christians, Paul wrote that they had previously been fornicators, idolaters, adulterers, homosexuals, thieves, covetous, drunkards and swindlers (see 1 Cor. 6:9-10). But now they have been washed and sanctified; they had been transformed. This, by itself, disproves the foolish notion that the Corinthians were indistinguishable from non-Christians.

Additionally, Paul instructed the Corinthian Christians "not to associate with any so-called brother if he should be an immoral person, or covetous, or an idolater, or a reviler, or a drunkard, or a swindler—not even to eat with such a one" (1 Cor. 5:11). Obviously, the Corinthian Christians were not guilty of these things themselves, otherwise Paul would have been telling them not to associate or eat with themselves.

Paul's first Corinthian letter was, in part, a response to a letter he'd received from them concerning several issues. They had asked him questions regarding what was right and wrong, indicating their own desire to do what was right. Was it wrong for single people to get married? How about those who had previously been married? What about eating meats that had been sacrificed to idols? Many of the Corinthian Christians, out of devotion to Christ, refused to eat such meats lest they offend the Lord, an indication of their living faith.

Paul wrote in 1 Corinthians 11:2: "Now I praise you because you remember me in everything, and hold firmly to the traditions, just as I delivered them to you." Are these people then indistinguishable from non-Christians?

The Corinthian Christians regularly partook of the Lord's Supper (albeit somewhat inappropriately), obedient to Jesus' command (see 1 Cor. 11:20-22). They also regularly gathered together for Christian worship (see 1 Cor. 12, 14), something not done by unbelievers in their day.

They were zealous of spiritual gifts (see 1 Cor. 14:12).

Just the fact that both of Paul's letters to the Corinthian Christians are so full of exhortations to holiness indicates that Paul believed they would heed what he wrote. He instructed them to excommunicate a hypocrite (see 1 Cor. 5:13) and receive monetary collections for poor Christians in Jerusalem (see 1 Cor. 16:1-4), something they had already been zealously doing (see 2 Cor. 8:10; 9:1-2). In this way, they displayed their love for the brethren, exactly what Jesus said would mark His true disciples (see John 13:35).

Paul's second letter indicates that many, if not most of them, had heeded the instructions of his first letter (see 2 Cor. 7:6-12). Between the two letters, Titus journeyed to Corinth and returned with a good report of their obedience (see 2 Cor. 7:13-16). The babes in Christ were growing up. Yes, there were still some problems in Corinth, and Paul would soon be visiting them personally to resolve what remained.

The conclusion? When Paul wrote that the Corinthian Christians were "walking like mere men," he obviously did not mean that they were completely indistinguishable from non-Christians in every respect. They were acting just like non-Christians do in one way, but in many other ways they were acting like devoted disciples of Christ.

What About Works That Will Burn?

Another argument that is often used to support the idea of a special class of carnal Christians is based on Paul's words in 1 Corinthians 3:12-15. In that passage, did not Paul assure the Corinthians that they would be saved even if all of their works were burned at the judgment? Does this not indicate that a person can be completely fruitless yet still be saved?

The context of that passage reveals the error of this argument. Clearly, Paul was writing about rewards that individual ministers will receive or forfeit, based on the quality of their works. Comparing the church to "God's building" (3:9), and stating that he had laid a foundation "which is Jesus Christ" (3:11), Paul wrote that every minister should "be careful how he builds upon" (3:10) that foundation. It is quite possible to build wrongly. Paul then figuratively mentioned six different building materials that could be used: "gold, silver, precious stones, wood, hay [and] straw" (3:12). The first three are of great value and incombustible, whereas the last three are of much lesser value and combustible.

According to Paul, the type of material being used by individual ministers to build God's building is not necessarily evident now. One day, however, it will be very evident, because "each man's work...is to be revealed with fire; and the fire itself will test the quality of each man's work" (3:13). Paul continued:

If any man's work which he has built upon it remains, he

shall receive a reward. If any man's work is burned up, he shall suffer loss; but he himself shall be saved, yet so as through fire (1 Cor. 3:14-15).

It has been debated as to what kind of works constitute "gold, silver and precious stones works," and what kind constitute "wood, hay and straw works." It is undoubtedly true, however, that ministers who "build" God's building with bricks of phony Christians and the mortar of a false gospel will find this passage to be very applicable when the Lord tests the quality of their work. Many unholy people who presently are within the church will ultimately find themselves in the fires of hell, and the minister who "won them to Christ" or assured them of their salvation by means of proclaiming a false grace will realize that all his efforts amounted to nothing in building the true "temple of God" (3:16). What he built will burn, and he shall "suffer loss" (3:15), receiving no reward. Yet he himself, if he is a true believer, "shall be saved, yet so as through fire" (3:15).

Clearly, Paul's intention in this passage was not to assure so-called "carnal Christians" that they could be completely fruitless and still be confident of their salvation. He was writing about the rewards that ministers will receive or forfeit based upon the quality of their work that will be revealed at the judgment.

Yes, true Christians may sometimes act carnally. Any time they yield to the flesh, they can be said to be acting like "mere men." However, there is no special group of "carnal Christians" in the body of Christ, heaven-bound but yielding completely to their fleshly nature. As Paul said in his letter to the Romans,

> For if you are living according to the flesh, you must die [or "perish" as the NLT says[10]]; but if by the Spirit you are putting to death the deeds of the body, you will live. For all who are being led by the Spirit of God, *these* are sons of God (Rom. 8:13-14, emphasis added).

And as he wrote to the Galatian Christians, "Now those who belong to Christ Jesus have crucified the flesh with its passions and desires" (Gal. 5:24).

What Would You Have Done If...

The story, probably fictitious, has been frequently told of a small church in a remote village of Central America. One Sunday morn-

---

10 Obviously, Paul was not warning them about dying physically, because everyone, no matter how he behaves, "must die" physically. Rather, Paul was warning about spiritual and eternal death.

ing, just as the regular service was about to begin, the doors into the back of the sanctuary burst open, and two unshaven men trooped in, wearing combat fatigues and brandishing machine guns. Belts of machine gun bullets were draped across their chests.

Fear gripped the hearts of the congregation. Communist guerrillas in their region had been known to unmercifully slaughter Christians. Was this their time?

One of the men called for silence and then spoke. "You Christians are always talking about going to see your Savior, the One you say is the Son of God. Well, today is your lucky day, because in a few minutes you are going to find out if your God really exists! Line up along the walls on either side of this church!

The congregation quickly moved through the pews to either side of the sanctuary.

"Now, before we kill you, we want to make sure that it is only true believers who die. Anyone here who really doesn't believe that Jesus is the Son of God may exit past us through the rear doors of the sanctuary. Move quickly!"

Many didn't hesitate. Within a minute, half the congregation was gone.

When the last person filed out, the doors were locked shut. The one guerrilla watched through a side window as those who exited the church ran from the premises. Then, as he laid down his gun, a smile filled his face, and he spoke once more: "Brethren, please forgive us. We wanted to worship the Lord with you this morning, but we only wanted to worship with true Christians. Now, let's praise the Lord together!" And what a church service they had that morning!

This story is usually told to provoke professing Christians to consider what they would have done if they had been present that morning. However, believing this story to be authentic requires us to overlook the fact that two machine-gun carrying Christians acted deceitfully while breathing murderous threats and denouncing Christ, just to worship God among true believers! By their actions, did they not deny Christ every bit as much as those who ran from the church that morning?

This being so, I would like to alter this fictitious story just slightly, changing the ending. Although my alteration is also fictitious, it is the way similar stories have ended thousands of times:

Within a minute, half the congregation was gone.

When the last person filed out, the doors were locked shut. The one guerrilla watched through a side window as those who exited the church ran from the premises. Then, as he aimed his machine gun at the remaining group of devoted disciples, an ugly grimace filled his face, and he spoke once more: "Prepare to meet your God." With those words his finger pulled the trigger. And what a church service they had that morning, in the presence of their Lord!

FIVE

The Antinomian "Christian"

It's 11:40 Sunday morning at your church. The hymns and choruses have been sung, the offering has been received, and now it's time for the Scripture reading and sermon. Your pastor walks to the pulpit, opens a large black book, takes a deep breath, and as he swings his arm high up into the air, authoritatively cries out, "A man is justified by *works*, and *not* by faith alone!"

What would be the reaction of most people in your church? Would they be shocked by the pastor's obvious heresy? Would they be angered by his contradiction of Paul's writings about salvation, those precious truths rediscovered during the Reformation? Would they label him a legalist? *Or would they realize that he had just read James 2:24?*

Those who would react adversely represent multitudes of professing Christians who are greatly mistaken. Not understanding the nature of saving faith, they suppose that works stand in opposition to faith, whereas, in reality, works are inseparably joined to true faith. As Martin Luther wrote, "It is impossible, indeed, to separate works from faith, just as it is impossible to separate heat and light from fire."[1]

---

1 John Dillenberger, ed., *Martin Luther* (New York: Doubleday, 1961), p. 24.

Luther coined a term to describe those who were convinced that, because salvation was a free gift of God's grace, obeying God's laws was unimportant. He called them *antinomians*, the roots of which are *anti*, against, and *nomos*, law.

Today the Protestant church is full of antinomians, and if Luther were alive, he would cry out against its heresy and call for a reformation. He would have no lack of scriptural support for his crusade, because Jesus, Paul, Peter, James, John and Jude all warned against the errors of antinomianism. In fact, Luther would have more scriptures to support his modern cause than he did for the truths of the Reformation. The New Testament's warnings against the errors of antinomianism are much more numerous than against the errors of legalism.

Two Deadly Errors

In Luther's day, the church was entrenched in legalism. Salvation was perceived by most church goers as something to be earned. By purchasing indulgences, viewing relics, doing penance and so on, a person could receive credits that would lessen his future sentence in purgatory by hundreds, even thousands, of years. The gospel had been lost.

While Luther studied the book of Romans, however, he discovered that salvation is a free gift received by faith. He was wonderfully born again, and immediately began challenging his contemporaries with the truths that had set him free. (His faith started working!) A firestorm of controversy was generated, but eventually, through Luther and other reformers' labors, many came to believe in the gospel of God's grace.

But there was an inherent danger in such a gospel, and the reformers knew it. It was possible that God's grace could be conceived as a license to sin. The importance of good works might be neglected, and a new heresy could replace the old one, just as deceptive and damning. Thus the reformers were cautious to proclaim, "It is faith, alone, which saves; but the faith that saves is not alone."

Today, hundreds of years later, what the reformers feared has come upon us. Unlike the legalists of Martin Luther's day, today's church goers don't need to be told that their dead works can't save them. Rather, they need to be told that that their dead faith can't save them. Too many have purchased shares of a false gospel that promise heaven without holiness. The grace in which they trust leads to a license to sin rather than obedience to Christ. Yet Jesus Christ, who is the same yesterday, today and forever, still warns antinomians everywhere, "Not everyone who says to Me, 'Lord, Lord,' will enter the kingdom of heaven; *but he who does the will of My Father who is in heaven*" (Matt. 7:21, emphasis added).

What is Legalism?

Perhaps no theological term has been more misunderstood and misused as the word *legalism*. Anyone who preaches self-denial, obedience or holiness today is in danger of being wrongly labeled a legalist. How often have professing Christians made statements such as, "I used to attend a very *legalistic* church where the pastor preached against R-rated movies"? Such a pronouncement reveals that the speaker does not really understand what legalism is. Legalism is not holding to a standard of holiness derived from God's Word. Rather, it is attempting to earn one's salvation by one's performance. The legalist doesn't think He needs Jesus to be saved. He thinks he can save himself. If someone said, "I used to attend a very legalistic church where the pastor preached that we could earn our place in heaven by not viewing R-rated movies," that would be the correct usage of the term, *legalism*.

The heresy of legalism is that it offers another way of salvation other than the one way that God has provided, through Christ. The folly of the legalist is that he hopes for what is impossible, that he can be good enough to merit heaven. Of course, the possibility of our being good enough to earn our place in heaven ended long ago: the first time God held us accountable for our sin. Theoretically, if a person could live a sinless life, he could get into heaven without the need of a Savior. But because all of us have transgressed, if we're going to be saved, we need another way of salvation. Obviously that way could only be through God's grace. The good news of the gospel is that God has extended His grace to us without compromising His standards of holiness through Jesus Christ, our substitute.

Perhaps the best definition of legalism is expressed by the following simple formula:

WORKS → SALVATION

The arrow should be read, "results in." The legalist thinks that his works will result in his salvation. Because his heart is unregenerate, void of faith in and love for God, the legalist produces only an outward conformity to the Law as he strives to earn God's favor.

Another form of legalism can be expressed by the formula:

FAITH + WORKS → SALVATION

This legalist adds faith and works together, thinking that the combination will insure his salvation. He is trusting, in part, in his works. This was the kind of legalism Paul opposed in his letter to the Galatians.

The biblical formula for the true means of salvation can be expressed:

FAITH → SALVATION + WORKS

Those who truly believe the gospel are not only saved, but transformed by God's grace, and manifest God's work in their lives by their joyful obedience. Unlike the legalist, the true believer's obedience springs from within, because his heart has been changed.

Finally, antinomianism is conveyed:

FAITH → SALVATION – WORKS

The antinomian supposes that his faith results in his salvation, even though the validating works of a transformed life are not manifested. Additionally, he often misunderstands at least five others things: (1) the nature of saving faith, (2) God's intent in saving people, (3) the full work of God's grace in the lives of those who believe, (4) the Christian's relationship to God's law, and (5) the true nature and necessity of repentance. Let's consider all five of these items in the remainder of this chapter.

The Nature of Saving Faith

The antinomian considers faith to be nothing more than mental acknowledgment. He supposes that his acceptance of certain theological truths constitutes saving faith. Because he *knows* Jesus died on the cross for everyone's sins, and *knows* that salvation is not of works but faith, he thinks he is saved.

Of course, even the devil knows that Jesus died on the cross for everyone's sins. Satan also knows that people are not saved by works but through faith. What would ever make us think that knowing those things makes us righteous in God's eyes?

True saving faith is much more than mental acknowledgment. The Bible defines faith as "the *assurance* of things hoped for, the *conviction* of things not seen" (Heb. 11:1, emphasis added). It is believing with one's *heart* that results in salvation (see Rom. 10:10). True faith is always manifested by outward actions.

Antinomians, however, often try to dissect works from faith, even setting them against each other. They piously state, because salvation is purely of God's grace, that they would never look to any of their works to provide assurance of their salvation, lest they "trust in their works."

Yet, as we shall soon see, that is not how Jesus, John the Baptist, the apostle John, Paul, Peter and James thought. For example, John wrote that the love we demonstrate for fellow believers is one of several means whereby we can determine if we are truly born again:

> We know [note that word, *know*] that we have *passed out of death into life*, because *we love the brethren*. He who does not love abides in death....But whoever has the world's goods, and beholds his brother in need and closes his heart against him, how does the love of God abide in him? Little children, let us not love with word or with tongue, but in deed and truth. *We shall know by this that we are of the truth, and shall assure our heart before Him*, in whatever our heart condemns us; for God is greater than our heart, and knows all things (1 John 3:14, 17-20, emphasis added).

John believed that our works can assure us of the work of God's grace in our lives. This is vastly different from trusting that one's works are earning him salvation. Our good works are not meritorious—they are validating. They provide additional assurance of our salvation beyond the assurance provided by the promises of the gospel. As we look at the works in our lives, we can say, "Praise God for this evidence of God's grace working in my life!" Our good works have "been wrought in God" (John 3:21).

John also wrote in his first epistle:

> No one who is born of God practices sin, because His seed abides in him; and he cannot sin, because he is born of God. By this the children of God and the children of the devil are obvious: anyone who does not practice righteousness is not of God, nor the one who does not love his brother (1 John 3:9-10).

Did John believe that the new birth affects how a person lives? Absolutely. Those who are truly born of God practice righteousness and love fellow believers. This is not to say that true believers never sin or always demonstrate perfect love (see 1 John 1:8-9; 4:17-18), but that righteousness and love are dominant characteristics in their lives, unlike those who are not saved, who are characterized primarily by unrighteous behavior and selfishness. John wrote repeatedly in his letter about living righteously and loving fellow believers to provide the assurance of salvation to his readers:

> *These things* [the contents of my letter] I have written to you who believe in the name of the Son of God, *in order that you may know that you have eternal life* (1 John 5:13, emphasis added).

John believed that professing Christians should examine their lives to gain assurance of God's grace working in them, because he also believed that there is a definite correlation between belief and behavior.

Paul on the Relationship Between Faith and Works

The apostle Paul didn't believe that works and obedience can be divorced from faith, or that these things stand in opposition to one another. Rather, he wrote in the book of Romans of "the obedience of faith" (Rom. 1:5; 16:26). The plain interpretation of that phrase is that faith is characterized by obedience. If I used a phrase, "the obedience of Bob," the clear implication is that Bob demonstrates obedience. If I used the phrase, "the joy of salvation," I would obviously be implying that salvation is characterized by joy. In neither case would I be saying that one serves a substitute for the other, as antinomians want us to believe that Paul's expression, "the obedience of faith" means that we don't need to have obedience, because faith serves as a great substitute. That would be like saying the expression, "the obedience of Bob" means that I don't need Bob because I have obedience, or, considering the other example, that I don't need salvation because I have joy, a perfectly acceptable substitute.

Paul not only thought the gospel was something to be *believed*, he also considered it something to be *obeyed*. He told the Thessalonian Christians that those who don't "*obey the gospel* of our Lord Jesus... will pay the penalty of eternal destruction" (2 Thes. 1:8-9, emphasis added).[2]

What is there about the gospel to obey? First, we are commanded by God to believe the gospel, making *believing* an act of obedience (see Mark 1:15). How then can some claim that obedience and faith stand in opposition to one another when believing is an act of obedience?

---

2 Peter used the same phrase when writing about the unsaved: "What will be the outcome for those who do not obey the gospel of God?" (1 Pet. 4:17). Likewise, Luke wrote in his account of the early church that "a great many of the priests were becoming obedient to the faith" (Acts 6:7).

Second, Jesus commanded people to *repent* and believe the gospel. He also commanded us to preach "repentance for the forgiveness of sins" (Luke 24:47), and this Paul did, declaring that people "should repent and turn to God, performing deeds appropriate to repentance" (Acts 26:20). Repenting is an act of obedience, a response to a divine commandment. Salvation begins in a person's life by an act of obedience that is also an act of faith.

Paul wrote to the Thessalonians, commending their *"work of faith and labor of love"* (1 Thes. 1:3, emphasis added). He did not view faith and works as two things that cannot be mixed. Like the apostle James, he also believed that true faith works. He wrote to the Galatian Christians, who were in danger of being seduced into thinking that circumcision was necessary for salvation,

> For in Christ Jesus neither circumcision nor uncircumcision means anything, but *faith working through love* (Gal. 5:6, emphasis added).

Like the apostle John, Paul believed that true faith worked through love. Love is a primary fruit of faith. Paul could be paraphrased, "For in Christ Jesus neither circumcision nor uncircumcision mean anything; they are human works, but faith starts a divine work in one's life so that his works of love originate from God."

Hebrews on Faith

The writer of the book of Hebrews believed that obedience to Jesus Christ is essential to salvation. He wrote,

> And having been made perfect, He became *to all those who obey Him* the source of eternal salvation (Heb. 5:9).

Of course, the writer could have also said that Jesus became the source of eternal salvation to all who believe in Him, and he would have been saying the same thing. To him, faith, something he mentioned over thirty times in his letter, naturally produced works. Every one of the "faith heroes" of chapter 11 *did* something because they believed.

In the third and fourth chapters of the book of Hebrews, notice how the writer used the words *unbelief* and *disobedience* synonymously:

> And so we see that they [the Israelites] were not able to enter [the promised land] because of *unbelief*....those who formerly had good news preached to them failed to enter

because of *disobedience* (Heb. 3:19; 4:6, emphasis added).

Because the majority of the Israelites didn't believe the good news, they didn't obey God. Because they didn't do what God commanded, they proved they didn't believe His promise.

John the Baptist and Jesus on Works

John the Baptist believed there is an inseparable correlation between belief and behavior. Read how he used the words *believe* and *obey* synonymously:

> He who believes [*pisteuo*] in the Son has eternal life; but he who does not obey [*apeitheo*] the Son shall not see life, but the wrath of God abides on him (John 3:36, emphasis added).

How much clearer could it be? And how can anyone say that it is wrong to examine our lives to determine our spiritual status lest we "trust in our works to save us"? Again, we should examine our works because Scripture is clear that it is quite possible to possess a spurious faith. Trusting in a non-working faith to save us is just as dangerous as trusting that our works will earn us salvation. The only intelligent safeguard against both these dangers is to examine our works for the validation of a true, saving faith.

Jesus also believed that belief affects behavior. He said that those who *believe* in Him would do the same *works* as He did[3] (see John 14:12). He foretold that those who "did the good deeds" would enjoy "a resurrection of life," and "those who committed the evil deeds" would suffer "a resurrection of judgment" (John 5:29). He also warned that only those who do the will of God will enter heaven, and that true and false believers can be known by their fruits (see Matt. 7:19-23). Unless Jesus was teaching that salvation is earned by works, the only possible correct interpretation of His warning is that saving faith is validated by obedience.

Jesus also warned that only those who do the will of His Father are His brothers and sisters (see Matt. 12:49-50). As we learned in the previous chapter, Jesus often said nothing at all about faith when He called people to salvation. He told seekers to deny themselves, take up their crosses and follow Him lest they forfeit their souls (see Mark

---

3 Some maintain that Jesus was only referring to His miracles when He spoke of His works in John 14:11-12. However, the context doesn't necessarily support this view, nor does experience. If all true believers are supposed to be characterized by performing the identical and even greater miracles than Christ performed, there are very few true Christians who have ever lived.

8:34-38). He called people to costly discipleship and sincere submission, a true faith.

Attempting to explain what it meant to believe in Him, Jesus went so far as to tell people that they needed to eat Him (see John 6:47-56), something we are reminded of every time we partake of the Lord's Supper. To believe in Jesus is to become one with Him. The very first act of faith by the new believer, water baptism, is a public declaration of his oneness with Jesus in His death, burial and resurrection.

To believe in Jesus is to join Him: "The one who joins himself to the Lord is one spirit with Him" (1 Cor. 6:17). To believe in Jesus is to abide in Him: "Abide in Me, and I in you....If anyone does not abide in Me, he is thrown away as a branch, and dries up; and they gather them, and cast them into the fire, and they are burned" (John 15:4,6). How could a person possess such a unity with Christ and it not affect his behavior?

James on Saving Faith

Perhaps the most classic definition of saving faith, and the one most troublesome to antinomians, is contained in the epistle of James in a passage we've already considered briefly in previous chapters:

> What use is it, my brethren, if a man says he has faith, but he has no works? Can that faith save him? (Jas. 2:14).

The obvious answer to James' rhetorical question is *No.* Faith without works cannot save.

Even in the light of such obvious truth, modern antinomians would like us to believe that faith without works can save a person. How do they maintain their conviction in spite of what James said? Their explanation of James' teaching is so complex it is highly unlikely that any of his original readers would have been able to understand it. For starters, some antinomians want us to believe that James was not talking about being saved from eternity in hell, but of being saved from a "sinful life of death on this earth."[4] Supposedly, James was trying to persuade his readers to believe that they had to have works with their faith if they wanted to be saved from a "sinful life of death" on this earth.

The phrase, "a sinful life of death," can only mean a life of sinfulness. And *being saved* from a "sinful life of death on this earth" can

---

4 This phrase is a quotation from a letter I received from a person who objected to my interpretation of James 2:14-26. Such ambiguous phrases seem to be the specialty of theologians, who, after politicians and poker players, are some of the world's greatest bluffers. Truly, there is no fog so thick as the fog of theologians.

only mean living an obedient life, or doing good works. Thus, some antinomians want us to believe that James was correcting a gross error in the theology of his readers: they actually thought they could live an obedient life with a faith that had no works of obedience! Is it possible that James thought his readers were so stupid that they didn't already know what would be self-evident to anyone? And do antinomians really think that we are so stupid to swallow such a far-fetched interpretation of James' clear teaching?

In further refutation of the antinomian argument, we note that the immediate context *before* and *after* James' words about the relationship between faith and works is the subject of future judgment (see Jas. 2:12-13; 3:1). James had eternal salvation in mind, not a temporal earthly salvation from "a sinful life of death."

Faith Working Through Love

This particular antinomian interpretation grows more absurd as one continues to read James' words:

> If a brother or sister is without clothing and in need of daily food, and one of you says to them, "Go in peace, be warmed and be filled," and yet you do not give them what is necessary for their body, what use is that? Even so faith, if it has no works, is dead, being by itself (Jas. 2:15-17).

Some antinomians would like us to believe that dead faith is still saving faith; it's just *dead* saving faith as opposed to *living* saving faith. But James has already stated that faith without works can't save anyone, and that is what dead faith is, a faith without works.

It is interesting that the example James used to illustrate dead faith is the picture of a professing Christian who does nothing to help an impoverished brother or sister. Like Jesus, John and Paul, James believed that the fruit of true faith is love for the brethren expressed by meeting pressing needs.

James goes on to write about the impossibility of true faith being void of works:

> But someone may well say, "You have faith, and I have works; show me your faith without the works, and I will show you my faith by my works." You believe that God is one. You do well; the demons also believe, and shudder. But are you willing to recognize, you foolish fellow, that faith without works is useless? (Jas. 2:18-20).

As James so rightly states, a person may claim to have faith, but he can't prove he has faith without works. On the other hand, another person may not verbally claim to have faith, but his works say what he doesn't need to claim. Actions speak louder than words. Thus, those who say they have faith that God is one (Deut. 6:4) but have no corresponding actions are fooling themselves. Demons believe that God is one, and they act like they believe it—they shudder! Only "foolish fellows," antinomians all, don't realize that faith without works is absolutely "useless" (Jas. 2:20). That means it is good for nothing.

Abraham's Living Faith

James continues his argument, citing Abraham, who was justified by faith, as an example of a person with living faith:

> Was not Abraham our father justified by works, when he offered up Isaac his son on the altar? You see that faith was working with his works, and as a result of the works, faith was perfected; and the Scripture was fulfilled which says, "And Abraham believed God, and it was reckoned to him as righteousness," and he was called the friend of God. You see that a man is justified by works, and not by faith alone (Jas. 2:21-24).

How could James have made it more clear? Abraham's faith was a living faith that obeyed God. It was not a faith void of works that justified him, but a faith that was validated by works. James goes so far as to make a statement that, taken out of its context, could be considered heretical: "A man is justified by works, and not by faith alone" (Jas. 2:24).

How do some antinomians attempt to wriggle out of the predicament into which James puts them? They theorize that James did not mean that Abraham was justified before *God* by his works, but before *men*. But this is absurd. Are we to believe that James' readers were convinced that a person could be justified in the sight of men without works, and that James considered their error to be so serious that he wrote to sternly refute them? Could this have really been the issue James addressed?

Notice also that James never said a word about Abraham being justified before men. Additionally, when Abraham almost sacrificed Isaac, there were no other people present to see his act of obedience, that which supposedly justified him in the sight of men. *God*, however, was watching, and He immediately said after Abraham's obedient act,

> Now I know that you fear God, since you have not withheld
> your son, your only son, from Me....because you have done
> this thing, and have not withheld your son, your only son,
> indeed I will greatly bless you, and I will greatly multiply
> your seed as the stars of the heavens, and as the sand which
> is on the seashore; and your seed shall possess the gate of
> their enemies. And in your seed all the nations of the earth
> shall be blessed, because you have obeyed My voice (Gen.
> 22:12, 16-18).

The whole incident was a test from God (see Gen. 22:1) to see
what Abraham would do. Moreover, James said that when Abraham
obeyed God, the Scripture was fulfilled which says, "And Abraham
believed God, and it was reckoned to him as righteousness" (Jas.
2:23). Before whom was Abraham reckoned righteous (or justified),
God or men? Obviously it was God.

This is not to say that Abraham wasn't reckoned righteous by
God years before he almost sacrificed Isaac, as Scripture tells us (see
Gen. 15:6; Rom. 4:3). But Abraham's amazing act of obedience in
almost sacrificing his son was indicative of the living faith he possessed from his first moment of faith. Now his faith was being *per-
fected* by his works. The kind of faith that resulted in Abraham's being declared righteous by God was a true faith, evidenced by his
obedience.

Doesn't James Contradict Paul?

But did not Paul write, "a man is justified by faith *apart from works*
of the Law" (Rom. 3:28, emphasis added)? Does this not contradict
what James said about our being justified by works if he was speaking, as Paul was, of being justified before God?

No, Paul and James were both speaking of being justified before
God, and their apparent contradictory statements are not difficult
to reconcile. Paul was addressing legalists who considered the Law
to be the means of salvation. Paul wanted them to know that salvation can't be earned by anyone's feeble attempt to keep the Law.
Salvation is a free gift that has been provided by God's grace and is
received by faith.

James, however, was addressing those who had corrupted the
truth of salvation by grace through faith, reducing it to a license to
sin. Their motto was "justification by faith alone," but like modern
antinomians, they had redefined faith to be nothing more than a verbal profession, a faith that can be void of any corresponding acts.

James wrote to refute that error, wording his explanation so that his point is unmistakable: "You see that a man is justified by works, and not by faith alone" (Jas. 2:24). The reason James could make such a statement is because our works demonstrate our faith by which we are justified before God.

Scripture teaches that at certain future judgments, the eternal destinies of individuals will be determined by their works (see Matt. 12:36-37; 25:31-46; John 5:28-29; Rev. 20:12-13). This is because works are what validate faith. So in that sense, as James stated, people's works justify them before God.

James concludes his teaching on the nature of saving faith by using one more biblical example of a person who was saved by a faith that worked:

> And in the same way was not Rahab the harlot also justified
> by works, when she received the messengers and sent them
> out by another way? For just as the body without the spirit
> is dead, so also faith without works is dead (Jas. 2:25-26).

What would have happened to Rahab if she had possessed a faith that was void of works (if such a thing were possible)? She would have perished with everyone else in Jericho. But her living faith stands today as an example for all who would be saved from the wrath of God. Rahab was no antinomian.

Some antinomians like to point to the thief on the cross as an example of a person who was saved by a faith that was void of works. However, they should read Scripture more closely. The repentant thief clearly demonstrated his living faith by his works during the last hours of his life. First, he openly confessed that he was a sinner. Second, he declared that Jesus was innocent and unworthy of death, going so far as to defend Him before the other thief, even rebuking him. Third, without shame he looked to Jesus as the source of salvation and, before a hostile, mocking crowd, publicly asked Him for it (see Luke 23:40-43). Of course, the repentant thief had a very limited opportunity to demonstrate his faith beyond what he did. Still, in just a few minutes, he displayed his faith more than many professing Christians do during their entire lifetime.

A second truth that antinomians often miss is:

God's Intent in Saving People

Long before the New Testament was written and Jesus walked on the earth, God clearly revealed His intent in saving people—He wanted to make them holy. For example, the Lord said through the prophet Jeremiah:

> "Behold, days are coming," declares the Lord, "when I will make a new covenant with the house of Israel and with the house of Judah, not like the covenant which I made with their fathers in the day I took them by the hand to bring them out of the land of Egypt, My covenant which they broke, although I was a husband to them," declares the Lord. "But this is the covenant which I will make with the house of Israel after those days," declares the Lord, "I will put My law within them, and on their heart I will write it; and I will be their God, and they shall be My people. And they shall not teach again, each man his neighbor and each man his brother, saying, 'Know the Lord,' for they shall all know Me, from the least of them to the greatest of them," declares the Lord, "for I will forgive their iniquity, and their sin I will remember no more" (Jer. 31:31-34).

This entire prophecy is quoted in Hebrews 8:8-12, and the writer of Hebrews leaves no doubt as to its application to all new covenant believers.

First, note that God promises to make a new covenant that will be unlike the old covenant (31:31-32). How would it be different? The old covenant was broken by the majority of Israel, but that would not be the case for those under the new covenant. The reason? Because God would do a supernatural work in their lives.

Specifically, He would put His law within them, writing it on their hearts. The result would be that He would be their God and they would be His people (31:33). Under the old covenant, the Lord intended that He would be the God of the Israelites and they would be His people, but it didn't work out that way, because they transgressed the covenant. They didn't obey Him, proving that He really wasn't their God, and they really weren't His people. Through Jeremiah, however, the Lord promised those under the new covenant that He *would* be their God and they *would* be His people. It would be so because they would obey Him. The source of their obedience would be His work within them.

Forgiven of their sins, everyone under the new covenant would really "know the Lord," another implication of their devoted relationship. John wrote, "And by this we know that we have come to know Him, if we keep His commandments. The one who says, 'I have come to know Him,' and does not keep His commandments, is a liar, and the truth is not in him" (1 John 2:3-4). God's intention for us from long ago was that we would truly know Him.

Another similar prophecy that has application to all new covenant believers is found in Ezekiel 36:27. There God promised, "And I will put My Spirit within you and cause you to walk in My statutes, and you will be careful to observe My ordinances." The result of putting the Holy Spirit within us would be our obedience. If God had only wanted to forgive us, He wouldn't have put His Holy Spirit within us. But He not only wanted to forgive us, He wanted to transform us. He not only wanted to make us legally righteous, He wanted to make us *practically* righteous. He not only wanted Jesus to become like us, He wanted us to become like Jesus. Just as the apostle Paul wrote: "For whom He foreknew [that is us], He also predestined to become conformed to the image of His Son" (Rom. 8:29). This was His intent from the beginning.

A third truth that antinomians often overlook is:

The Full Work of God's Grace in the
Lives of Those Who Believe

The previous topic leads well into this one. Antinomians believe in God's grace to forgive us, but fail to realize that God gives much more in His grace. The same grace that forgives us also transforms us.

Grace has been defined as unmerited favor, and so it is. In spite of our rebellion, God has sent His Son to die as a sacrificial substitute and offer us riches beyond measure. We are undeserving of such grace. Yet some have, as Jude said, "turn[ed] the grace of our God into licentiousness" (Jude 1:4). That is, they consider God's favor to be a license to sin, cheapening what has cost Him so much, continuing on their own path of self-gratification.

This, of course, is not the response God expects from those who have received His grace. He expects that our hearts will be melted as we fall on our faces before Him, ashamed, repentant, and full of gratitude. As Paul wrote, God's grace instructs "us to deny ungodliness and worldly desires and to live sensibly, righteously and godly in the present age" (Titus 2:12).

Clearly, from the earliest days of the church, there were antinomians, although not labeled as such. Paul refuted antinomian logic and its perverted views of God's grace throughout his letters. For example, He wrote to the Romans:

What shall we say then? Are we to continue in sin that grace might increase? May it never be! How shall we who died to sin still live in it? (Rom. 6:1-2).

Here was antinomian logic at its worst: Let us give God more opportunity to extend His grace by continuing in sin! To Paul, the thought of such a course of life is as abhorrent as it is impossible. "How shall we who died to sin still live in it?" (Rom. 6:2). Paul appeals to the transforming power of God's grace in the new birth. Those who have truly believed in Jesus have died to sin.

Paul explains in the next few verses exactly how this happens: By virtue of our being in Christ who died and was resurrected, so we too have died and come back to life to "walk in newness of life" (Rom. 6:4). When we died in Christ, sin's power was broken over us. Sin was a spiritual force that held us captive, but now we are no longer sin's slaves because, "he who has died is freed from sin" (Rom. 6:7). Although still capable of being tempted by sin and yielding to it, our situation is not like it was prior to our new birth. Then sin was part of our spiritual nature and had power over us. It was next to impossible, if not impossible, for us to be obedient to God. Now, however, it is *very* possible for us to obey God, and obviously those who have submitted themselves to Christ in obedient faith will act holy now that they are able.

Grace to be Holy

The promise of the good news of God's grace is not only that we can be forgiven, but that we can be made holy. Scripture indicates that there is an initial transformation at the new birth, a work of God that cleans us up dramatically. After that, there is an ongoing work of God in our lives, often called in Scripture *sanctification*. Consider the wonderful message contained within the following scripture:

> Or do you not know that the unrighteous shall not inherit the kingdom of God? Do not be deceived; neither fornicators, nor idolaters, nor adulterers, nor effeminate, nor homosexuals, nor thieves, nor the covetous, nor drunkards, nor revilers, nor swindlers, shall inherit the kingdom of God. And such were some of you; but you were washed, but you were sanctified, but you were justified in the name of the Lord Jesus Christ, and in the Spirit of our God (1 Cor. 6:9-11).

Within the Corinthian church, there were former sinners who had previously been bound by some of the most addictive sins known to humanity. But they had been set free and transformed by the Holy Spirit. Isn't it sad that as the grace of God longingly waits to forgive and set free homosexuals, thieves, adulterers and drunkards, the church organizes support groups to help "Christians" understand and cope with their addictions? While God's eternal word testifies of the sin-delivering power of the gospel, the church buys into secular theories and pop psychology. Unlike so many in the church today, Paul was not ashamed of the gospel, because he knew it was "the power of God for salvation to everyone who believes" (Rom. 1:16). The Greek word he used for "salvation," *sozo*, can be translated *deliverance*. God's power in the gospel can deliver anyone of anything.

Yet so much of the church today is either ashamed or ignorant of the delivering power in the gospel. Under the guise of love, sin addicts are "compassionately" told that God in His grace accepts them as they are. It is certainly true that God loves everyone as they are, but He will only accept them if they will believe in His Son and turn from sin. If they do, He will not leave them as they are, but will set them free. I've personally witnessed homosexuals, alcoholics, drug addicts, fornicators and adulterers be set free from their sin instantly when they repented and called on Jesus. Is God not that powerful? According to 1 Corinthians 6:9-11, He is!

Speaking the Truth in Love

If we really loved people who are bound by sin, we would tell them the truth. Do we think that we are more loving than God as we compassionately counsel people to cope as they continue practicing the sin from which He desires to deliver them? Was Jesus being too harsh when He told the woman who had been caught in adultery, "Go your way. From now on sin no more" (John 8:11)? Should He have been more compassionate and said, "I accept you just as you are. You are obviously a sex addict, and no doubt it has a lot to do with how you were raised as a child. Your actions reveal that you are still longing for the love that your father never gave you. So don't feel guilty. Guilt can be very damaging to our personalities. I suggest that you go your way and join a support group for recovering sex addicts. With time, I hope that you will be able to overcome your addiction with the help of a higher power."?

Jesus' message to all of us, once we've encountered Him, is, "Go and sin no more." By the power of the Holy Spirit in an authentic new birth, sin's power is broken, making obedience possible. Those who have been truly born again are new creations in Christ (see 2 Cor. 5:17) who can say with certainty, "I have been crucified with Christ; and it is no longer I who live, but Christ lives in me" (Gal. 2:20). God is at work within them, "both to will and to work for His good pleasure" (Phil. 2:13), and He promises to perfect the good work He began in them (see Phil. 1:6).

As I've previously stated, if all God wanted to do was forgive us, He would have never put His Holy Spirit in us. Clearly, at least part of His purpose in giving us the Holy Spirit was to make us holy. God's grace does more than forgive us—it delivers and transforms us.

A fourth concept that antinomians often misunderstand it:

The Christian's Relationship to God's Law

A favorite antinomian expression is, "I'm so glad I'm not under the Law, but under grace." Although this is a biblical expression, the antinomian rips it from its context. He uses it to mean, "I'm so glad that I don't have to be concerned when I commit a certain sin" or, "I'm so glad I don't always have to be worrying about what God approves or disapproves, as they had to under the Law." Such interpretations reveal a grave error in interpreting an important biblical expression.

The New Testament does indeed inform us that those who are in Christ are not "under the Law, but under grace" (Rom. 6:14). However, Scripture makes it very clear that, whatever this expression means, it *does not* mean that those who are under grace have a license to sin. By taking a few scriptures out of context, antinomians force a meaning on a biblical expression that contradicts the whole tenor of Scripture. For example, consider Paul's words in Romans 3:31:

> Do we then nullify the Law through faith? May it never be!
> On the contrary, we establish the Law.

Clearly, some of what Paul writes in Romans is a defense against a Jewish argument that his gospel of grace would lead people to sin. We can almost hear Paul's antagonists shouting at him: "If people are saved by faith and not by obeying the Law as you say, then you are nullifying God's Law!"

"On the contrary," Paul responded. "You who have been trying to be saved by keeping the Law have never come close to obeying it fully yourselves. But those who have faith in Jesus are born again. God's law is written in their hearts, sin's power is broken over their lives, and they are indwelt by God's Spirit. By virtue of these things and others, they begin keeping the letter *and* spirit of the moral aspects of the Law. Do we then nullify the Law through faith? May it never be! On the contrary, we establish the Law."

What Did Paul Mean?

Later in Romans, Paul used the expression under our consideration, "we are not under law but under grace." But read the context of his statement:

> What then? *Shall we sin because we are not under law but under grace? May it never be!* Do you not know that when you present yourselves to someone as slaves for obedience, you are slaves of the one whom you obey, either of sin resulting in death, or of obedience resulting in righteousness? (Rom. 6:15-16, emphasis added).

Though we are not under law, this in no way implies that God has given us the liberty to sin. Paul pointed out the incompatibility of such an idea by making reference to what every *true* believer does at the moment of his conversion: He presents himself to God as His obedient slave, and the result is righteousness. The only other alternative available to the human race is to present themselves as slaves to sin, which everyone has done prior to believing in Jesus, and the result is spiritual and eternal death.

The problem is that so many professing Christians have never presented themselves to God as obedient slaves. They've heard a gospel that promises them heaven without repentance. Making Jesus Christ Lord is considered an optional step on the sure road to heaven. Surely it must be an optional step, they think, otherwise salvation would not be of grace. Besides, doesn't the Bible say that we are not under the Law, but grace?

But as Paul so clearly stated, nothing could be further from the truth. Making Jesus Lord is the *only* first step on the road to heaven. Presenting yourself as His obedient slave is the *only* true response of saving faith and the *only* way to receive God's gift of righteousness.

The Law of Christ

Just because we are not under God's Law given through Moses does not mean that we are not under God's laws given through Christ. Paul clearly stated in the above Romans passage that we should not sin. Obviously, if we can be guilty of sin, there must be a standard to which we are held. Law must exist for sin to exist. "Where there is no law, neither is there violation" (Rom. 4:15).

Under the new covenant, there is a law that is binding upon us. It is not a means of earning salvation because our salvation is of God's grace. Yet it is obviously meant to be obeyed, otherwise it would not have been given. That law is what Scripture calls the "law of Christ." The law of Christ includes everything Christ commanded, just as "the Law of Moses" includes everything Moses commanded. Remember that Jesus told us to make disciples, teaching them to obey all His commandments (see Matt. 28:18-20).

Let's consider another portion of Scripture, where Paul clearly states that he is not under the Law of Moses, but definitely under the law of Christ:

> For though I am free from all men, I have made myself a slave to all, that I might win the more. And to the Jews I became as a Jew, that I might win Jews; to those who are under the Law, as under the Law, *though not being myself under the Law*, that I might win those who are under the Law; to those who are without law, as without law, *though not being without the law of God but under the law of Christ*, that I might win those who are without law (1 Cor. 9:19-21, emphasis added).

How, exactly, does the law of Christ compare with the Law of Moses? A study of Christ's commandments reveals that, in some cases, He expressly laid aside certain old covenant laws. In other cases, He instituted new laws that did not exist under the old covenant. And in other cases, He explained the spirit of, and endorsed, certain old covenant laws. Let's consider examples of all three.

An example of the first is Jesus' abolishing the dietary restrictions of the old covenant. We read in Mark's Gospel that He "declared all foods clean" (Mark 7:19). We can eat bacon under the new covenant without guilt.[5]

An example of the second was Christ's instituting the commandment of water baptism, something that was not required of any of God's old covenant people (see Matt. 28:19). Jesus also once gave us what He called a *new* commandment, to love one another as He has loved us (see John 13:34).

An example of the third would be Jesus' endorsement of the seventh commandment, the prohibition of adultery. While preaching

---

5 This truth is endorsed by God's vision to Peter in Acts 10:10-15 and by Paul's words in 1 Timothy 4:3-5.

His Sermon on the Mount, Jesus explained the spirit of that prohibition, revealing God's original intent. It seems very likely that many in His audience considered themselves holy so far as adultery was concerned, yet all the while they were habitually lusting in their hearts. But as Jesus indicated, if it is wrong to have a sexual relationship with your neighbor's wife, it is obviously also wrong to mentally undress her.

All of us who are truly in Christ have an obligation, an inward motivation, and the ability to obey the law of Christ. We are under His law. Jesus' commandments embody all the moral requirements of the old covenant law.[6]

Finally, a fifth scriptural concept that antinomians often disregard is:

The True Nature and Necessity of Repentance

Some antinomians completely ignore the New Testament's inclusion of repentance as a necessary requirement for salvation. Some argue that to tell unsaved people that they need to repent is to tell them that their works contribute to their salvation, which amounts to legalism. But this is simply not true. Repentance is indeed a work, but like every other work, it contributes nothing so far as a payment for salvation. Like every other work in the life of a true believer, repentance is a work that follows faith, and is the first work of a living faith. Repentance is the only proper response to the gospel.

Other antinomians, who are a little more knowledgeable of Scripture, realize the claim that repentance should be excluded from gospel preaching is tantamount to saying that the preaching of John the Baptist, Jesus, Peter and Paul was defective. Therefore, their strategy has been to redefine repentance. By their new definition, repentance is no more than a change of mind about Jesus, and one that, amazingly, may not necessarily affect a person's behavior. So let us search for the definition of repentance within the Bible. What did the preachers of the New Testament mean when they called people to repent?

Paul believed that true repentance required not just a change of mind, but a change of behavior. Recounting his initial vision and subsequent ministry of the ensuing decades, Paul testified before King Agrippa,

> Consequently, King Agrippa, I did not prove disobedient
> to the heavenly vision, but kept declaring both to those of
> Damascus first, and also at Jerusalem and then throughout

---

6 In the next two chapters, we will look more closely at the "law of Christ," and how it resembles the law of Moses.

all the region of Judea, and even to the Gentiles, that they should repent and turn to God, *performing deeds appropriate to repentance* (Acts 26:19-20, emphasis added).

John the Baptist also believed that repentance was more than just a change of mind about certain theological facts. He called on his audiences to repent. When they asked him what they should do, he enumerated specific changes of behavior (see Luke 3:3, 10-14). He derided the Pharisees and Sadducees for only going through the motions of repentance, and warned them of hell's fires if they didn't truly repent:

> You brood of vipers, who warned you to flee from the wrath to come? Therefore *bring forth fruit in keeping with repentance*....the axe is already laid at the root of the trees; *every tree therefore that does not bear good fruit is cut down and thrown into the fire* (Matt. 3:7-10, emphasis added).

Jesus preached the same message of repentance as John (see Matt. 3:2; 4:17). He once stated that Nineveh repented at Jonah's preaching (see Luke 11:32). Anyone who has ever read the book of Jonah knows that the people of Nineveh did more than change their minds. They also changed their actions, turning from sin.

What is biblical repentance? It is a willful change of behavior in response to authentic faith born in the heart.

The Necessity of Repentance

How important is repentance? Can a person be saved without repenting? According to Scripture, the answer is *No*.

John the Baptist proclaimed a gospel (and Luke calls it "the gospel") whose central message was repentance (see Luke 3:1-18). Those who didn't repent would go to hell (see Matt. 3:10-12; Luke 3:17).

Jesus preached repentance from the start of His ministry (see Matt. 4:17). He warned people that unless they repented, they would perish (see Luke 13:3, 5).

When Jesus sent out His twelve disciples to preach in various cities, "they went out and preached that men should *repent*" (Mark 6:12, emphasis added).

After His resurrection, Jesus told the twelve to take the message of repentance to the whole world, because it was the key that opened the door to forgiveness:

And He said to them, "Thus it is written, that the Christ should suffer and rise again from the dead the third day; and that *repentance* for forgiveness of sins should be proclaimed in His name to all the nations, beginning from Jerusalem" (Luke 24:46-47, emphasis added).

The apostles obeyed Jesus' instructions. When the apostle Peter was preaching on the day of Pentecost, his convicted listeners, after realizing the truth about the Man whom they had recently crucified, asked Peter what they should do. His response was that they, first of all, should repent (see Acts 2:38).

Peter's second public sermon at Solomon's portico contained the identical message. Sins would not be wiped away without repentance:[7]

> *Repent* therefore and return, that your sins may be wiped away (Acts 3:19a, emphasis added).

As we have already learned from Paul's testimony before King Agrippa, his gospel always contained the message of repentance. In Athens, Paul warned his audience that everyone must stand in judgment before Christ, and those who have not repented will be unprepared for that great day:

> Therefore having overlooked the times of ignorance, God is now declaring to men that *all everywhere should repent*, because He has fixed a day in which He will judge the world in righteousness through a Man whom He has appointed, having furnished proof to all men by raising Him from the dead (Acts 17:30-31, emphasis added).

In his farewell sermon to the Ephesian elders, Paul listed repentance along with faith as an essential ingredient of salvation:

> I did not shrink from...solemnly testifying to both Jews and Greeks of *repentance* toward God and faith in our Lord Jesus Christ (Acts 20:20a, 21; emphasis added).

The writer of the book of Hebrews said that "repentance from dead works" is the most fundamental doctrine of Christ (see Heb. 6:1).

---

7 Likewise, when God revealed to Peter that Gentiles could be saved simply by believing in Jesus, Peter declared to Cornelius' household, "I most certainly understand now that God is not one to show partiality, but in every nation the man who fears Him and *does what it right*, is welcome to Him" (Acts 10:34b-35, emphasis added). Peter also declared in Acts 5:32 that God gave the Holy Spirit "to those who obey Him." All true Christians are indwelt by the Holy Spirit (see Rom. 8:9; Gal. 4:6).

Hopefully, this list of scriptural proofs is enough to convince any-one that a relationship with God begins with repentance. *There is no for-giveness of sins without it.* If you did not repent when you first "accepted Jesus," performing "deeds appropriate to repentance," you were not saved. If you have not repented since then, you are still not saved.

Of What Does God Expect Us to Repent?

When a person first believes the gospel, he should initially repent of all known sin. Of course, he can't repent of everything he does that's wrong because he doesn't know everything he is doing that's wrong. God holds us accountable only for what we know (see Luke 23:34; 1 Tim. 1:13). As the new believer grows in his understanding of God's will (see Eph. 5:10), there will be ongoing repentance. That is the process of sanctification.

In some cases, there will be a need to make restitution and/or ask forgiveness for previous wrongs. Obviously, if a person stole twenty dollars yesterday, believes in Jesus today, and still keeps the stolen money, he is still a thief. He has in his possession what belongs to another. How can he claim to be a follower of Christ? The conscience of a true new believer will not allow him rest until he returns what he has stolen.

Of course, some wrongs are impossible to make right. But every stolen item that can be returned should be. Every wrong that can be righted should be. Letters may need to be written or phone calls made, asking forgiveness from offended parties.

If every professing Christian in the world would repent, it would cause a revolution.

Legalism and *antinomianism*—two words that describe equally fa-tal theologies. Which of these two words have you heard more often spoken from the lips of professing Christians? How many of them have never even heard of antinomianism? Although the New Testa-ment warns against antinomianism many more times than it does against legalism, antinomianism remains the prevailing theology in many modern Protestant circles.

Antinomians often mistakenly speak of authentic Christians as le-galists. Authentic Christians don't mind though, because unlike an-tinomians, they expect persecution, knowing that, "Indeed, all who desire to *live godly* in Christ Jesus *will be persecuted*" (2 Tim. 3:12, em-phasis added). They seek praise from God rather than man, looking forward to the day when they will hear their Lord say, "Well done, *good and faithful slave; you were faithful*...enter into the joy of your *master*" (Matt. 25:21, emphasis added). It is only those who have been good and faithful to their *Master* who will enter into His joy.

SIX

Jesus' Greatest
Salvation Sermon

About two thousand years ago, the Son of God, then living on earth in human form, spoke to a multitude of people who had gathered to hear Him on a mountainside along the Sea of Galilee. Today we refer to the words He spoke that day as the "Sermon on the Mount."

Jesus was the greatest communicator who ever existed, and He was teaching people whom we would consider to be uneducated. Thus, His teaching was simple and easy to understand. He used everyday objects to illustrate His points.

Today, however, many think that we need someone who has a Ph.D. to interpret what Jesus said. And unfortunately the basic premise of some of those interpreters is that Jesus *couldn't* have meant what He said. Thus they've concocted elaborate theories to explain what Jesus *really* meant, theories that the people whom He originally spoke to wouldn't have guessed at in a thousand years, nor would they have understood those theories if someone had explained them. For example, some modern "scholars" want us to believe that Jesus' words had no application to either His audience or to modern Christians. Rather, they say that His words will be applicable only during the time when we're living in His future kingdom. This is an astounding theory, in light of the fact that, as Jesus addressed His audience, He used the word *you* (not *them*) in this short sermon over one hundred times.

The purpose of this chapter and the next is to study Jesus' Sermon on the Mount. As we do, we will discover that it was a message about salvation, holiness and the relationship between the two. It is a sermon that repeatedly warns against antinomianism. Caring dearly for the spiritually hungry people who had gathered to hear Him, Jesus wanted them to understand what was most important—how they could inherit the kingdom of heaven. It is imperative that we, too, pay attention to what He said. This was the one about whom Moses wrote: "The Lord God shall raise up for you a prophet like me from your brethren; to Him you shall give heed in everything He says to you. And it shall be that every soul that does not heed that prophet shall be utterly destroyed from among the people" (Acts 3:22-23).

Let us begin at the beginning.

The Beatitudes

In the first section of Jesus' sermon, what are called the Beatitudes, Jesus promised specific blessings to people who possess certain character traits. Many different traits are listed and many specific blessings are promised. Casual readers sometimes read the Beatitudes like people peruse their horoscopes, thinking that each person should find himself in one, and only one, Beatitude. As we read more closely, however, we soon realize that Jesus was not listing different kinds of people who will receive varied blessings. Rather, He was speaking of one kind of person who will receive one all-encompassing blessing: inheriting God's kingdom. There is no other reasonable way to interpret His words.

Let's read the first twelve verses of the Sermon on the Mount:

> When Jesus saw the crowds, He went up on the mountain; and after He sat down, His disciples came to Him. He opened His mouth and began to teach them, saying,
> "Blessed are the poor in spirit, for theirs is the kingdom of heaven.
> "Blessed are those who mourn, for they shall be comforted.
> "Blessed are the gentle, for they shall inherit the earth.
> "Blessed are those who hunger and thirst for righteous-

ness, for they shall be satisfied.

"Blessed are the merciful, for they shall receive mercy.

"Blessed are the pure in heart, for they shall see God.

"Blessed are the peacemakers, for they shall be called sons of God.

"Blessed are those who have been persecuted for the sake of righteousness, for theirs is the kingdom of heaven.

"Blessed are you when people insult you and persecute you, and falsely say all kinds of evil against you because of Me. Rejoice and be glad, for your reward in heaven is great; for in the same way they persecuted the prophets who were before you" (Matt. 5:1-12).

The Blessings and Character Traits

First, consider all the blessings promised. The blessed shall (1) inherit the kingdom of heaven, (2) receive comfort, (3) inherit the earth, (4) be satisfied, (5) receive mercy, (6) see God, (7) be called God's sons, and (8) inherit the kingdom of heaven (a repeat of #1) where they shall be rewarded.

Does Jesus want us to think that *only* the poor in spirit and those who have been persecuted for righteousness (#1 and #8) will inherit God's kingdom? Will *only* the pure in heart see God and *only* the peacemakers be called sons of God, but neither shall inherit God's kingdom? Will the peacemakers *not* receive mercy and the merciful *not* be called sons of God? Obviously that is not what Jesus wants us to think.

Now consider the different traits Jesus describes: (1) poor in spirit, (2) mournful, (3) gentle, (4) hungering for righteousness, (5) merciful, (6) pure of heart, (7) peacemaking, and (8) persecuted.

Does Jesus want us to think that a person can be pure in heart yet unmerciful? Can one be persecuted for the sake of righteousness but not be one who hungers and thirsts after righteousness? Again, obviously not.

Therefore, it is only safe to conclude that the numerous blessings promised are the manifold blessings of one big blessing—inheriting God's kingdom. Moreover, the many character traits of the blessed are the manifold traits shared by *all* the blessed.

Clearly, the Beatitudes describe the character traits of Jesus' true followers, in which, by enumerating those traits, He encouraged His followers with promises of the many blessings of salvation. The blessed are saved people, so Jesus was describing the traits of people who are going to heaven. *People who do not fit Jesus' description are not blessed and will not inherit the kingdom of heaven.* Thus it is fitting that we should ask ourselves if we fit Jesus' description. This is a sermon about salvation, holiness, and the relationship between the two.

The Character Traits of the Blessed

The eight characteristics Jesus listed of blessed people are not necessarily all easily understood, and they are thus variously interpreted. For example, what is virtuous about being "poor in spirit"?

Personally, I'm inclined to think that Jesus was describing the first essential trait a person must possess if he is going to be saved. That is, he realizes his own spiritual poverty. One must first see his need for a Savior before he can be saved.

This first trait eliminates all self-sufficiency and any thought of meriting salvation. The truly blessed person is one who realizes that he has nothing to offer God, and that his own righteousness is as "filthy rags" (Is. 64:6, KJV). He sees himself among the company of those who are "separate from Christ...having no hope and without God in the world" (Eph. 2:12).

Jesus did not want anyone to think that by his own self-effort he might attain to the standards He was about to enumerate. No, people are *blessed*, that is, *blessed by God* if they possess the characteristics of the blessed. They have tasted of God's grace. They are blessed, not only because of what awaits them in heaven, but because of the work God has done in their lives on earth. If I see the traits of the blessed in my life, it should remind me not of what I've done, but of what God has done in me by His grace.

If the first characteristic is listed first because it is the first necessary trait of the heaven-bound, perhaps the second trait is also listed meaningfully: "Blessed are those who mourn" (Matt. 5:4).

Could Jesus have been describing heartfelt repentance and remorse? I think so, especially since Scripture is clear that godly sorrow results in a repentance that is necessary for salvation (see 2 Cor. 7:10). The mournful tax collector who humbly bowed his head in the Temple, beating his breast and crying out for God's mercy, was indeed a blessed person. He, unlike the proud Pharisee who simultaneously prayed in the Temple, left that place justified, forgiven of his sins (see Luke 18:9-14).

If Jesus was not speaking of the initial mourning of the repentant person who is just coming to Christ, then perhaps He was describing the sorrow all true Christians sense as they continually face a world that is in rebellion against the God who loves them. Paul expressed it as "great sorrow and unceasing grief in [his] heart" (Rom. 9:2).

The third characteristic, gentleness, is listed in Scripture as one of the fruits of the Spirit (see Gal. 5:22-23). Gentleness is not a self-generated attribute. Those who have received the grace of God and the indwelling of the Spirit are also blessed to be made gentle. Harsh and violent "Christians" beware. You are not among those who will inherit the earth. You are not among the blessed ones.

Hungering for Righteousness

The fourth characteristic, hungering and thirsting for righteousness, describes the God-given inward longing that every true born-again person possesses. He is grieved by unrighteousness in the world and in himself. He hates sin (see Ps. 97:10; 119:128, 163) and loves righteousness.

Too often, when we read the word *righteousness* in Scripture, we immediately translate it, "the legal righteousness imputed to us by Christ," but that is not always what the word means. Quite often it means, "the quality of living right by God's standards." That is obviously the meaning Jesus intended here, because there is no reason for a Christian to hunger for what he already possesses. He already has an imputed righteousness.

Those who have been born of the Spirit long to *live* righteously, and they have assurance that they will one day "be satisfied" (Matt. 5:6), certain that God, by His grace, will complete the work He's begun in them (see Phil. 1:6).

Jesus' words here also foresee the time of the new earth, "in which righteousness dwells" (2 Pet. 3:13). Then there will be no sin. Everyone will love God with all his heart and love his neighbor as himself. We who now hunger and thirst for righteousness will then be satisfied. Finally our prayer will be answered, "Your will be done on earth as it is in heaven" (Matt. 6:10).

Mercy and Purity

The fifth trait, mercifulness, is also one that every born-again person naturally possesses by virtue of his having the merciful God living within him. Those who possess no mercy are not blessed of God and reveal that they are not partakers of His grace. The apostle James concurs: "Judgment will be merciless to one who has shown no mercy" (Jas. 2:13). If you stand before God and receive a merciless judgment, do you think you will go to heaven or hell?[1]

Jesus once told a story of a servant who had received great mercy from his master, but who was then unwilling to extend some mercy to his fellow servant. When his master discovered what had happened, He "handed him over to the torturers until he should repay all that was owed him" (Matt 18:34). All his formerly-forgiven debt was reinstated. Then Jesus warned His disciples, "My heavenly Father will also do the same to you, if each of you does not forgive his brother from your heart" (Matt. 18:35). Again, non-merciful people will not receive mercy from God. They are not among the blessed.

The sixth trait of the heaven-bound is purity of heart. True followers of Christ are not just outwardly holy. By God's grace, their hearts have been made pure. They truly love God from their hearts, and it affects their meditations and motives. Jesus promised that they shall see God.

Again may I ask, are we to believe that there are true Christian believers who are *not* pure in heart and who therefore will *not* see God? Is God going to say to them, "You can come into heaven, but you can't ever see Me"? No, obviously every true heaven-bound person has a pure heart.

Blessed to be Peacemakers

Peacemakers are listed next. They will be called sons of God. Again, Jesus must have been describing every true follower of Christ, because everyone who believes in Christ is a son of God (see Gal. 3:26).

Those who are born of the Spirit are peacemakers in at least three ways.

First, they've made peace with God, one who was formerly their enemy.

Second, they live in peace, as far as possible without disobeying God, with other people. They're not characterized by dissensions and strife. Paul wrote that those who make a practice of strife, jealousy, outbursts of anger, disputes, dissensions and factions will not inherit God's kingdom (see Gal. 5:19-21). True believers will go the extra mile to avoid a fight and keep peace in their relationships. They do not claim to be at peace with God while at odds with a brother (see Matt. 5:23-24; 1 John 4:20).

Third, by sharing the gospel, true followers of Christ also help others make peace with God and their fellow man.

---

1 Interestingly, the very next verse in the book of James is, "What use is it, my brethren, if a man says he has faith, but he has no works? Can that faith save him?" (Jas. 2:14).

The Persecuted

Finally, Jesus called *blessed* those who are persecuted for the sake of righteousness. Obviously, He was speaking of people who are *living* righteously, as they are the ones whom nonbelievers persecute. Those are the sort of people who will inherit God's kingdom.

What kind of persecution was Jesus talking about? Torture? Martyrdom? No, He specifically spoke of the persecution of being insulted and spoken against on His account. This means that when a person is a true Christian, it is obvious to nonbelievers, otherwise nonbelievers wouldn't say evil things against him. How many so-called Christians are so indistinguishable from nonbelievers that not a single unbeliever speaks against them? They are not really Christians at all. Jesus warned, "Woe to you when all men speak well of you, for in the same way their fathers used to treat the false prophets" (Luke 6:26). When all men speak well of you, that's a sign that you're a false believer. The world hates true Christians (see also John 15:18-21; Gal. 4:29; 2 Tim. 3:12; 1 John 3:13-14).

Does anyone hate you? This is a sermon about salvation, holiness, and the relationship between the two.

Salt and Light

In the next few verses, Jesus continued describing His true followers, the blessed ones, comparing them to salt and light. Both have certain obvious characteristics. Salt is salty and light shines. If it isn't salty, it isn't salt. If it doesn't shine, it's not light.

> You are the salt of the earth; but if the salt has become tasteless, how can it be made salty again? It is no longer good for anything, except to be thrown out and trampled under foot by men. You are the light of the world. A city set on a hill cannot be hidden; nor does anyone light a lamp and put it under a basket, but on the lamp stand, and it gives light to all who are in the house. Let your light shine before men in such a way that they may see your good works, and glorify your Father who is in heaven (Matt. 5:13-16).

In Jesus' time, salt was used primarily as a preservative of meats. As obedient followers of Christ, we are what preserves this sinful world from becoming completely rotten and corrupt. But if we become like the world in our behavior, we are truly good for nothing. Jesus warned the blessed to remain salty, preserving their unique characteristics. They must remain distinct from the world around them, lest they become "unsalty," deserving to be "thrown out and trampled under foot." This is one of many clear warnings against backsliding directed at true believers that is found in the New Testament. If salt is truly salt, it is salty. Likewise, followers of Jesus act like followers of Jesus, otherwise they aren't followers of Jesus, even if they once were.

Christ's true followers are also the light of the world. Light *always* shines. If it isn't shining, it isn't light. In this analogy, light represents our good works (see Matt. 5:16). Christ admonished His followers to do their good works so that others would see them. That way they would glorify their heavenly Father because He is the source of their good works.

Notice Jesus didn't say we should *create* light, but to let the light we have shine before others so that they'll see our light. He wasn't exhorting those who have no works to drum some up, but exhorting those who have good works not to hide their goodness. Christ's followers *are* the light of the world. They are blessed, by God's grace, to be lights in darkness.

The Importance of Keeping God's Commandments

Now we begin a new paragraph (in the NASB). Here, Jesus began talking about the Law and its relationship to His followers.

> Do not think that I came to abolish the Law or the Prophets; I did not come to abolish but to fulfill. For truly I say to you, until heaven and earth pass away, not the smallest letter or stroke shall pass from the Law until all is accomplished. Whoever then annuls one of the least of these commandments, and teaches others to do the same, shall be called least in the kingdom of heaven; but whoever keeps and teaches them, he shall be called great in the kingdom of heaven. For I say to you that unless your righteousness surpasses that of the scribes and Pharisees, you will not enter the kingdom of heaven (Matt. 5:17-20).

If Jesus warned His audience against thinking that He was abolishing the Law or the Prophets, then we can safely conclude that at least some in His audience were making that assumption. Why they were making such an assumption we can only guess. Perhaps it was His stern rebukes of the scripture-twisting scribes and Pharisees that tempted some to think He was abolishing the Law and Prophets.

Regardless, Jesus clearly wanted everyone in His audience to realize the error of such an assumption. He was God, the divine in-spirer of the entire Old Testament, so certainly He was not going to abolish everything He'd said through Moses and the Prophets. On the contrary, He would fulfill the Law and Prophets.

Exactly how would He fulfill the Law and Prophets? Some think that Jesus was talking only about fulfilling the messianic predictions. Although Jesus certainly did (or will yet) fulfill every messianic pre-diction, that is not entirely what He had in mind. Clearly, the context indicates He was also talking about *all* that was written in the Law and Prophets, down to "smallest letter or stroke" (v. 18) of the Law, and to the "least of" (v. 19) the commandments.

Others theorize Jesus meant that He would fulfill the Law by ful-filling its requirements on our behalf through His obedient life and sacrificial death. But this, as the context also reveals, is not what He had in mind. In the verses the follow, Jesus mentions nothing about His life or death as being a reference point for the fulfilling of the Law. Rather, in the very next sentence, He states that the Law will be valid at least until "heaven and earth pass away" and "all is ac-complished."

So what did Jesus mean when He declared that He would fulfill the Law? Jesus would fulfill the Law by revealing God's true and original intent in it, filling back "to the full" what the scribes and Pharisees had effectively emptied from it. He would fully endorse and explain it, and completing what was lacking in peoples' under-standing of it.[2] The Greek word translated *fulfill* in verse 17 is also translated in the New Testament as *complete, finish, fill*, and *fully carry out*. That is exactly what Jesus was about to do, beginning just four sentences later.

No, Jesus did not come to abolish the Law, but to fulfill it, that is, "fill it to the full." Concerning the commandments found in the Law and Prophets, Jesus couldn't have made His point more forcefully. He expected everyone to obey them. They were as important as ever. In fact, how one esteems the commandments will determine how he is esteemed in heaven: "Whoever then annuls one of the least of these commandments, and so teaches others, shall be called least in the kingdom of heaven; but whoever keeps and teaches them, he

2 This would be true of what is often referred to as the "ceremonial law" as well as the "moral law," al-though much of His fuller explanation concerning the ceremonial law would be given by His Holy Spirit to the apostles after His resurrection. We now understand why there is no need to sacrifice animals under the new covenant, because Jesus was the Lamb of God. Neither do we follow the old covenant dietary laws because Jesus declared all foods to be clean (see Mark 7:19). We don't need the intercession of an earthly high priest because Jesus is now our High Priest, and so on. Unlike the ceremonial law, however, no part of the moral law was ever annulled or altered by anything Jesus did or said, before of after His death and resurrection. Rather, Jesus expounded upon and endorsed God's moral law, as did the apostles by the inspiration of the Spirit after His resurrection.

shall be called great in the kingdom of heaven" (5:19).[3]

Then we come to verse 20: "For I say to you, that unless your righteousness surpasses that of the scribes and Pharisees, you shall not enter the kingdom of heaven."

Notice that this is not a new thought, but a concluding statement that is connected with previous verses by the conjunction *for*. How important is keeping the commandments? *One must keep them better than the scribes and Pharisees in order to enter the kingdom of heaven.* Again we see that this is a sermon about salvation and holiness, and how they are related.

Of What Kind of Righteousness Was Jesus Speaking?

When Jesus stated that our righteousness must surpass that of the scribes and Pharisees, was He not alluding to the legal righteousness that would be imputed to us as a free gift? No, He was not, for at least two good reasons. First, the context does not fit this interpretation. Before and after this statement (and throughout the entire Sermon on the Mount), Jesus was talking about keeping the commandments, that is, living righteously. The most natural interpretation of His words is that we must live more righteously than the scribes and Pharisees.

Second, if Jesus was talking about the imputed, legal righteousness that we receive as a gift for believing in Him, why didn't He at least hint at it? Why did He say something that would be so easily misunderstood by the uneducated people to whom He was speaking, who would have never guessed that He was talking about imputed righteousness?

Our problem is that we don't want to accept the obvious meaning of the verse, because it sounds to us like legalism. But our real problem is that we don't understand the inseparable correlation between imputed righteousness and practical righteousness. The apostle John did, however. He wrote: "Little children, let no one deceive you; the one who practices righteousness is righteous" (1 John 3:7). Nor do we understand the correlation between the new birth and practical righteousness as John did: "Everyone also who practices righteousness is born of Him" (1 John 2:29).

Jesus could have added to His statement of 5:20, "And if you repent, are truly born again, and receive through a living faith My free gift of righteousness, your practical righteousness will indeed

---

3 Although Jesus' words here are a strong motivation not to annul or teach others to disregard any commandment, including lesser ones, His words also offer hope that heaven's population will include people who have been guilty of that very thing.

exceed that of the scribes and Pharisees as you cooperate with the power of My indwelling Spirit."

The Righteousness of the Scribes and Pharisees

The other important question that is naturally raised by Jesus' statement in Matthew 5:20 is this: How righteous (practically speaking) were the scribes and Pharisees?

At another time, Jesus referred to them as "whitewashed tombs which on the outside appear beautiful, but inside they are full of dead men's bones and all uncleanness" (Matt. 23:27). That is, they appeared outwardly righteous but were inwardly evil. They did a great job at keeping the letter of the Law, but ignored the spirit of it, often justifying themselves by twisting or even altering God's commands.

This Jesus brought to light in the next portion of the Sermon on the Mount. He quoted several of God's commandments, and then showed the difference between keeping the letter and spirit of them. Jesus showed how the scribes and Pharisees interpreted and outwardly obeyed each law, and then revealed what was God's true intent in each case. He began each example with the words, "You have heard," and then told God's view of what they had heard. The sixth commandment is the subject of His first example:

> You have heard that the ancients were told, "You shall not commit murder" and "Whoever commits murder shall be liable to the court." But I say to you that everyone who is angry with his brother shall be guilty before the court; and whoever shall say to his brother, "Raca," shall be guilty before the supreme court; and whoever shall say, "You fool," shall be guilty enough to go into the fiery hell. If therefore you are presenting your offering at the altar, and there remember that your brother has something against you, leave your offering there before the altar, and go your way; first be reconciled to your brother, and then come and present your offering. Make friends quickly with your opponent at law while you are with him on the way, in order that your opponent may not deliver you to the judge, and the judge to the officer, and you be thrown into prison. Truly I say to you, you shall not come out of there, until you have paid up the last cent (Matt. 5:21-26).

The scribes and Pharisees prided themselves that they were not murderers. That is, they never actually killed anyone. In their minds, they were keeping the sixth commandment. They would have *loved* to kill, however, if it wasn't prohibited, as revealed by the fact that they did everything *but* murder those they hated. Jesus listed a few examples of their murderous behavior. From their mouths they spewed forth vicious words of contempt toward those with whom they were angry. They were inwardly bitter, unforgiving and irreconcilable, embroiled in lawsuits, either suing or being sued for their murderously selfish actions.[4] The scribes and Pharisees were murderers at heart who had only restrained themselves from the physical act.

The truly righteous person, however, is much different. His standard is much higher. He knows God expects him to love his brother, and if his relationship with his brother isn't right, his relationship with God isn't right. He won't hypocritically go through the motions of his religion, pretending to love God while he hates a brother (see Matt. 5:23-24). As the apostle John would later write, "The one who does not love his brother whom he has seen, cannot love God whom he has not seen" (1 John 4:20).

The scribes and Pharisees thought that only by the act of murder could they incur guilt. But Jesus warned that the *attitude* of a murderer makes one worthy of hell. True Christians are blessed of God to the degree that He puts His love in them, making them lovers (see Rom. 5:5), all by His grace.

God's Definition of Adultery

The seventh commandment was the object of Jesus' second example of how the scribes and Pharisees kept the letter while neglecting the spirit of the Law:

> You have heard that it was said, "You shall not commit adultery"; but I say to you, that everyone who looks on a woman to lust for her has committed adultery with her already in his heart. And if your right eye makes you stumble, tear it out, and throw it from you; for it is better for you that one of the parts of your body perish, than for your whole body to be thrown into hell. And if your right hand makes you stumble, cut it off, and throw it from you; for it is better

---

4 It is possible that Jesus was intimating that the scribes and Pharisees, so at home in the courtroom, needed to realize that they were heading for God's courtroom, and that they were quite disadvantaged to have Him as their "opponent at law." He thus warned them to settle out of court, lest they face the eternal consequences.

for you that one of the parts of your body perish, than for your whole body to go into hell (Matt. 5:27-30).

First, note once again that this is a sermon about salvation and holiness, and the relationship between the two. Jesus warned about hell, and what one must *do* to stay out of it. That is crystal clear.

The scribes and Pharisees couldn't ignore the seventh commandment, so they outwardly obeyed it, remaining faithful to their wives. Yet they fantasized about making love to other women. They would mentally undress women they watched in the marketplace. They were adulterers at heart, and thus were transgressing the spirit of the seventh commandment. (How many professing Christians are no different?)

God, of course, intended for His people to be completely sexually pure. Obviously, as I've stated earlier in this book, if it is wrong to have a sexual relationship with your neighbor's wife, it is also wrong to dream of yourself having a sexual relationship with her.

Were any among Jesus' audience convicted? Probably they were. What should they do? They should immediately repent as Jesus instructed. Whatever it took, no matter what the cost, those who were lustful should stop lusting, because those who are lustful go to hell.

Of course, no reasonable person thinks Jesus meant that lustful people should literally pluck out an eye or cut off a hand. A lustful person who cuts out his eye simply becomes a one-eyed luster. Jesus was dramatically and solemnly emphasizing the importance of obeying the spirit of the seventh commandment. Eternity depended on it.

Are you convicted? Then "cut off" whatever it is that is causing you to stumble. If it's cable TV, get the cable disconnected. If it's regular TV, then throw out your TV. If it's what you see when you go to a certain place, stop going there. If it's a magazine subscription, cancel it. If it's the Iinternet, get off line. None of those things are worth spending eternity in hell. No one in hell is going to say, "Yeah, I'm in hell, but I sure enjoyed a lot of sexually-explicit movies when I was on the earth. I've got no regrets, even though my sin will have eternal consequences.

God's View of Divorce

Jesus' next example is very much related to the one that we just considered, which is probably why it is mentioned next. It should be considered a further elaboration rather than a new subject. The subject is, "Another thing people do that is equivalent to adultery":

And it was said, "Whoever sends his wife away, let him give her a certificate of divorce"; but I say to you that everyone who divorces his wife, except for the cause of unchastity, makes her commit adultery; and whoever marries a divorced woman commits adultery (Matt. 5:31-32).

Here is another illustration of how the scribes and Pharisees kept the letter of the law while rejecting the spirit of it.

Let's create an imaginary Pharisee in Jesus' day. Across the street from him lives an attractive woman after whom he has been lusting. He flirts with her when he sees her each day. She seems attracted to him, and his desire for her grows. He would love to see her unclothed, and imagines her regularly in his sexual fantasies. Oh, if he could only have her!

But he has a problem. He is married and so is she, and his religion forbids adultery. He doesn't want to break the seventh commandment (even though he's already broken it every time he's lusted). What can he do?

There is a solution! If they both were divorced from their present spouses, he could marry the mistress of his mind! But is it lawful to get a divorce? Yes! There is a scripture for it! Deuteronomy 24:1 talks about giving your wife a divorce certificate when you divorce her. Divorce must be lawful under certain circumstances! But what are those circumstances? He reads closely what God said:

When a man takes a wife and marries her, and it happens that she finds no favor in his eyes because he has found some indecency in her, and he writes her a certificate of divorce and puts it in her hand and sends her out from his house... (Deut. 24:1).

Ahah! He can divorce his wife if he finds some indecency in her! And he has! She's not as attractive as the woman across the street![5]

And so he lawfully divorces his wife by giving her the required certificate (you can pick one up in the lobby of the local office of the Pharisees' Club), and quickly marries the woman of his fantasies, herself just legally divorced. And all without incurring an ounce of guilt because God's Law has been obeyed.

---

5 This is not a far-fetched example. According to Rabbi Hillel, who had the most popular teaching regarding divorce in Jesus' day, a man could lawfully divorce his wife if he found someone prettier, because that made his current wife "indecent" in his eyes. Rabbi Hillel also taught a man could divorce his wife if she put too much salt on his food, or spoke to another man, or didn't produce a son for him.

But, of course, God sees things differently. The "indecency" of which He spoke in Deuteronomy 24:1-4 for lawful divorce was something very immoral, probably something just short of adultery.[6] That is, a husband could lawfully divorce his wife if he discovered that she was promiscuous before or during their marriage.

In God's mind, the imaginary man I've just described is no different than an adulterer. He has broken the seventh commandment. In fact, he's even more guilty than the average adulterer. He is guilty of "double adultery." How is that? First, he's committed adultery himself. Jesus later said, "Whoever divorces his wife, except for immorality, and marries another woman commits adultery" (Matt. 19:9).

Second, because his now-divorced wife must seek another husband to survive, in God's mind the Pharisee has done the equivalent of forcing his wife to have sex with another man. Thus, he incurs guilt for her "adultery."[7] Jesus said, "Everyone who divorces his wife, except for the cause of unchastity, *makes* her commit adultery" (Matt. 5:32, emphasis added).

Jesus may even have been charging our lustful Pharisee with "triple adultery" if His statement, "and whoever marries a divorced woman commits adultery" (Matt. 5:32), means that God holds the Pharisee accountable for the "adultery" of his former wife's new husband.[8]

This was a hot issue in Jesus' day, as we read in another place where some Pharisees questioned Him, "Is it lawful for a man to divorce his wife for any cause at all?" (Matt. 19:3). Their question reveals their hearts. Obviously, at least some of them wanted to believe any cause was a lawful cause for divorce.

I must also add what a shame it is when Christians take these same scriptures about divorce, misinterpret them, and place heavy shackles on God's children. Jesus was not talking about the Christian who was divorced when he or she was a sinner, and who, upon finding a wonderful potential mate who also loves Christ, marries that person. That is not anywhere close to being equivalent to adultery. And if that is what Jesus was talking about, we'll have to change the gospel, because no longer does it provide forgiveness for all the sins

---

6 Under the Old Covenant, those who committed adultery were to be stoned.

7 Of course, God doesn't hold her accountable for adultery when she remarries; she was just the victim of her husband's sin. Obviously, Jesus' words make no sense unless she does remarry. Otherwise, there is no sense in which she could be considered to be an adulteress.

8 Again, God would not hold the new husband accountable for adultery. He's doing a virtuous thing, marrying and providing for a divorced woman. However, if a man encouraged a woman to divorce her husband so he could marry her, then he would be guilty of adultery, and that is more likely the sin Jesus had in mind here.

of sinners. From now on we'll have to preach, "Jesus died for you, and if you repent and believe in Him, you can have all your sins forgiven. *However*, if you've been divorced, make sure you never get remarried or else you'll be living in adultery, and the Bible says that adulterers will go to hell. Also, if you've been divorced *and* remarried, before you come to Christ you need to commit one more sin and divorce your present spouse. Otherwise you'll continue to live in adultery, and adulterers aren't saved."[9] Is that the gospel?

On Being Truthful

Jesus' third example of the unrighteous conduct and scriptural misapplication of the scribes and Pharisees is related to God's commandment to tell the truth. The scribes and Pharisees had developed a very creative way to lie. We learn from Matthew 23:16-22 their belief that they were not obligated to keep their vows if they swore by the temple, the altar, or heaven. However, if they swore by the *gold* in the temple, the *offering* on the altar, or by *God* in heaven, they *were* obligated to keep their vow! It was an adult equivalent of a child's thinking he is exempt from having to tell the truth as long as his fingers are crossed behind his back.

This item of hypocrisy was next in Jesus' most famous sermon:

> Again, you have heard that the ancients were told, '"You shall not make false vows, but shall fulfill your vows to the Lord." But I say to you, make no oath at all, either by heaven, for it is the throne of God, or by the earth, for it is the footstool of His feet, or by Jerusalem, for it is the city of the great King. Nor shall you make an oath by your head, for you cannot make one hair white or black. But let your statement be, "Yes, yes" or "No, no"; and anything beyond these is of evil (Matt. 5:33-37).

Of course, there is nothing wrong with making a vow, which is simply a promise. Jesus was not contradicting the Old Testament Law that He inspired, saying that it is now wrong to make any vows. Rather, He was correcting the practice of the scribes and Pharisees of swearing with an oath. God's original commandment concerning vows said nothing about making an oath by swearing. God simply intended for His people to keep their word. When people have to swear with an oath to convince others to believe them, it is an outright admission that they often lie. Our word should be good, need-

---

9 There are, of course, other situations that could be addressed. For example, the Christian woman whose unsaved husband divorces her is certainly not guilty of adultery if she remarries a Christian man.

ing no oath-swearing. Does your righteousness exceed that of the scribes and Pharisees in this area?

The Sin of Revenge

The next item on Jesus' list of grievances was a Pharisaic perversion of a very well-known verse in the Old Testament.

> You have heard that it was said, "An eye for an eye, and a tooth for a tooth." But I say to you, do not resist him who is evil; but whoever slaps you on your right cheek, turn to him the other also. And if anyone wants to sue you, and take your shirt, let him have your coat also. And whoever shall force you to go one mile, go with him two. Give to him who asks of you, and do not turn away from him who wants to borrow from you (Matt. 5:38-42).

The Law of Moses declared that when a person was found guilty in court of injuring another person, his punishment should be equivalent to the harm he caused. If he knocked out someone's tooth, in fairness and justice, his tooth should be knocked out. This commandment was given to insure that justice would be served in court cases for major offenses. Once again, however, the scribes and Pharisees had twisted it, turning it into a commandment that made getting revenge a holy obligation. Apparently, they'd adopted a "zero tolerance" policy, seeking revenge for even the smallest offenses.

God, however, has always expected more from His people. Revenge is something He expressly forbids (see Deut. 32:35). The Old Testament taught that God's people should show kindness to their enemies (see Ex. 23:4-5; Prov. 25:21-22). Jesus endorsed this truth by telling us to turn the other cheek and go the extra mile when we are dealing with evil people. When we are wronged, God wants us to be merciful, returning good for evil.

But does Jesus expect us to allow people to take gross advantage of us, allowing them to ruin our lives if they desire? Is it wrong to take a nonbeliever to court, seeking justice for an illegal act committed against us? No. Jesus was not talking about obtaining due justice for major offenses in court (something endorsed by the Mosaic Law that He inspired), but about getting personal revenge for petty, ordinary infractions. Notice that Jesus did not say that we should offer our neck for strangling to someone who has just stabbed us in the back. He didn't say we should give someone our house when they demand our car. Jesus was simply telling us to show tolerance and mercy to a high degree when we daily encounter petty offenses and the normal challenges of dealing with selfish people. He doesn't expect us to "go the extra hundred miles," but "go the extra one mile." He wants us to be more kind than selfish people expect, and be unselfish with our money, generously giving and lending it. To this standard, the scribes and Pharisees didn't come close. Does your righteousness exceed theirs in this area?

Loving Our Neighbors

Finally, Jesus listed one more God-given commandment that the scribes and Pharisees had altered to accommodate their hateful hearts:

> You have heard that it was said, "You shall love your neighbor, and hate your enemy." But I say to you, love your enemies, and pray for those who persecute you in order that you may be sons of your Father who is in heaven; for He causes His sun to rise on the evil and the good, and sends rain on the righteous and the unrighteous. For if you love those who love you, what reward have you? Do not even the tax-gatherers do the same? And if you greet your brothers only, what do you do more than others? Do not even the Gentiles do the same? Therefore you are to be perfect, as your heavenly Father is perfect (Matt. 5:43-48).

In the Old Testament, God had said, "Love your neighbor" (Lev. 19:18), but the scribes and Pharisees had conveniently assumed that if God wanted them to love their neighbors, He must have meant for them to hate their enemies. It was their holy obligation. According to Jesus, however, that is not at all what God meant, and that is not what He said.

Jesus would later teach in the story of the Good Samaritan that we should consider *every* person to be our neighbor. God wants us to love *everyone*, including our enemies. That is God's standard for His children, a standard by which He Himself lives. He sends crop-growing sun and rain, not only on good people, but also on evil people. We should follow His example, showing kindness to undeserving people. When we do, it shows that we are "sons of [our] Father who is in heaven" (Matt. 5:45). Authentic born-again people act like their Father.

The love God expects us to show our enemies is not an emotion or an approval of wickedness. God is not requiring us to have warm fuzzy feelings about those who oppose us. He is not telling us to say what is untrue, that our enemies are really wonderful people. But He does expect that we will love them and take willful action to that end, at least by greeting them and praying for them.

What About You?

By now you realize that the scribes and Pharisees weren't very righteous at all. They had some degree of outward righteousness, but, like too many professing Christians, they were hateful, lustful, selfish, revengeful, unmerciful, greedy, Scripture-twisting liars. According to Jesus, however, true believers are characterized as gentle, hungering for righteousness, merciful, pure in heart, peacemaking, and persecuted. Thus, this part of the Sermon on the Mount should either fill you with assurance that you've been truly born again, or fill you with terror because you realize you are no different than those whom Jesus condemned. If you are in the former category, you, like everyone else in that category, know you still have room for improvement. But perfection is your goal because it is God's goal for you, as Jesus said (see Matt. 5:48; see also Phil. 3:12-14).

If you are in the latter category, you can repent and become a slave of Jesus' by believing in Him. You will instantly experience being moved by God into the former category by His grace!

SEVEN

Jesus' Greatest Salvation Sermon Continues

How many pastors would consider it complimentary if someone labeled them a "holiness preacher"? How many professing
Christians would use such a term in a way that is not derogatory?
Why is holiness such a negative topic in the minds of so many people who claim to believe in a book that contains the words *holy* or
holiness over six-hundred times, which promises them a future in a
holy city where resides the "holy One," whose very name is *holy*, who
gives them His *Holy* Spirit, and whose *holy* throne is surrounded by
four living creatures who day and night do not cease to say, "Holy,
holy, holy, is the Lord God, the Almighty"? (see Rev. 21:2; Is. 40:25;
Lev. 22:32; 1 Thes. 4:8; Ps. 47:8; Rev. 4:8, emphasis added).

If the first portion of the Sermon on the Mount has taught us anything, it has taught us that Jesus was a holiness preacher. That was
His topic—holiness and how it relates to salvation.

The Sermon on the Mount is recorded in Matthew's Gospel, chapters 5, 6 and 7. So far we've considered only chapter 5. There, in the
Beatitudes, we learned the characteristics of the heaven-bound. We
also discovered that Jesus did not come to abolish the Law, and that
keeping the commandments is as important as ever. We learned that
we will not enter the kingdom of heaven unless our righteousness
exceeds that of the scribes and Pharisees, who kept the letter but

ignored the spirit of the Law.

The second part of the Sermon on the Mount, Matthew 6 and the first half of chapter 7, consists of more commandments Christ gave to His followers. Does keeping them have anything to do with salvation? It certainly does. The entire last half of chapter 7 makes that point unmistakably clear, as we will see.

Let's continue reading what Jesus commanded His true followers, those who believed He was God's Son, the Messiah. We can, and should, ask the very revealing question: *If Jesus' audience didn't believe in Him, why else would they obey Him?* Why would they even listen to Him make demands that would affect every area of their lives? The answer is obvious: *Because they believed, they wanted to obey.* They would show their faith by their works.

Chapter Six Begins

Notice in this first section that Jesus assumes His followers will practice righteousness, and warns them to make sure their motive is to please God rather than impress men:

> Beware of practicing your righteousness before men to be noticed by them; otherwise you have no reward with your Father who is in heaven. When therefore you give alms, do not sound a trumpet before you, as the hypocrites do in the synagogues and in the streets, that they may be honored by men. Truly I say to you, they have their reward in full. But when you give alms, do not let your left hand know what your right hand is doing that your alms may be in secret; and your Father who sees in secret will repay you (Matt. 6:1-4).

Jesus fully expected that His followers would give alms to the poor (as we learned in chapter three of this book). The Law commanded it (see Ex. 23:11; Lev. 19:10; 23:22; 25:35; Deut. 15:7-11), and the scribes and Pharisees did it with the blowing of trumpets, ostensibly to call the poor to their public distributions. Yet how many professing Christians (and professing Christian churches) give *nothing* to the poor? They haven't even made it to the point of needing to examine their motives for alms giving. If selfishness motivated the scribes and Pharisees to advertise their alms giving, what is it that motivates professing Christians to *ignore* the plight of the poor? Does our righteousness surpass that of the scribes and Pharisees?

As Paul would echo in 1 Corinthians 3:10-15, we can do good

works that will go unrewarded if our motives are not pure. True followers of Christ should have pure motives in every good deed, but not all do. Paul wrote that it is possible even to preach the gospel from impure motives (see Phil. 1:15-17). The best way to be sure our giving is purely motivated is to give as secretively as possible.

Jesus also expected that His followers would pray and fast. That was a given. He did not say, "*If* you pray," but "*When* you pray." The danger was that they might allow their motives to become tainted, as were the motives of unregenerate people who prayed and fasted. If that happened, they would lose the reward they would have received had their motives been pure. So He admonished them:

> And when you pray, you are not to be as the hypocrites; for they love to stand and pray in the synagogues and on the street corners, in order to be seen by men. Truly I say to you, they have their reward in full. But you, when you pray, go into your inner room, and when you have shut your door, pray to your Father who is in secret, and your Father who sees in secret will repay you. And when you are praying, do not use meaningless repetition, as the Gentiles do, for they suppose that they will be heard for their many words. Therefore do not be like them; for your Father knows what you need, before you ask Him...

> And whenever you fast, do not put on a gloomy face as the hypocrites do, for they neglect their appearance in order to be seen fasting by men. Truly I say to you, they have their reward in full. But you, when you fast, anoint your head, and wash your face, so that you may not be seen fasting by men, but by your Father who is in secret; and your Father who sees in secret will repay you (Matt. 6:5-8, 16-18).

Again, how many professing Christians rarely spend time in prayer and have never fasted? How does their righteousness compare with that of the scribes and Pharisees, who practiced both (albeit for the wrong reasons)?

Holy Praying

Jesus also told His disciples how they should pray. His model prayer is a telling revelation of His expectations for their devotion, obedience and priorities:[1]

---

[1] Some unfortunately claim that this is not a prayer that Christians should employ because it is not prayed "in Jesus' name." Applying this logic, however, we would have to conclude that many prayers of the apostles recorded in the book of Acts and epistles were not "Christian prayers."

Pray, then, in this way: "Our Father who art in heaven, hallowed be Thy name. Thy kingdom come. Thy will be done,
on earth as it is in heaven. Give us this day our daily bread"
(Matt. 6:9-11).

The true disciple's foremost concern should be that God's name
be hallowed. That is, that God's name be respected, revered, and
treated as holy.

Of course, those who pray that God's name be hallowed should
be holy, hallowing God's name themselves. It would be hypocritical to do otherwise. Thus this prayer reflects our desire that others
would submit themselves to God as we have. And, as I asked in a
previous chapter, to what degree does a person reflect his longing for
God's name to be hallowed when he entertains himself by viewing
actors who continually blaspheme the name of God and His Son?
According to my observations, this is something that many professing Christians do with regularity. Would you be offended by a movie
where the actors used *your* name as a swear word?

The second request of the prayer is similar: "Thy kingdom come."
The idea of a kingdom implies the idea of a King who rules His kingdom. The Christian disciple longs to see his King, the one who rules
his life, rule over the whole earth. Oh, that everyone would bow
their knee to King Jesus in obedient faith!

The third request echoes the first and second: "Thy will be done,
on earth as it is in heaven." Again, how can we sincerely pray such a
prayer without being submitted to God's will in our own lives? The
true disciple desires that God's will be done on earth just as it is in
heaven—perfectly and completely.

That God's name be hallowed, that His will be done, that His
kingdom would come, should be more important to us than sustain-
ing food, our "daily bread." This fourth request is placed fourth for
a reason. Even in itself, it reflects a right ordering of our priorities,
and no hint of greed is found here. This praying disciple serves God
and not mammon.

The Model Prayer Continues

So far the theme of holiness streams from every supplication of
the Lord's Prayer. And it continues to flow from its final lines:

"And forgive us our debts, as we also have forgiven our
debtors. And do not lead us into temptation, but deliver us

from evil. For Thine is the kingdom, and the power, and the glory, forever. Amen." For if you forgive men for their transgressions, your heavenly Father will also forgive you. But if you do not forgive men, then your Father will not forgive your transgressions (Matt. 6:12-15).

Jesus' true disciple desires to be holy, so when he sins, it troubles him greatly.[2] He realizes that his disobedience has offended God, and he feels ashamed. He wants the stain of unholiness to be removed, and thankfully, his gracious heavenly Father is willing to forgive him. But he must ask for forgiveness, the fifth request found in the Lord's prayer.

Our being forgiven, however, is conditional upon our forgiving others. Because we've been forgiven of so much, we have an obligation to forgive everyone who requests our forgiveness, and to love even those who don't. If we refuse to forgive, God won't forgive us. Do unforgiven people gain entrance into God's eternal kingdom? Again we see that this is a sermon about holiness, salvation, and the relationship between the two.

The sixth and final request, too, is one obviously related to holiness: "Do not lead us into temptation, but deliver us from evil" [or "the evil one"]. So much does the true disciple long for holiness that he asks God not to lead him into a situation where he might be tempted, lest he succumb. Additionally, he requests that God would rescue him from any evil that might entrap him. This final request of Jesus' model prayer is certainly nothing less than a cry for God's help to be holy.

Why are all six requests of this prayer appropriate? The final line tells us: God is a great King who rules over His kingdom in which we are His servants. He is all-powerful, and no one should dare resist His will. All glory will belong to Him forever: "For Thine is the kingdom, and the power, and the glory, forever" (Matt. 6:13). He is worthy to be obeyed.

What is the dominant theme of the Lord's prayer? Holiness. Christ's disciples desire that God's name be hallowed, that His reign would be established over the earth, and that His will be perfectly done everywhere. This is more important to them than even their daily bread. They want to be pleasing in His sight, and when they fail, they want forgiveness from Him. As forgiven people, they extend forgiveness to others. They long to be perfectly holy, to the

---

2 This verse is one of many that tell us that true disciples are not perfect or sinless. However, it also proves that true believers are concerned when they do sin.

degree that they desire to avoid temptation, because temptation increases their chances of sinning.

The Disciple and His Material Possessions

The next topic of the Sermon on the Mount is perhaps the most disturbing section for professing Christians whose primary motivation in life is the accumulation of things:

> Do not lay up for yourselves treasures upon earth, where moth and rust destroy, and where thieves break in and steal. But lay up for yourselves treasures in heaven, where neither moth nor rust destroys, and where thieves do not break in or steal; for where your treasure is, there will your heart be also. The lamp of the body is the eye; if therefore your eye is clear, your whole body will be full of light. But if your eye is bad, your whole body will be full of darkness. If therefore the light that is in you is darkness, how great is the darkness! No one can serve two masters; for either he will hate the one and love the other, or he will hold to one and despise the other. You cannot serve God and mammon (Matt. 6:19-24).

Jesus commanded that we not lay up for ourselves treasures upon earth. What then constitutes a "treasure"? Literal treasures are normally kept in treasure chests, stored away somewhere, never used for anything practical. Jesus defined them as things that attract moths, rust and thieves. Another way of saying it would be, "nonessentials." Moths eat what is in our attic and the far ends of our closets, not what we wear frequently. Rust eats away at the toys and "tools" we never use, piled in the corners of basements, garages and storage sheds. Thieves break in and steal things people really don't need: art, jewelry, expensive gadgets, and what can be pawned. They normally don't take beds, stoves, food or tennis shoes (at least they don't in wealthy nations such as ours).

The point is that we are God's and so is everything we "own." We are stewards of God's money, so every decision to spend money is a spiritual decision. What we do with our money reflects who is controlling our lives. When we accumulate "treasures," hoarding money and buying what is not essential, we reveal that Jesus is not in control, because if He was, we would do better things with the money He's entrusted to us.

What are those better things? Jesus commands us to lay up treasure in heaven. How can we do that? He tells us in Luke's Gospel: "Sell your possessions and give to charity; make yourselves purses which do not wear out, an unfailing treasure in heaven, where no thief comes near, nor moth destroys" (Luke 12:33). By giving to charity, we lay up treasure in heaven. Jesus is telling us to take what is sure to depreciate to the point of being worthless, and invest it in something that will never depreciate. How many professing Christians are doing that? Why do the large majority of professing Christians in North America, who enjoy one of the highest standards of living in the world, not even give anywhere close to a tenth of their income, which was required under the Law?[3]

The Bad Eye

What did Jesus mean when He spoke about the eye being "the lamp of the body"? His words must have something to do with how we view money and material things, because that is what He was talking about before and after.

Just as He first contrasted the person who lays up earthly treasures with the person who lays up heavenly treasures, Jesus was again contrasting two kinds of people, one with a clear eye whose body is full of light, and one with a bad eye whose body is full of darkness. In the verses that immediately follow, He also contrasts two people, saved and unsaved, one who serves God and one who serves money. Thus it is safe to conclude that the person with the clear eye corresponds to the one who lays up treasures in heaven and who serves God, while the one with the bad eye corresponds to the one who lays up treasures on earth and serves money.

From other scriptures, we learn that an "evil eye" is an idiom for having a greedy heart (see Matt. 20:15 and Prov. 28:22). A "clear eye" is the opposite, so it must signify one who does not have a greedy heart. A person with a clear eye is full of light, that is, truth, whereas the person with the evil eye is full of darkness. Remember, he is the same person who is laying up treasures on earth. He is the same person whose god is money.

What does it mean to have money as your god? It means that money has a place in your life that only God should rightfully have. Money is directing your life. It consumes your energy, thoughts and

---

3 According to a Gallup poll, only 25% of evangelical Christians tithe. Forty percent claim that God is the most important thing in their lives, yet those who make between $50-75,000 per year give an average of 1.5 percent of their incomes to charity, including religious charity. Meanwhile, they spend an average of 12% of their incomes on leisure pursuits. George Barna reports in his book, *The Second Coming of the Church*, that his polls indicate that non-Christians are actually more likely than born-again Christians to give to nonprofit organizations and the poor.

time. It is the main source of your joy. You love it.[4] That is why Paul equated greed with idolatry, stating that no greedy person will inherit God's kingdom (see Eph. 5:5; Col. 3:5-6).

In this passage, Jesus is not contrasting two kinds of Christians. He is contrasting a true believer with an unbeliever. Those who are laying up treasures on earth are full of darkness and not serving God, but money. They reveal their unbelief by what they do. Again, this is a sermon about holiness, salvation, and the relationship between them.

The Covetous Poor

A preoccupation with material things is not only wrong if those things are luxury items. A person can be wrongly preoccupied with material things even when those things are basic necessities. Jesus continued:

> For this reason I say to you, do not be anxious for your life, as to what you shall eat, or what you shall drink; nor for your body, as to what you shall put on. Is not life more than food, and the body than clothing? Look at the birds of the air, that they do not sow, neither do they reap, nor gather into barns, and yet your heavenly Father feeds them. Are you not worth much more than they? And which of you by being anxious can add a single cubit to his life's span? And why are you anxious about clothing? Observe how the lilies of the field grow; they do not toil nor do they spin, yet I say to you that even Solomon in all his glory did not clothe himself like one of these. But if God so arrays the grass of the field, which is alive today and tomorrow is thrown into the furnace, will He not much more do so for you, O men of little faith? Do not be anxious then, saying, "What shall we eat?" or "What shall we drink?" or "With what shall we clothe ourselves?" For all these things the Gentiles eagerly seek; for your heavenly Father knows that you need all these things. But seek first His kingdom and His righteousness; and all these things shall be added to you. Therefore do not be anxious for tomorrow; for tomorrow will care for itself. Each day has enough trouble of its own (Matt. 6:25-34).

Most readers of this book will not be able to relate at all to the

---

4 On another occasion, Jesus made the same statement about the impossibility of serving God and mammon, and Luke tells us, "Now the Pharisees, who were lovers of money, were listening to all these things, and they were scoffing at Him" (Luke 16:14).

people Jesus was addressing. When was the last time you worried about having food, drink or clothing?

However, Jesus' words certainly have application to us. If it is wrong to be preoccupied with the *essentials* of life, how much more wrong is it to be preoccupied with *nonessentials*? Jesus expects His disciples to be primarily focused on seeking two things: His kingdom and His righteousness. When a professing Christian can't afford to tithe, but *can* afford dog food, cable TV, payments on a new car or furniture, designer fashions, or junk food, is he living up to Christ's standard of seeking first His kingdom and righteousness? No, he's only fooling himself if he thinks he's a follower of Jesus.

Specks and Logs

Jesus' next set of commandments to His followers concerns the sins of judging and fault finding:

> Do not judge lest you be judged. For in the way you judge, you will be judged; and by your standard of measure, it will be measured to you. And why do you look at the speck that is in your brother's eye, but do not notice the log that is in your own eye? Or how can you say to your brother, "Let me take the speck out of your eye," and behold, the log is in your own eye? You hypocrite, first take the log out of your own eye, and then you will see clearly to take the speck out of your brother's eye (Matt. 7:1-5).

What does it mean to judge another person? A judge is someone who looks for faults in people who are brought to court. That's the judge's job, and there's nothing wrong about what he does, as long as he judges according to proven facts. Judges are *supposed* to judge people, measuring them by the standard of the law of the land. If there were no judges, criminals would never be brought to justice.

Many people seem to think, however, that they have been appointed as judges, and thus they are always looking for faults in others. *That* is wrong. Furthermore, they often judge people without knowing all the facts, jumping to wrong conclusions. To make matters worse, these self-appointed judges usually measure people by standards that they themselves fall short of, making themselves hypocrites. "He who is without sin among you, let him be the first to throw a stone" (John 8:7).

This is the kind of behavior Jesus was talking about. The apostle James wrote, "Do not complain, brethren, against one another, that you yourselves may not be judged; behold, the Judge is standing right at the door" (Jas. 5:9). This is one of the most prevalent sins in the church, and those who are guilty of judging others place themselves in a dangerous position of being judged. When we speak against a fellow believer, pointing out his faults to others, we're playing the part of a judge. We're breaking the golden rule, because we don't want others to speak ill of us in our absence. And when we speak to a fellow believer about his faults while we have greater faults, we are the man with the *log in his eye.*

Notice, however, that Jesus did not forbid spiritually appraising other people. He said in the very next verse:

> Do not give what is holy to dogs, and do not throw your pearls before swine, lest they trample them under their feet, and turn and tear you to pieces (Matt. 7:6).

In order to obey this commandment, we must appraise if someone is a "spiritual dog" or "spiritual pig." that is, someone who does not appreciate valuable spiritual things, such as God's Word. And we will shortly read how Jesus commanded His followers to appraise all spiritual leaders by examining their fruit.

Encouragement to Pray

Finally we come to the last section of Jesus' sermon. It begins with some encouraging prayer promises:

> Ask, and it shall be given to you; seek, and you shall find; knock, and it shall be opened to you. For everyone who asks receives, and he who seeks finds, and to him who knocks it shall be opened. Or what man is there among you, when his son shall ask him for a loaf, will give him a stone? Or if he shall ask for a fish, he will not give him a snake, will he? If you then, being evil, know how to give good gifts to your children, how much more shall your Father who is in heaven give what is good to those who ask Him (Matt. 7:7-11).

"Aha!" a reader somewhere is saying. "Here's a part of the Sermon on the Mount that has nothing to do with holiness."

That all depends on what it is we're asking, knocking and seeking for in prayer. As those who "hunger and thirst for righteousness," we long to obey all that Jesus has commanded in the preceding sermon, and that longing is certainly reflected in our prayers. In fact, the model prayer that Jesus previously shared in this same sermon was the expression of a desire for God's will to be done and for holiness. Additionally, Luke's version of these same prayer promises under consideration ends with, "If you then, being evil, know how to give good gifts to your children, how much more shall your heavenly Father give the *Holy* Spirit to those who ask Him?" (Luke 11:13). Apparently, Jesus was not thinking of motor homes and sailboats when He promised us "good gifts." In His mind, the Holy Spirit is a "good gift," because the Holy Spirit makes us holy and helps us spread the gospel that makes other people holy. And holy people go to heaven.

A Summarizing Statement

Now we arrive at a verse that should be considered a statement that summarizes practically everything Jesus said up to this point. Many commentators miss this, but it is important that we don't. This particular verse is obviously a summarizing statement, as it begins with the word *therefore*. It is thus connected to previous instructions, and the question is: How much of what Jesus has said does it summarize? Let's read it and think:

> Therefore, however you want people to treat you, so treat them, for this is the Law and the Prophets (Matt. 7:12).

This statement can't be a summary of just the few verses before it about prayer, otherwise it would make no sense.

Remember that early in His sermon, Jesus had warned against the error of thinking that He had come to abolish *the Law or the Prophets* (see Matt. 5:17). From that point in His sermon until the verse at which we've now arrived, He did essentially nothing but endorse, explain and expand God's Old Testament commandments. Thus, He now summarizes *everything* He's commanded, all of which He derived from the Law and Prophets: "Therefore, whatever you want others to do for you, do so for them, for this is *the Law and the Prophets*" (7:12). The phrase, "the Law and the Prophets," connects everything Jesus said between Matthew 5:17 and 7:12.

The relation between salvation and keeping what we now know as "the golden rule" is made clear in the two verses that follow:

> Enter by the narrow gate; for the gate is wide, and the way is broad that leads to destruction, and many are those who enter by it. For the gate is small, and the way is narrow that leads to life, and few are those who find it (Matt. 7:13-14).

Obviously the narrow gate and the way that leads to life, which few find, is symbolic of salvation. The wide gate and broad way that leads to destruction, the route of the majority, symbolizes damnation. If everything Jesus said prior to this statement means anything, if this sermon has any logical progression, if Jesus possessed any intelligence as a communicator, then the most natural interpretation would be that the narrow way is the way of following Jesus, obeying His commandments. The broad way would be the opposite. How many professing Christians are traveling the narrow way that Jesus revealed from Matthew 5:17 to 7:12? If you are going along with the crowds, you can be sure you are on the broad way.

It is disturbing to many professing Christians that Jesus said nothing about faith or believing in Him in this salvation sermon. However, to those who understand the inseparable correlation between belief and behavior, faith and works, this sermon presents no problem. People who obey Jesus show their faith by their works. Those who don't obey Him don't believe He is the Son of God. Not only is our salvation an indication of God's grace toward us, so is the transformation that has taken place in our lives. Our holiness is really His holiness.

How to Recognize False Religious Leaders

Next, Jesus warned His audience about false prophets, religious leaders who lead the unsuspecting down the broad road to destruction. They are those whose message is not truly from God, and so false teachers fall under this category as well. How can they be recognized as being false? By the same way a person can be recognized as being a false believer:

> Beware of the false prophets, who come to you in sheep's clothing, but inwardly are ravenous wolves. You will know them by their fruits. Grapes are not gathered from thorn bushes, nor figs from thistles, are they? Even so, every good tree bears good fruit; but the bad tree bears bad fruit. A good tree cannot produce bad fruit, nor can a bad tree produce good fruit. Every tree that does not bear good fruit is cut down and thrown into the fire. So then, you will know them by their fruits. Not everyone who says to Me, "Lord, Lord," will enter the kingdom of heaven; but he who does the will of My Father who is in heaven. Many will say to Me on that day, "Lord, Lord, did we not prophesy in Your name, and

in Your name cast out demons, and in Your name perform many miracles?" And then I will declare to them, "I never knew you; depart from Me, you who practice lawlessness" (Matt. 7:15-23).

False teachers are very deceptive. They have some exterior indications of being genuine. They may call Jesus their Lord, prophesy, cast out demons and perform miracles. But the "sheep's clothing" only hides the "ravenous wolf." They aren't of the true sheep. How can it be known if they are true or false? Their true character can be known by examining their "fruits."

What are the fruits of which Jesus was speaking? They are the fruits of obedience to all He has taught. Those who are true, teach and do the will of the Father. Those who are false, teach what is not true and "practice lawlessness" (7:23). Our responsibility, then, is to compare their teaching and lives with what Jesus taught and commanded.

False teachers abound today in the church, and we should not be surprised, because both Jesus and Paul forewarned us that, as the end approaches, we should expect nothing less (see Matt. 24:11; 2 Tim. 4:3-4). The most prevalent false prophets of our day are those who teach that heaven awaits the unholy. They are responsible for the eternal damnation of millions of people. Of them, John Wesley wrote,

> How terrible is this!—when the ambassadors of God turn agents for the devil!—when they who are commissioned to teach men the way to heaven do in fact teach them the way to hell....If it be asked, "Why, who ever did...this?"...I answer, Ten thousand wise and honourable men; even all those, of whatever denomination, who encourage the proud, the trifler, the passionate, the lover of the world, the man of pleasure, the unjust or unkind, the easy, careless, harmless, useless creatures, the man who suffers no reproach for righteousness' sake, to imagine he is in the way to heaven. These are false prophets in the highest sense of the word. These are traitors both to God and man....They are continually peopling the realms of the night; and whenever they follow the poor souls they have destroyed, "hell shall be moved from beneath to meet them at their coming!"[5]

Interestingly, Wesley was specifically commenting about the false

---

5 *The Works of John Wesley* (Baker: Grand Rapids, 1996), by John Wesley, reprinted from the 1872 edition issued by the Wesleyan Methodist Book Room, London, pp. 441, 416.

teachers whom Jesus warned against in Matthew 7:15-23.

Notice that Jesus again plainly said, contrary to what so many false teachers tell us today, that those who don't bear good fruit will be cast into hell (see 7:19). This applies not just to teachers and prophets, but to everyone. Jesus said, "Not everyone who says to Me, 'Lord, Lord,' will enter the kingdom of heaven; but he who does the will of My Father who is in heaven" (Matt. 7:21). Forgive me for saying it again, but this is a sermon about the correlation between salvation and holiness. People who aren't obeying Jesus are heading for hell.

Also notice the connection Jesus made between what a person is inwardly and what he is outwardly. "Good" trees produce good fruit. "Bad" trees *can't* produce good fruit. The source of the good fruit that shows up on the outside is the nature of the person. God has changed the nature of those who have truly believed in Jesus.[6]

The Final Summary

Jesus concludes His entire sermon with a summarizing example. As you would expect, it is an illustration of the relation between obedience and salvation:

> Therefore everyone who hears these words of Mine, and acts upon them [literally, "does them"], may be compared to a wise man, who built his house upon the rock. And the rain descended, and the floods came, and the winds blew, and burst against that house; and yet it did not fall, for it had been founded upon the rock. And everyone who hears these words of Mine, and does not act upon them [literally, "does not do them"], will be like a foolish man, who built his house upon the sand. And the rain descended, and the floods came, and the winds blew, and burst against that house; and it fell, and great was its fall (Matt. 7:24-27).

Jesus' final illustration is not a formula for "success in life" as some use it. The topic of the context is not how to prosper financially during tough times by having faith in Jesus' promises. This is the summary of all that Jesus has said in His Sermon on the Mount.

---

6 I can't resist taking the opportunity to also comment here about a common expression people use when trying to excuse sins in others: "We don't know what is in their hearts." In contradiction to this, Jesus said that the outside reveals the inside. In another place, He told us that "the mouth speaks out of that which fills the heart" (Matt. 12:34). When a person speaks words of hate, it indicates hatred fills his heart. Jesus also told us that "from within, out of the heart of men, proceed the evil thoughts, fornications, thefts, murders, adulteries, deeds of coveting and wickedness, as well as deceit, sensuality, envy, slander, pride and foolishness" (Mark 7:21-22). When a person commits adultery, we *do* know what is in his heart: adultery.

Those who do what He says are wise and will endure; they need not fear the wrath of God. Those who don't obey Him are foolish and will suffer greatly, paying "the penalty of eternal destruction" (2 Thess. 1:9).

Answer to an Objection

Is it not possible that Jesus' Sermon on the Mount was only applicable to those followers of His who lived prior to His sacrificial death and resurrection? Were they not under the Law as their temporary means of salvation, but after Jesus died for their sins, were then saved by faith, thus invalidating the means of salvation expounded in this sermon?

This theory is a bad one. No one has ever been saved by his works. It has always been by faith, prior to and during the Old Covenant. Paul argues in Romans 4 that Abraham and David were justified by faith and not works.

Moreover, it was an impossibility that any of Jesus' audience could be saved by works, because they had all sinned and fallen short of God's glory (see Rom. 3:23). Only God's grace could save them, and only faith can receive His grace.

Unfortunately, too many in the church today view all of Jesus' commandments as serving no higher purpose than to make us feel guilty so we'll see the impossibility of earning salvation by works. Now that we've "gotten the message" and have been saved by faith, we can ignore most of His commandments. Unless, of course, we want to get others "saved." Then we can pull out the commandments again to show people how sinful they are so they will be saved by a "faith" that is void of works.

Jesus did not tell His disciples, "Go into all the world and make disciples, and make sure they realize that, once they've felt guilty and are then saved by faith, My commandments have served their purpose in their lives." Rather, He said, "Go therefore and make disciples of all the nations...*teaching them to observe all that I commanded you*" (Matt. 28:19-20, emphasis added).

EIGHT

Sanctification: Perfecting Holiness

Come to Me, all who are weary and heavy-laden, and I will give you rest. Take My yoke upon you, and learn from Me, for I am gentle and humble in heart; and you shall find rest for your souls. For My yoke is easy, and My load is light (Matt. 11:28-30).

Very few professing Christians would debate that the above scripture is an invitation to salvation from the lips of Jesus. It is used frequently in evangelistic sermons. Jesus was offering rest to the weary. He was obviously not speaking of *physical* rest for those who are physically weary. Rather, He was promising rest for souls (v. 29) that are burdened with sin and guilt. He was offering salvation. But how is this salvation received? Jesus said it is received by taking His yoke upon us.

Perhaps the favorite antinomian interpretation of what it means to take Jesus' yoke is the following: Supposedly, Jesus is wearing a *double* yoke that He wants to share with us. The "proof" of this interpretation is that Jesus refers to the yoke as "*My* yoke," indicating that it must be a yoke around His own neck. "And of course," the antinomian thinks, "Jesus can't mean that He wants to *transfer* that yoke from His neck to my neck, so He must be wearing a double yoke, meant for two oxen! He thus wants me to be "yoked" to Him by faith, inseparably joined together on our journey to heaven."

But this far-fetched interpretation misses the point entirely. Taking Jesus' yoke is symbolic of submitting to His authority. He doesn't have a double-yoke around His neck that He wants us to share. He, the Master, is holding a yoke in His hands, standing before all the wild oxen who are presently laboring under a load of guilt, yoked to sin. To them He cries out, "If you want rest, there's only one way to get it. Take *My* yoke upon you. I want to be *your* Master, but you must submit to Me. Become My disciple; learn of Me, and the heavy burden on your soul will be lifted. The yoke I will place on you will be easy, and the burden I'll give you to pull will be light, because My Holy Spirit will enable you to obey Me. Once you've believed in Me and submitted to My lordship, you'll be spiritually reborn; then My commandments will not be burdensome" (see 1 John 5:3). This is Jesus' consistent salvation message.

"Bearing the yoke" is symbolic of coming under the authority of another. Scripture frequently uses the yoke imagery in this way.[1] Those who truly believe in Jesus submit to His authority. The yoked ox has one reason for existence: his master's service. He may not know exactly what his master wants him to do, but his will is submitted. He's ready to go to work.

Sanctification Defined

This chapter is about sanctification, or the growing holiness experienced by those who've been born again. To be sanctified means "to be set apart for holy use," so it is a word that beautifully describes God's plan for every true believer. The New Testament uses the word in two tenses: past and present. Believers have *been sanctified* and are *being sanctified*. The past tense reveals God's intention—He has forgiven our sins and given us His Holy Spirit to set us apart for His own holy use.[2] The present tense reveals the ongoing process of the fulfillment of His intention—we are continually and increasingly being used for God's holy purposes.[3]

Unfortunately, to many professing Christians, sanctification is nothing more than a theory, because they've never been born again, which is absolutely essential for sanctification. Yet many are con-

---

1 See, for example, Gen. 27:40; Lev. 26:13; Deut. 28:48; 1 Kin. 12:10-11; Is. 14:25; 47:6; 58:6, 9; Jer. 2:20; 5:5; 27:8-12; 28:2-4, 14; 30:8; Ezek. 30:18; 34:27; Hos. 10:11; 11:4; Nah. 1:13; Gal. 5:1; 1 Tim. 6:1.

2 1 Cor. 1:2; 6:11; Heb. 2:11; 10:10, 14 are examples of the first uses of the word *sanctification*.

3 Rom. 6:19, 22; 1 Thes. 4:3; 1 Thes. 5:23; Heb. 12:14; 1 Pet. 1:2 are examples of this second usage of the word *sanctification*.

vinced they've been made righteous in Christ even though there is no evidence of sanctification in their lives. Scripture tells us, however, that with righteousness also comes sanctification:

> But by His doing you are in Christ Jesus, who became to us...*righteousness* and *sanctification*, and redemption....And such were some of you; but you were washed, but you were *sanctified*, but you were *justified* [made righteous] in the name of the Lord Jesus Christ, and in the Spirit of our God (1 Cor. 1:30; 6:11, emphasis added).

John wrote,

> If you know that He is righteous, you know that everyone also who practices righteousness is born of Him....Little children, let no one deceive you; the one who practices righteousness is righteous, just as He is righteous (1 John 2:29; 3:7).

Many professing Christians will gladly listen to sermons that fall under the category of "sanctification sermons," through which they're admonished to "turn over" various areas of their lives to Christ's lordship. However, listening to those sermons becomes an end in itself, because they really never intend to "turn over" any area of their lives to Christ's lordship, especially if doing so requires any self-denial. Yet they somehow convince themselves that there is some virtue in listening to convicting sermons, regardless of whether they adjust their lives accordingly. James warned against this very thing: "But prove yourselves doers of the word, and not merely hearers who delude themselves" (Jas. 1:22).

Hearers who aren't doers are deluded because they think they're saved when they aren't. Those kinds of professing Christians are the chief frustration of many godly pastors, who wonder why people in their congregations never change or demonstrate any growth in holiness. The reason is because those people have never taken Jesus' yoke and have never been born again. They may *think* they've been born again because they once prayed a salvation prayer and now understand that salvation is by grace, not works. But they're not, because they've never submitted themselves to Jesus. All attempts to get them to act more like Christ will be essentially futile until they take that first step.

The foundation of sanctification is submission to God; sanctification will never happen in anyone's life without submission. Once we've submitted, however, the sanctification process continues in our lives as we learn God's will and spiritual truth. We first take on Jesus' yoke; then we "learn from Him" as He said (Matt. 11:29). We "*grow* in the grace and *knowledge* of our Lord and Savior Jesus Christ" (2 Pet. 3:18, emphasis added).

At first, we don't fully know God's will or all that God has done for us through Christ, nor do we realize all that needs changed in our lives. But as Paul wrote, we are "trying to learn what is pleasing to the Lord" (Eph. 5:10). This is why Paul's prayers for Christians are petitions for their increased spiritual understanding and knowledge.[4] And that is why Paul often admonished his readers using the words, "Do you not know that..?"[5] He expected that the believers to whom he was writing would act differently if they knew some theological truth, such as the fact that their bodies were temples of the Holy Spirit.

That is why it is so important for followers of Christ to avail themselves to all that God has provided for them to learn spiritual truth. They should study the Scriptures themselves, and true followers of Christ will, because they'll have a desire to learn about spiritual things. They should also avail themselves to instruction from those in the church whom God has specifically called to teach His Word. They should be a part of a local church that has a vision for making disciples. That is what Jesus wants. He said, "Go therefore and make disciples...teaching them to observe all that I commanded you" (Matt. 28:19-20). True disciples are learning.

Going on to Perfection

Paul wrote in his second letter to the Corinthians: "Therefore, having these promises, beloved, let us cleanse ourselves from all defilement of flesh and spirit, perfecting holiness in the fear of God" (2 Cor. 7:1). This indicates to us that true believers are not necessarily perfect, as some extremists would have us believe. Defilements of flesh and spirit remain in the lives of true believers. We must, however, read Paul's words within the context of the rest of the New Testament. Although true Christians may still be partially defiled, they are characterized predominately by righteousness. Notice that Paul did not admonish his readers to *begin* acting holy. Rather, he admonished them to *perfect* their holiness. You can only perfect what

---

4 See, for example, Eph. 1:15-19; 3:14-19; Phil. 1:9-11; Col. 1:9-12; Philem. 1:6.

5 See Rom. 6:3; 6:16; 7:1; 11:2; 1 Cor. 3:16; 5:6; 6:2-3, 9,15-16, 19; 9:13, 24.

you are already doing fairly well. Paul's words indicate that the Corinthian Christians were already acting holy, and now their holiness needed perfecting. That is what biblical sanctification is—perfecting holiness.

Paul's words also help us to understand that the ongoing process of sanctification in our lives is not something God does apart from us. We must cleanse *ourselves* from fleshly and spiritual defilements. The writer of Hebrews says, "Pursue...the sanctification without which no one will see the Lord" (Heb. 12:14). God does not override our free will, and Scripture couldn't be more clear about our responsibility in the sanctification process.[6]

On the other hand, we should not think that sanctification is something we must do apart from God's involvement. Paul also wrote, "For I am confident of this very thing, that He who began a good work in you will perfect it until the day of Christ Jesus" (Phil. 1:6). Perhaps the balance between our part and God's part is best expressed by Paul in Philippians 2:12-13:

> So then, my beloved, just as you have always obeyed, not as in my presence only, but now much more in my absence, *work out your salvation with fear and trembling; for it is God who is at work in you,* both to will and to work for His good pleasure (emphasis added).

Paul was writing to true believers, those who obeyed even in his absence. Obviously, God was at work within them by His indwelling Spirit. Thus, they had a solemn obligation to cooperate with what He was doing in their lives. *Sanctification occurs as we cooperate with God.*

The Chronology of Sanctification

In this chapter and the next, we'll consider the process of sanctification, and how it involves God and us. Let's begin at the beginning.

God's work, of course, began long before anyone was sanctified. He preordained the plan of salvation through His Son, who fulfilled that plan, dying for our sins and rising from the dead. Through the means of a God-ordained messenger who shares the gospel, and by the convicting power of the Holy Spirit, the sinner is awakened and convicted of his sin and need for salvation.

At the point of conviction, human responsibility enters the pic-

6 In the next chapter, I list hundreds of scriptures that reveal human responsibility in sanctification.

ture. We have a choice to make, and the only proper response on our part is to repent of our sins and believe in Jesus. God commands us to repent and believe in Jesus,[7] so repenting and believing must be something that is our responsibility, not God's.

However, the moment we repent and believe the gospel, God goes to work again. He immediately indwells us by His Holy Spirit, regenerating our spirits, and breaks sin's power over our lives, releasing us from its clutches. Our spirits are reborn, re-created in Christ's likeness, and we become new creations in Him (see 1 Pet. 1:3; Eph. 4:24; 2 Cor. 5:17). God becomes our spiritual Father.

The result is an immediate degree of holiness manifested in the life of the new believer. From scriptures such as 1 Cor. 6:9-10, Gal. 5:19-21, Eph. 5:5-6, 1 John 3:15 and Rev. 21:8, we can be certain that the new birth brings an end to the practice of certain grievous sins such as fornication, adultery, immorality, impurity, sensuality, effeminacy, homosexuality, coveting, thievery, swindling, drunkenness, carousing, reviling, enmity, strife, jealousy, outbursts of anger, disputes, dissensions, factions, envying, idolatry, sorcery, murder and lying.

This is not to say that a true believer *couldn't* commit any of those sins. Any believer could, if he decided, commit any of those sins, because God has not taken away his free will. However, he will find that he possesses an inward resistance and abhorrence of sin that he did not possess previously. His ability to resist temptation is greatly increased. If he does yield to temptation, he will feel greatly convicted and sorrowful until he confesses his sin to God. Again, the *practice* of such sins is a guarantee that one will not inherit God's kingdom, as Scripture repeatedly warns.

Is All Sin the Same in God's Eyes?

Some would argue that "all sin is the same," and thus say that the habitual, unrepentant practice of the above-listed sins can't be considered any different than the habitual, unrepentant practice of any other sin. This logic, however, doesn't change the scriptures I've listed, nor does it strengthen any counter-argument against what I've said. If all sin is the same in God's sight, then we must greatly extend Paul's exclusionary lists to include *every* sin, and thus conclude that

---

7 See, for example, Mark 1:15; John 14:1; Acts 17:30; Rev. 3:3.

no one is truly saved! Yet, thankfully, ingratitude, worry, and sleeping during sermons are not included in any of Paul's exclusionary lists!

Clearly, all sin is not the same in God's sight. Jesus spoke of lesser and (thus by implication) greater commandments (see Matt. 5:19). He spoke of a "greater sin," and (thus by implication) a lesser sin (see John 19:11). He considered one particular commandment to be "great and foremost" (Matt. 22:38), and another to be second only to it. He mentioned one sin that is uniquely unforgivable (see Matt. 12:31-32). He rebuked the Pharisees, who neglected "the *weightier* provisions of the law: justice and mercy and faithfulness," and emphasized the lighter requirements of the law, such as tithing (Matt. 23:23, emphasis added).

The fact that some sins are more grievous in God's eyes than others is reflected in the Law of Moses, where some transgressions summoned more severe punishment. We also note that God initially gave Israel *ten* commandments, rather than eleven or forty. This indicates that He considers some commandments to be more important than others.

In Ezekiel 8, we read how the Lord showed Ezekiel four successive scenes of certain sins being practiced in Israel. Each sinful practice God called an even "greater abomination" than the previous one.

The apostle John stated that there is a sin "not leading to death," and a sin "leading to death" (1 John 5:16-17).

Clearly, all sin is not the same in God's eyes. All sin separates us from God, and all sin grieves God, but all sin is not equally grievous to Him. Everyone knows that both murder and giving someone a black eye are wrong. However, everyone also knows the former is more serious than the latter.

The Initial and Ongoing Transformation

If you're born again, God has taken care of what is most grievous to Him. You've experienced an initial transformation. But God isn't satisfied with just that. His goal for you is perfection, and so you can expect an ongoing transformation. The chart on the next page illustrates this:

ALL OF HUMANITY | GOD

UNSAVED	SAVED	PERFECTION
fornication	love	
adultery	joy	
immorality	peace	
impurity	patience	
senuality	kindness	
effeminacy	goodness	
homosexuality	faithfulness	
coveting	gentleness	
thievery	self-control	
swindling		
drunkenness	Matt. 7:2	
caarousing	Gal. 5:22-24	
reviling	Jas. 2:26	
enmity, strife	1 John 3:7-15	
jealousy		
outbursts of anger		
disputes		
dissensions		
factions, envying		
idolatry, sorcery		
murder		
lying		
Matt. 5:20-30		
1 Cor. 5:11; 6:9-10;		
Gal. 5:19-21		
Eph. 5:5-6		
1 John 3:7-10, 15		
Rev. 21:8		

Vertical labels between columns: Conversion • The New Birth • Salvation • Conversion • The New Birth • Salvation

Matthew 5:48

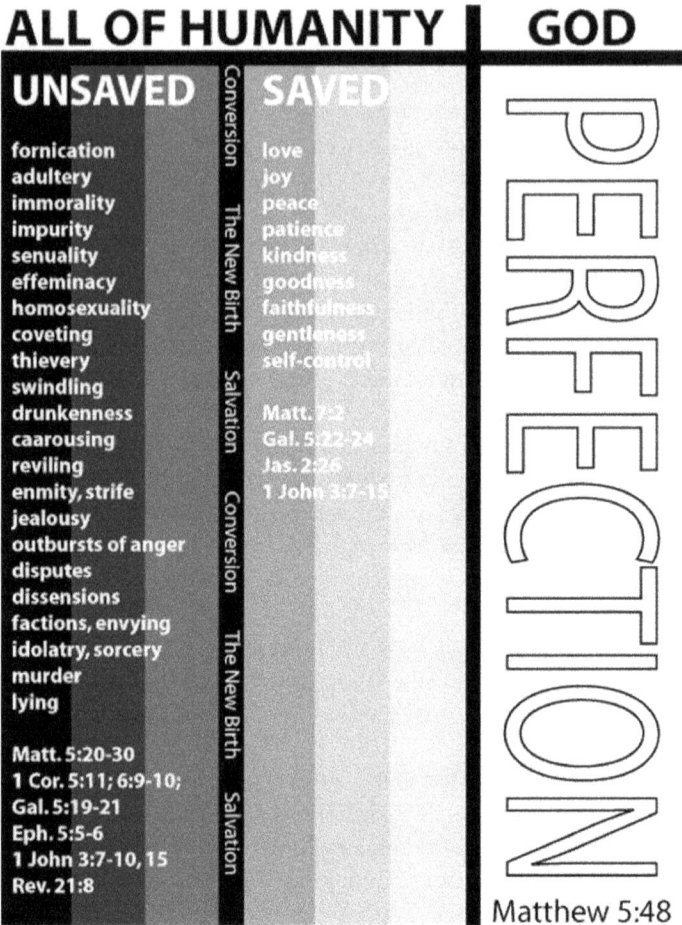

On the left two-thirds of the chart, all of humanity is divided into two groups, the unsaved and the saved. There are, of course, no other categories. You are either in one or the other.

As you travel from left to right, you progress from wickedness to holiness. The UNSAVED category includes people who are the most wicked (on the extreme left), and the least wicked (on the extreme right of the UNSAVED column). Not all non-Christians are equally evil.

However, as you continue to the right, you cross a thick line, which represents conversion and the new birth. Once you cross that line, you are among the saved. However, the saved on the extreme left are less holy than those who have progressed further to the right. Not all Christians are equally holy.

Nevertheless, the difference that is made as one crosses the line of conversion is dramatic, which is why the line of conversion is so thick. There is no "thin line" between the saved and unsaved. The apostle John wrote that it is obvious who is saved and unsaved (see 1 John 3:10).

As a saved person is sanctified by cooperating with the Holy Spirit, he moves progressively toward the right, closer to the right-hand third of the chart, which is labeled PERFECTION. At present, of course, only God is perfect.

Notice that under the UNSAVED column, I've listed sins that, if practiced, are proof that a person is not born again, and some scriptures that say so.

Under the SAVED column, I've listed the fruit of the Spirit and some relevant scriptures. Fruit can ripen and mature, and so can all of the fruit of the Spirit in our lives. We can all grow in love, peace, patience and so on.

Hopefully, you've not found yourself described in the unsaved column. If you have, you need to repent and believe in Jesus, crossing the line of conversion. If you do, you will immediately be born again and experience God's initial transformation.

Once we are born again, God accomplishes His ongoing work of transforming us through a number of means that we will consider. We must first understand, however, that God's success is very dependent upon our cooperation. He does not override our free will. On the other hand, He provides lots of motivation for us to cooperate.

What is it that motivates us to strive against sin and become progressively more like Jesus? There are at least three motivations with which God supplies us: love, hope and fear. All of those motivations are legitimate and scriptural. More specifically, they are (1) love for God, (2) hope of reward, and (3) fear of discipline.

Love for God

Obedience that springs from love would seem to be the highest and most pleasing kind of obedience to God. Ideally, we should obey Him only because we love Him, and every true believer will do this to some extent. Jesus spoke of the obedience of love, saying:

> If you love Me, you will keep My commandments....He who has My commandments and keeps them, he it is who loves Me; and he who loves Me shall be loved by My Father, and I will love him, and will disclose Myself to him (John 14:15, 21).

Likewise, the apostle John wrote,

> For this is the love of God, that we keep His commandments;
> and His commandments are not burdensome (1 John 5:3).

How can we not love Him when we understand what He has done for us? How can we not feel a sense of gratitude for His amazing self-denial on our behalf? How can we not seek to please Him who loves us so much?

Let's imagine for a moment that you are crossing the street on a busy corner and carelessly step in front of an oncoming bus. A fellow pedestrian lunges at you, just barely pushing you out of harm's way, but he himself is hit by the bus. He is rushed to the hospital, where he learns that he will be confined to a wheelchair for the rest of his life.

Would you not feel a debt of gratitude to him who saved you at such great personal cost? Would you not feel an obligation to repay what you could never repay? Your love for the one who showed you so much love would motivate you to do what you could to please him. If he desired something, you would do what you could to provide it. So it is with those who believe in Jesus. They can't help but love Him, and because they do, they strive to please Him by their obedience.

Hope of Reward

A second motivation God provides to those who obey Him is the hope of reward. Clearly, salvation is given to us by God's grace. This is not to say, however, that other blessings aren't given in response to our works. Both present and future blessings are repeatedly promised in Scripture as rewards to the obedient. Paul wrote that, "godliness is profitable for all things, since it holds promise for the present life and also for the life to come" (1 Tim. 4:8). Indeed, God is "a rewarder of those who seek Him" (Heb. 11:6).

Hope of reward could be considered a selfish motivation, hardly virtuous compared to being motivated by pure love for God. Would not the Lord prefer that we serve Him because we love Him, rather than for personal benefit (as is so clearly exemplified by the testing of Job, for example)?

I would tend to think so. Nevertheless, God is the one who initiated the program of rewards for obedience. Like any good parent, He might prefer that His children obey Him motivated by pure love, but He knows, like most parents, that filial love is often insufficient.

Parents frequently promise their children rewards for good behavior, and it works. Besides, the earthly rewards we receive glorify the goodness of our God who loves to bless His children.

We must also keep in mind that selfishness is serving ourselves at the expense of others. Thus, not all that benefits self is necessarily selfish. Without a hint of disapproval, Scripture describes true Christians as those who "by perseverance in doing good *seek for glory and honor and immortality*" (Rom. 2:7, emphasis added). Most of us, I suppose, believed in Christ (at least initially) out of concern for ourselves—we want to go to heaven and miss hell. Yet our act of believing in Christ can hardly be considered selfish. Our receiving eternal life did not cause someone else's exclusion from the same blessing. If anything, our receiving eternal life *increased* the possibility that others would be saved. Consequently, receiving salvation because of concern for self cannot be classified as selfish. So it is also true of the rewards God promises to the godly. They don't come at the expense of others. Neither God's grace nor His rewards are limited. We're not competing against others for a piece of the pie.

This being so, desire for reward should not be considered sinful, wrong, or selfish, especially since God is the initiator and promiser of the rewards. If it were wrong for us to desire a reward God promises, then He is guilty of enticing us to do wrong, making Him a sinner. That, of course, is impossible.

Repayment According to Deeds

Throughout Scripture, the godly are promised special rewards for their obedience. For example, we know that in the future kingdom at Christ's return, God is going to repay every one us according to our deeds:

> For the Son of Man is going to come in the glory of His Father with His angels; and will then *recompense every man according to his deeds* (Matt. 16:27, emphasis added).

> Behold, I am coming quickly, and My reward is with Me, *to render to every man according to what he has done* (Rev. 22:12, emphasis added).

The recompense and rewards of which Jesus spoke not only include general repayments that all the saved or unsaved shall mutually share, such as heaven or hell. The promised repayments also include specific and individual rewards based upon each person's individual deeds. Paul, writing of his and Apollos' ministries, stated,

> Now he who plants and he who waters are one; but each
> will receive his *own* reward according to his *own* labor (1
> Cor. 3:8, emphasis added; see also vv. 9-15).

Our future rewards will be based on our own works, taking into consideration our particular gifts, talents, and opportunities. Jesus' Parable of the Talents makes this ever so clear (see Matt. 25:14-30). God expects more from those He's given more. Jesus said, "From everyone who has been given much shall much be required" (Luke 12:48).

The Time of Reward

Scripture doesn't always make it clear exactly *when* the godly will be rewarded. Some promises are clearly for this life, while others are for the next. Some are ambiguous. First, let's consider a few that apparently promise rewards in this life:

> Honor your father and mother (which is the first commandment with a promise), *that it may be well with you, and that you may live long on the earth* (Eph. 6:2-3, emphasis added).

> And do not judge and you will not be judged; and do not condemn, and you will not be condemned; pardon, and you will be pardoned. Give, and it will be given to you; good measure, pressed down, shaken together, running over, *they* [the KJV says 'men']⁸ will pour into your lap. For by your standard of measure it will be measured to you in return (Luke 6:37-38, emphasis added).

> For, "Let him who means to *love life and see good days* refrain his tongue from evil and his lips from speaking guile" (1 Pet. 3:10, emphasis added).

> But one who looks intently at the perfect law, the law of liberty [the law of love], and abides by it, not having become a forgetful hearer but an effectual doer, *this man shall be blessed in what he does* (James 1:25, emphasis added).

Here are a few examples of promises that clearly have application to our future lives:

---

8 This seems to be a clue that the rewards promised here will be in this life.

> But when you give a reception, invite the poor, the crippled, the lame, the blind, and you will be blessed, since they do not have the means to repay you; for *you will be repaid at the resurrection of the righteous* (Luke 14:13-14, emphasis added).

> Rejoice, and be glad, for *your reward in heaven is great,* for so they persecuted the prophets who were before you (Matt. 5:12, emphasis added).

> Sell your possessions and give to charity; make yourselves purses which do not wear out, an unfailing *treasure in heaven,* where no thief comes near, nor moth destroys (Luke 12:33, emphasis added).

What heavenly rewards might be in store for us, only God knows. As vague as heaven is to us, so are the special rewards that await us there. Earthly rewards, however, should be understood to be anything we would consider a blessing. Don't limit God's blessings to only happy inward feelings or shivers down your spine!

Finally, here are a few promises whose time of fulfilled reward is ambiguous:

> But love your enemies, and do good, and lend, expecting nothing in return; and *your reward will be great,* and you will be sons of the Most High; for He Himself is kind to ungrateful and evil men (Luke 6:35, emphasis added).

> But when you give alms, do not let your left hand know what your right hand is doing that your alms may be in secret; and your Father who sees in secret *will repay you....* But you, when you pray, go into your inner room, and when you have shut your door, pray to your Father who is in secret, and your Father who sees in secret *will repay you....*But you, when you fast, anoint your head, and wash your face so that you may not be seen fasting by men, but by your Father who is in secret; and your Father who sees in secret *will repay you* (Matt. 6:3-4, 6, 17-18, emphasis added).

> With good will render service, as to the Lord, and not to men, knowing that whatever good thing each one does, *this he will receive back from the Lord,* whether slave or free (Eph. 6:7-8, emphasis added).

God is keeping track of even the smallest good deeds, with plans to reward them:

> For whoever gives you a cup of water to drink because of your name as followers of Christ, truly I say to you, he shall not lose his reward (Mark 9:41).

Do you desire to enjoy more blessings from your heavenly Father, both now and in heaven? Of course you do! Then obey Him more, and you will be rewarded. Jesus said, "*Blessed* are those who hear the word of God, and observe it" (Luke 11:28, emphasis added).

Fear of Discipline

Apart from love of God and hope for reward, there is at least one other way God motivates His children to be obedient: through fear of discipline. I would suspect that this third motivation is the one God prefers to use the least of the three. Nevertheless, it is certainly valid and scriptural. Most parents use all three means to motivate their children to be obedient, and none should be considered blame-worthy.

Against this, some contend that fearing God is incompatible with loving Him. Does not Scripture say, "perfect love casts out fear"? (1 John 4:18).

The fear of which John wrote that is cast out by love is not the fear of holy reverence for God. It is the fear of eternal punishment that begins on "the day of judgment" (1 John 4:17). Having understood and received the love of God, and now abiding in His love (see John 15:10), we need not fear the hell that we formerly deserved.

Loving and fearing God are not incompatible according to the New Testament. Believers are *commanded* to fear God (see 1 Pet. 2:17). They are told to be subject to one another "in the fear of Christ" (Eph. 5:21), to "work out [their] salvation with fear and trembling" (Phil. 2:12), and to perfect their holiness "in the fear of God" (2 Cor. 7:1). Peter admonished the recipients of his first letter to conduct themselves *with fear* during their earthly sojourn, knowing that God would impartially judge each one of them according to their works (see 1 Pet. 1:17).

Discipline at Corinth

Unfortunately, God's discipline is a foreign concept to many professing Christians, but it is certainly not foreign to the Bible. From

Adam and Eve to Ananias and Sapphira, from the Israelites who died in the wilderness to the Christians who were sick in Corinth, God's discipline is revealed in Scripture. Sometimes His discipline can be severe when there is good cause for it. Consider Paul's important words to the Corinthian believers:

> Therefore whoever eats the bread or drinks the cup of the Lord in an unworthy manner, shall be *guilty* of the body and the blood of the Lord. But let a man examine himself, and so let him eat of the bread and drink of the cup. For he who eats and drinks, eats and drinks *judgment* to himself, if he does not judge the body rightly. *For this reason many among you are weak and sick, and a number sleep. But if we judged ourselves rightly, we should not be judged. But when we are judged, we are disciplined by the Lord in order that we may not be condemned along with the world* (1 Cor. 11:27-32, emphasis added).

First, note that as a result of God's discipline, which Paul also refers to as God's judgment, some of the Corinthians were weak and sick. Some had even died.

The reason for God's judgment? They were partaking of the Lord's Supper in an "unworthy manner" (11:27). What did Paul mean? From the context, we can safely conclude that he was referring to partaking of the Lord's Supper while in disobedience to the Lord. For example, Paul wrote that we should first *examine* ourselves before Communion, and warned that we are in danger of judgment if we don't "judge the body rightly" (11:29). It would seem reasonable to conclude that "judging the body rightly" would be equivalent to other related phrases within the context, namely, those that say we should examine and judge ourselves. We know that it is the "deeds of the body" that get us into trouble (see Rom. 8:12-14; 1 Cor. 9:27). "Judging the body rightly" must mean recognizing and subduing the sinful nature within that wars against the Spirit. We can avoid God's judgment if we would judge ourselves, that is, not yield to the sinful nature, continually examine ourselves, and confess our sins if need be.

Can Christians Go to Hell?

God disciplines us, as Paul wrote, "in order that we may not be condemned along with the world" (11:32). The world, of course, is going to be condemned to eternal damnation. Thus, God disciplines sinning believers so they don't go to hell (indicating, again, that heaven is only for the holy).

This raises several important questions. The first is this: Is there really a danger that a true believer could end up in hell?

The answer is *yes*. If a true believer returns to committing the "exclusionary sins," those which, if practiced, Scripture guarantees will result in one's exclusion from God's kingdom (see 1 Cor. 5:11; 6:9-10, Gal. 5:19-21, Eph. 5:5-6), he forfeits eternal life. God has not taken away our free will nor our capacity to sin. Contrary to what many modern teachers say, the Bible teaches that any believer who consistently follows after the old sinful nature, what Scripture calls *the flesh*, is in danger of spiritual death. Writing to Christians, Paul said:

> So then, *brethren*, we are under obligation, not to the flesh, to live according to the flesh—for if you are living according to the flesh, *you must die;* but if by the Spirit you are putting to death the deeds of the body, *you will live.* For all who are being led by the Spirit of God, *these* are sons of God (Rom. 8:12-14, emphasis added).

For at least two reasons we must conclude that Paul was addressing spiritually alive Christian believers.

First, notice that he addressed them as *brethren*.

Second, they had the capacity to put to death the deeds of the body by the Spirit, which is something only believers, indwelt by the Spirit, could do.

Note that Paul warned the Roman Christians that if they lived according to the flesh, they *must* die. Was he referring to physical or spiritual death? It seems logical to conclude that he was referring to spiritual death, since everyone, even those who "are putting to death the deeds of the body," is going to die physically sooner or later. Is it not also true that those who "live according to the flesh" often continue to enjoy physical life for a long, long time?

The only proper conclusion that can be drawn from these facts is that true Christian believers can die spiritually by "living according to the flesh." Thus Paul's "exclusionary lists" of 1 Cor. 6:9-10, Gal. 5:19-21 and Eph. 5:5-6 should not be considered only applicable to those who do not profess faith in Christ. They are just as applicable to those who do profess faith in Christ. (In fact, within their context, the "exclusionary lists" are written as warnings to believers.) It is those who are led by the Spirit, as opposed to the flesh, who are the true children of God, as Paul so clearly stated (see Rom. 8:14).

More Proof that Christians Can Die Spiritually

Paul wrote similar words to the Galatian Christians. After warning them that those who practice the "deeds of the flesh" will not inherit God's kingdom, he stated:

> Do not be deceived, God is not mocked; for whatever a man sows, this he will also reap. For the one who sows to his own flesh shall from the flesh reap corruption, but the one who sows to the Spirit shall from the Spirit reap *eternal life.* And let us not lose heart in doing good, for in due time we shall reap *if* we do not grow weary (Gal. 6:7-9, emphasis added).

Notice the two people who are contrasted. One sows to his flesh and the other to the Spirit. The first reaps corruption (the NIV translates it "destruction") and the other reaps eternal life. If corruption (destruction) is the opposite of eternal life, then it must refer to spiritual death. Please note that reaping eternal life is only promised to those who sow to the Spirit and who continue sowing to the Spirit. Those who sow to the flesh will *not* reap eternal life, but destruction. As Paul warned, "Do not be deceived" about this (Gal. 6:7). Yet so many today are.

Sowing to the flesh was a personal concern of the apostle Paul, who, like every other true Christian, still possessed a sinful nature. He wrote to the Corinthians:

> And everyone who competes in the games exercises self-control in all things. They then do it to receive a perishable wreath, but we an imperishable. Therefore I run in such a way, as not without aim; I box in such a way, as not beating the air; but *I buffet my body and make it my slave, lest possibly, after I have preached to others, I myself should be disqualified* (1 Cor. 9:25-27, emphasis added).

Like Olympic athletes, we must also exercise self-control if we hope to receive our imperishable prize. Paul stated that he buffeted his body and made it his slave, because if he didn't, he was in danger of being "disqualified."[9] When one is disqualified, there is no hope that he might win. The immediate context of Paul's words makes it clear that he was not expressing concern over the possibility of losing further opportunities for service or heavenly rewards, but of losing his ultimate salvation. In fact, in the verses that follow (1

---

9 The Greek word translated "disqualified" here in the NASB (*adokimos*), is the same word Paul used in 2 Cor. 13:5 to describe those in whom Christ does not dwell: "Test yourselves to see if you are in the faith; examine yourselves! Or do you not recognize this about yourselves, that Jesus Christ is in you—unless indeed you fail the test [*adokimos*]?"

Cor. 10:1-14), Paul warned the Corinthian Christians not to follow the tragic example of the Israelites who, although they were so initially blessed and privileged, ultimately perished in the wilderness because they did not continue in obedient faith. Unlike the Israelites who perished, the believers in Corinth should flee from greed, idolatry, immorality (sins Paul previously listed in his "exclusionary list of 6:9-10), testing God, and grumbling, admonishing them, "Let him who thinks he stands take heed lest he fall" (1 Cor. 10:12).

James Adds His "Amen"

Consider also what James wrote to Christian believers about persevering under trial. Those who successfully persevere are the ones who will receive "the crown of life," that is, salvation.[10] Those who return to a life of sin will die:

> Blessed is a man who perseveres under trial; for once he has been approved, he will receive the crown of life, which the Lord has promised to those who love Him. Let no one say when he is tempted, "I am being tempted by God"; for God cannot be tempted by evil, and He Himself does not tempt anyone. But each one is tempted when he is carried away and enticed by his own lust. Then when lust has conceived, it gives birth to sin; and when sin is accomplished, *it brings forth death.* Do not be deceived, my *beloved brethren* (Jas. 1:12-16, emphasis added).

James stated that it is not God who is tempting us, but "each one is tempted when he is carried away and enticed by his own lust [desires]" (1:14). The result is that "when lust has conceived, it gives birth to sin" (1:15). Finally, when sin is "accomplished," or as the NIV and NKJV say, when it is "full-grown," it brings forth death. How long it takes for sin to become "full-grown" and result in death is a matter of conjecture. Certainly, a single sin by a believer does not result in instant spiritual death. Persisting in sin, however, or habitually walking after the flesh, does eventually result in spiritual death. James warns us not to be deceived about this.

Again, how could James be warning about physical death as opposed to spiritual death, as some claim? Everyone is going to die physically, sinner and saint.

---

10 The "crown of life" is often interpreted as being a special, literal crown that only some Christians will receive. Note, however, that it is promised to all those who love the Lord, which is true of all authentic believers. Our love for the Lord is proven by our persevering under trial.

Additionally, how can some claim that James is addressing unbelievers in this passage? It isn't possible for sin to "bring forth death" in them, because they are already "dead in [their] trespasses and sins" (Eph. 2:1). James was clearly addressing Christians, *"beloved brethren"* (Jas. 1:16, emphasis added).

James also wrote at the end of his epistle:

> My brethren, if any *among you* strays from the truth, and one *turns him back,* let him know that he who turns a sinner from the error of his way *will save his soul from death,* and will cover a multitude of sins (Jas. 5:19-20).

Notice that James was addressing *brethren.* He stated that "if *any among you* strays from the truth," so he must have meant fellow believers who were previously in the truth but who strayed from it. That they had not strayed in doctrine only is clear from James' words, "he who turns a *sinner* from the error of his *way*" (5:20). These people had strayed from holiness.

However, if we turn back one who has strayed as James described, we "will save his soul from death." Note that James didn't say we would save his *body* from death, but rather, his *soul*. Again, the only honest conclusion we can draw is that James believed that a spiritually alive person could ultimately die spiritually by returning to the practice of sin.

Peter Joins the Chorus

Not only did Paul and James agree on this issue, but so did Peter. Warning about the seduction of believers by false teachers, he wrote,

> For speaking out arrogant words of vanity they entice by fleshly desires, by sensuality, *those who barely escape from the ones who live in error*, promising them freedom while they themselves are slaves of corruption; for by what a man is overcome, by this he is enslaved. For if *after they have escaped the defilements of the world by the knowledge of the Lord and Savior Jesus Christ, they are again entangled in them and are overcome, the last state has become worse for them than the first.* For it would be better for them not to have known the way of righteousness, than having known it, to turn away from the holy commandment delivered to them. It has happened to them according to the true proverb, "A dog returns to its own vomit," and, "A sow, after washing, returns to wallowing in the mire" (2 Pet. 2:18-22, emphasis added).

First, note that Peter wrote that the false teachers entice "those who barely escape from the ones who live in error" (2:18). Peter was clearly writing of true Christians, because they *did* escape, although "barely" from the ones who live in error, the nonbelievers. Peter also said that they had "escaped the defilements of the world by the knowledge of the Lord and Savior Jesus Christ" (2:20). That can only mean that they were born again and were no longer practicing sin. (Notice what Peter considered to be the mark of the true believer.) They were spiritually alive.

But, Peter wrote, they were "again entangled" in what previously defiled them and were "overcome" (2:20). The result was that the "last state has become worse for them than the first" (2:20). If that was the case, could they still have been spiritually alive and heaven-bound? Obviously not. Peter compared them to dogs returning to their vomit and pigs going back to the mud. Are we to think that such people are spiritually alive, children of God, indwelt by the Holy Spirit, and on the sure road to heaven?[11]

John's Testimony

The apostle John obviously believed that a spiritually alive person could become spiritually dead:

> If anyone sees his *brother* committing a *sin not leading to death*, he shall ask and God will for him give life to those who commit sin not leading to death. *There is a sin leading to death; I do not say that he should make request for this.* All unrighteousness is sin, and there is a sin not leading to death. We know that no one who is born of God sins; but He who was born of God keeps him and the evil one does not touch him (1 John 5:16-18).

First, note that John was speaking of fellow Christians sinning.

Second, note that John did not believe that any and every sin a Christian might commit would immediately result in his death, as some extremists say. However, John did believe that there was a "sin leading to death" and that there was no point in praying for a brother who committed that sin. We could debate about what exactly that

---

11 This passage also helps us to understand what "backsliding," as it is often called, actually is. In order to truly "backslide," a person first has to "frontslide." What is often referred to as backsliding today is nothing more than when a sinner verbally professes faith in Christ and then grows more sinful. He never manifested any indication that he had "escaped the defilements of the world by the knowledge of the Lord and Savior Jesus Christ" (2:20). He cannot be rightfully accused of "leaving his first love" (see Rev. 2:4), because Jesus never was his first love.

sin is, but may it suffice for now to say that such a sin exists.

Did John mean that there is a sin unto physical death? Many think so, primarily because their theology leaves no possibility for a spiritually alive person to die spiritually. However, when we consider the context before and after John's statement, *eternal life* is clearly what he had in mind when he was writing (see 1 John 5:13, 20). The sin unto death is the sin that ends eternal life.

Jesus Warned His Followers of Hell

Jesus, too, believed that present salvation was no absolute guarantee of future salvation. He warned His *own disciples* to "fear Him who is able to destroy both soul and body in hell" (Matt. 10:28). Consider also His words recorded in Luke 12:35-46, also addressed to His own disciples:

> "Be dressed in readiness, and keep your lamps alight. And be like men who are waiting for their master when he returns from the wedding feast, so that they may immediately open the door to him when he comes and knocks. Blessed are those slaves whom the master shall find on the alert when he comes; truly I say to you, that he will gird himself to serve, and have them recline at the table, and will come up and wait on them. Whether he comes in the second watch, or even in the third, and finds them so, blessed are those slaves. And be sure of this, that if the head of the house had known at what hour the thief was coming, he would not have allowed his house to be broken into. You too, be ready; for the Son of Man is coming at an hour that you do not expect."

> And Peter said, *"Lord, are You addressing this parable to us, or to everyone else as well?"* And the Lord said, "Who then is the faithful and sensible steward, whom his master will put in charge of his servants, to give them their rations at the proper time? Blessed is that slave whom his master finds so doing when he comes. Truly I say to you, that he will put him in charge of all his possessions. But if that slave says in his heart, 'My master will be a long time in coming,' and begins to beat the slaves, both men and women, and to eat and drink and get drunk; the master of that slave will come on a day when he does not expect him, and at an hour he does not know, and will cut him in pieces, and *assign him a*

place with the unbelievers" (emphasis added).

Matthew recorded this same admonition by Jesus, including His
further elaboration on the final destination of the unfaithful servant:
"Weeping shall be there and the gnashing of teeth" (Matt. 24:51).
Thus, according to Jesus, one who formerly served the Lord, his
Master, can still be damned if he returns to a lifestyle of sin.

Notice that the apostate slave in this parable was characterized
by hating his fellow slaves and drunkenness, two sins that mark a
person as unsaved (see 1 John 3:13-15; 1 Cor. 6:10).

Notice also that Jesus was clearly addressing this parable to His
own disciples, as revealed by Luke 12:22 and 41. Present salvation
is not guarantee of future salvation. We must continue in a living
faith. The two parables that follow in Matthew's Gospel, that of the
Ten Virgins and the Talents, also serve to illustrate this fact (see Matt.
25:1-30).

Jesus' point is so unmistakably clear in this parable that some
who subscribe to the false doctrine of unconditional eternal security
are forced to conclude that "outer darkness," where there is "weeping and gnashing of teeth," describes a place in heaven where less
faithful Christians will temporarily mourn their loss of heavenly
rewards![12]

Jesus also once warned the church in Sardis of the danger of
born-again members dying spiritually. Apparently, the majority of
the Christians in Sardis had returned to the practice of sin; thus they
were in grave danger that they would not be clothed in white gar-
ments, that Jesus would not confess them before His Father, and that
their names would be erased from the book of life. Yet there was still
time for them to repent. Read slowly and honestly:

> I *know your deeds,* that you have a name that you are alive,
> *but you are dead.* Wake up, and strengthen the things that
> remain, which were about to die; for I have not found your
> deeds completed in the sight of My God. *Remember there-
> fore what you have received and heard; and keep it, and repent.
> If therefore you will not wake up, I will come like a thief, and
> you will not know at what hour I will come upon you. But you
> have a few people in Sardis who have not soiled their garments;*
> and *they* will walk with Me in white; for *they* are worthy.
> He who overcomes shall thus be clothed in white garments;

---

[12] In a later chapter, I provide a quotation from one of the most well-known Evangelical teachers in America, stating this absurd theory.

and I will not erase his name from the book of life, and I will confess his name before My Father, and before His angels (Rev.
3:1-5, emphasis added).

In light of all Jesus, Peter, James, John and Paul taught, how is
it that so many modern teachers maintain that if a person is truly
saved, he can never forfeit his salvation, no matter how he lives?
This is the devil's original lie, when he said to a spiritually alive person who was considering sin, "You surely shall not die!" (Gen. 3:4).
Why don't more Christians recognize Satan's original lie being perpetrated through modern false doctrine?[13]

When a Believer Stops Believing

The practice of unrighteousness is not the only danger for believers. If a true believer stops believing, he will forfeit his salvation,
since salvation is only promised to those who believe and continue
to believe. In reference to salvation, the New Testament Greek often
uses the word *believe* in a continuous tense. Salvation is for those who
believe and continue believing, not to those who believed at some
moment in the past. For this reason and others, the New Testament is
full of admonitions that exhort believers to continue along the paths
of righteousness. Jesus warned His own disciples that "it is the one
who has endured to the end who will be saved" (Matt. 10:22).

Notice the conditional *if* in Paul's words to the Colossian Christians:

And although you were formerly alienated and hostile in
mind, engaged in evil deeds, yet He has now reconciled you
in His fleshly body through death, in order to present you
before Him holy and blameless and beyond reproach—*if
indeed you continue in the faith firmly established and steadfast,
and not moved away from the hope of the gospel* that you have
heard, which was proclaimed in all creation under heaven
(Col. 1:21-23, emphasis added).

Some Calvinists claim Paul meant that all true Christians will continue to persevere in faith until death, and if at some point they stop
believing, that proves they never truly believed in the first place and
were never actually saved. Because of the many fruit-bearing believers who apparently do fall away, some also maintain that a phony
Christian, who, of course, is not indwelt by the Holy Spirit, can appear to be a true believer. He may even demonstrate more fruit than

---

13 Two other related scriptures worth reading are Ezekiel 18:24-32 and 33:12-19.

some authentic Christians, yet he will ultimately go to hell because he never really possessed saving faith! Thus, the Calvinist who is consistent in his theology must always live with the possibility that his faith may yet prove to be bogus if he ever stops believing. If the only genuine faith is faith that perseveres until death, then a Calvinist can never be certain of his salvation, because he won't know if his faith is genuine until his final breath. Only then will he know if his faith persevered until death, thus proving itself to be true.

This theory is obviously not what Paul had in mind in Colossians 1:23. He wanted the Colossian Christians to know that they were presently reconciled to God, and that they would maintain their blameless standing before Him if they continued to believe.

Notice Paul's conditional *if* regarding the Corinthian's salvation:

> Now I make known to you, brethren, the gospel which I preached to you, which also you received, in which also you stand, by which also you are saved, *if you hold fast the word which I preached to you...* (1 Cor. 15:1-2, emphasis added).

Paul assured them of their salvation, predicated on their faith. They would remain saved if they held fast to the gospel. He did not say that time would tell if they really were saved if they persevered in faith until death.

Guard Your Heart Against Unbelief

The writer of the book of Hebrews warned of the real dangers of allowing unbelief or sin to creep into our lives. Note that he addressed his words to Christian brethren:[14]

> Take care, *brethren*, lest there should be in any one of you an evil, unbelieving heart, in falling away from the living God. But encourage one another day after day, as long as it is still called "Today," lest any one of you be hardened by the deceitfulness of sin. For we have become partakers of Christ, *if we hold fast the beginning of our assurance firm until the end* (Heb. 3:12-14, emphasis added).

---

14 Contrary to what some want us to believe, the author was not addressing *Hebrew brethren* who were only considering if they might believe in Jesus. He wrote to brethren who were already "partakers of Christ" (3:14), not brethren who were *considering* partaking of Christ. Additionally, he admonished them to "hold fast the beginning of [their] assurance firm until the end" (3:14), something only a believer who already has assurance can do. Moreover, the author warned these brethren to take care, lest there should be in any one of them an "evil, unbelieving heart in falling away from the living God" (3:12). Those who are not born again presently have evil, unbelieving hearts, and thus are in no danger of their hearts becoming evil and unbelieving. Finally, these brethren were in danger of "falling away from the living God," whereas Hebrew brethren who were only considering Christ had not even come to God yet.

We are "partakers of Christ" as long as we "hold fast" in faith. Sin has the ability to deceive and harden us, so we should beware of both unbelief and sin creeping into our lives.

Later in his epistle, the author of the book of Hebrews quoted one of the most well-known verses in the Old Testament, Habakkuk 2:4, and then added his inspired commentary:

> "But My righteous one shall live by faith; *And if he shrinks back, My soul has no pleasure in him*." But we are not of those *who shrink back to destruction,* but of those who have faith to the preserving of the soul (Heb. 10:38-39, emphasis added).

How much clearer could it be?

Grafted in and Broken Off

Among many other scriptures, Romans 11:13-24 also stands out as proof that true believers can forfeit their salvation if they abandon their faith. This, any honest reader will have to admit:

> But I am speaking to you who are Gentiles. Inasmuch then as I am an apostle of Gentiles, I magnify my ministry, if some-how I might move to jealousy my fellow countrymen and save some of them. For if their rejection be the reconciliation of the world, what will their acceptance be but life from the dead? And if the first piece of dough be holy, the lump is also; and if the root be holy, the branches are too. But if some of the [Jewish] branches were broken off, and you, being a wild olive [a Gentile], were grafted in among them and became partaker with them of the rich root of the olive tree, do not be arrogant toward the branches; but if you are arrogant, remember that it is not you who supports the root, but the root supports you. You will say then, "Branches were broken off so that I might be grafted in." Quite right, *they were broken off for their unbelief,* but *you stand by your faith.* Do not be conceited, but fear; for *if God did not spare the natural branches, neither will He spare you.* Behold then the kindness and severity of God; to those who fell, severity, but to you, God's kindness, *if you continue in His kindness; otherwise you also will be cut off.* And they also, if they do not continue in their unbelief, will be grafted in; for God is able to graft them in again. For if you were cut off from what is by nature a wild olive tree, and were grafted contrary to nature into

a cultivated olive tree, how much more shall these who are the natural branches be grafted into their own olive tree? (Rom. 11:13-24, emphasis added).

Clearly, there exists the possibility of losing one's position in God's tree of salvation. We stand by our faith and are guaranteed our place only if we "continue in His kindness" (11:22).[15]

Back to God's Discipline

With all this in mind, let's go back now to Paul's words about God's discipline in 1 Corinthians 11:27-34 and ask another question: Does God's discipline guarantee that a sinning Christian will repent and not be condemned along with the world?

Obviously the answer is *no* for several reasons. First, because of the many scriptures we've just considered, all of which indicate that a true believer can forfeit his salvation by abandoning his faith or returning to the practice of unrighteousness. Any believer who strays is, without a doubt, the object of God's love, and Scripture teaches that He disciplines those He loves (see Heb. 12:6). However, since it's clearly possible for believers to return to unrighteousness or unbelief and die spiritually, we can only conclude that God's discipline doesn't always bring back those who stray.

Second, God never overrides our free will so far as our own salvation is concerned. If we don't want to serve Him, we don't have to, and the Bible contains scores of examples of those whom God disciplined who did not repent. King Asa, for example, was a man who initially was a very godly king. Later in his life, however, he sinned, and refused to repent even while suffering God's discipline, dispensed by means of a disease in his feet. He ultimately died from his disease (see 2 Chron. 14-16).

It is quite possible, according to the author of the book of Hebrews, for God's children to respond wrongly to His discipline:

> You have forgotten the exhortation which is addressed to you as sons, "My son, do not regard lightly the discipline of the Lord, nor faint when you are reproved by Him"....

---

15 Those who are still not persuaded that a Christian can forfeit his salvation should consider all of the following New Testament passages: Matt. 18:21-35; 24:4-5, 11-13, 23-26, 42-51; 25:1-30; Luke 8:11-15; 11:24-28; 12:42-46; John 6:66-71; 8:31-32, 51; 15:1-6; Acts 11:21-23; 14:21-22; Rom. 6:11-23; 8:12-14, 17; 11:20-22; 1 Cor. 9:23-27; 10:1-21; 11:29-32; 15:1-2; 2 Cor. 1:24; 11:2-4; 12:21-13:5; Gal. 5:1-4; 6:7-9; Phil. 2:12-16; 3:17-4:1; Col. 1:21-23; 2:4-8, 18-19; 1 Thes. 3:1-8; 1 Tim. 1:3-7, 18-20; 4:1-16; 5:5-6, 11-15, 6:9-12, 17-19, 20-21; 2 Tim. 2:11-18; 3:13-15; Heb. 2:1-3; 3:6-19; 4:1-16; 5:8-9; 6:4-9, 10-20; 10:19-39; 12:1-17, 25-29; Jas. 1:12-16; 4:4-10; 5:19-20; 2 Pet. 1:5-11; 2:1-22; 3:16-17; 1 John 2:15-2:28; 5:16; 2 John 6-9; Jude 20-21; Rev. 2:7, 10-11, 17-26; 3:4-5, 8-12, 14-22; 21:7-8; 22:18-19.

> Furthermore, we had earthly fathers to discipline us, and
> we respected them; shall we not much rather be subject to
> the Father of spirits, and live? (Heb. 12:5, 9).

When we are disciplined by our Father, we can "regard [it] light-ly," that is, ignore it, or "faint," that is, be overcome by it and quit. God, however, desires that we subject ourselves to His discipline and "live." Clearly, the implication is that if we don't subject ourselves, we will not live, but die. The author must have been writing about spiritual life (and, by implication, spiritual death), simply because even obedient Christians all eventually die physically, not to men-tion the fact that many who are not subject to "the Father of spirits" continue to live physically for a long time.

This leads us to the next question: What about premature physi-cal death? If that is a form of God's discipline, the purpose of which is that we "may not be condemned along with the world," wouldn't the Lord bring every sinning Christian home to heaven before he died spiritually?

If that was always the case, then it would be impossible for a person to forfeit his salvation. If a person was saved, he would never need to be concerned about abandoning his faith or returning to the practice of sin, because he could rest in the assurance that the Lord would cut his life short before he died spiritually and lost his salva-tion. This idea, however, stands opposed to the many scriptures that clearly indicate that a truly saved person can forfeit his salvation. So what is the answer?

Perhaps an example from human experience might help us: A citizen might break the law and suffer the discipline of the govern-ment. If he, however, flees the country, he has taken himself out of the jurisdiction of the government. Consequently, he neither suffers its wrath nor enjoys the benefits shared by all its citizens.

Or another example: A son might disobey his father and suffer his loving discipline. But if the son runs away from home to constantly indulge in what his father would disapprove of, he need not fear his father's discipline. He's removed himself from the family. So, too, those who abandon their faith or return wholeheartedly to follow the flesh, the comfort of promised discipline and, if need be, prema-ture death, does not apply. They have forfeited all that was theirs. They, of course, may well die prematurely, but their final destination is not heaven.

Those among God's children, however, who stumble into sin but whose hearts are still inclined to serve God, place themselves in a position to be disciplined by their Father if they do not judge themselves by confession and repentance. These children are generally obedient: not running away or abandoning their family, but are disobedient to some degree. If they persist in their disobedience, not confessing and repenting of their sin, they may be judged by means of premature physical death, but are still saved when they die.

For example, God may call one of His children to be a pastor. If that child of God resists the call, he may suffer God's discipline in some form. If he persists in disobedience, he may suffer premature death, yet he will still go to heaven. He was not "living according to the flesh," but was "by the Spirit putting to death the deeds of the body." He had fruit in his life, but was falling short of what God expected. So he is not like the Christian who has abandoned his faith or returned to the practice of sin.

We might ask, "What is so terrible about dying prematurely and going to heaven? Wouldn't that be more of a reward than a chastisement?"

Such a question reveals our lack of understanding of how greatly God will reward the godly in the next life. If giving even a cup of cold water will be rewarded; if by patiently enduring "momentary, light affliction" we can expect in return "an eternal weight of glory far beyond all comparison" (2 Cor. 4:17); if by sharing with those in need we can lay up "treasure in heaven" (Luke 12:33), then every extra second we can serve God on earth should be considered an unparalleled opportunity. How sad it is when we waste time that we can never regain. In the future, we will look back with much regret. How much more will this be true of those who died prematurely and had no further opportunities to serve the Lord on earth?

Is All Sickness an Indication of God's Discipline?

Clearly, from what Paul wrote to the Corinthians, weakness, sickness and premature death can all be manifestations of God's discipline. Although it would be unsafe to conclude that all weakness, sickness or premature death is a sure indication of God's discipline, there are many other scriptures besides 1 Corinthians 11:27-32 that attest to the possibility.[16] Thus any Christian who finds himself suffering physically would be wise to spend some time in self-examination. If we *are* suffering God's discipline, it would seem unlikely that we would find lasting physical relief apart from repentance and

16 See, for example, Ex. 15:26; Num. 12:1-15; Deut. 7:15; 28:22, 27-28, 35, 58-61; 1 Sam. 5:1-12; 1 Kings 8:35-39; 2 Kings 5:21-27; 2 Chron. 16:10-13; 21:12-20; 26:16-21; Ps. 38:3; 106:13-15; 107:17-18; Is. 10:15-16; Jn. 5:5-14; Acts 5:1-11; 1 Cor. 5:1-5; 11:27-34; Jas. 5:13-16; Rev. 2:20-23.

God's forgiveness.

God's discipline can certainly come in forms other than physical illness. God can arrange circumstances in an infinite number of ways to accomplish His purposes. Jacob, who once impersonated his brother in order to deceive his father, woke up one morning married to a woman who had impersonated his fiancée! Many disobedient Christians have awakened to similar circumstances, as the Lord gently taught them about sowing and reaping.

Above all, we should not forget that God's discipline is an indication of His love for us. The disciplined Christian should not entertain any thoughts that would say otherwise. Jesus said, *"Those whom I love, I reprove and discipline;* be zealous therefore, and repent" (Rev. 3:19, emphasis added). The writer of the book of Hebrews tells us that God deals with us as any good father would his son:

> For consider Him who has endured such hostility by sinners against Himself, so that you may not grow weary and lose heart. You have not yet resisted to the point of shedding blood in your striving against sin; and you have forgotten the exhortation which is addressed to you as sons,
>
> "My son, do not regard lightly the discipline of the Lord,
>   Nor faint when you are reproved by Him;
>   For those whom the Lord loves He disciplines,
>   And He scourges every son whom He receives."
>
> It is for discipline that you endure; God deals with you as with sons; for what son is there whom his father does not discipline? But if you are without discipline, of which all have become partakers, then you are illegitimate children and not sons. Furthermore, we had earthly fathers to discipline us, and we respected them; shall we not much rather be subject to the Father of spirits, and live? For they disciplined us for a short time as seemed best to them, but He disciplines us for our good, that we may share His holiness. All discipline for the moment seems not to be joyful, but sorrowful; yet to those who have been trained by it, afterwards it yields the peaceful fruit of righteousness (Heb. 12:3-11).

Taking into consideration what we've just read, it would seem that we should be more concerned about *not being* disciplined than *being* disciplined! The author of Hebrews wrote that "all have become partakers" of God's discipline, and those who haven't are "illegitimate children and not sons" (12:8).

God desires that we share His holiness. This has been His intention from the beginning. Being disciplined is no fun, but after we've endured it, it yields righteousness in our lives. The Psalmist wrote, "Before I was afflicted I went astray / But now I keep Thy word....It is good for me that I was afflicted / That I may learn Thy statutes" (Ps. 119:67, 71).

When the Church Administers God's Discipline

There is one other aspect of God's discipline that we need to consider. It, too, is something God uses to motivate us to be holy. It is discipline administered by the church.

Unfortunately, Jesus' words on the subject are rarely obeyed, primarily because the focus of so many churches and professing Christians is not personal or corporate holiness. Nevertheless, true Christians who are striving together to please the Lord won't ignore what Jesus said:

> And if your brother sins, go and reprove him in private; if he listens to you, you have won your brother. But if he does not listen to you, take one or two more with you, so that by the mouth of two or three witnesses every fact may be confirmed. And if he refuses to listen to them, tell it to the church; and if he refuses to listen even to the church, let him be to you as a Gentile and a tax-gatherer (Matt. 18:15-17).

One can't help but wonder what would happen if these commands were obeyed in every church. No doubt that in many, attendance would significantly drop. Clearly, as fellow members of Christ's body, we have a responsibility, not only for our own holiness, but we also share some responsibility for the holiness of other believers and the purity of Christ's church.

It seems reasonable to think that Jesus' words regarding church discipline have application to those times when a brother sins against us *personally*, and not when a brother sins in general. This interpretation is buttressed somewhat by Jesus' words recorded in Luke 17:3-4: "Be on your guard! If your brother sins, rebuke him; and if he repents, forgive him. And if he sins *against you* seven times a day, and returns to you seven times, saying, 'I repent,' forgive him" (emphasis added).

Notice Jesus said, "If he sins *against you*." Also, Jesus told us to forgive any repentant brother whom we rebuke. We can only forgive the personal offenses of others, not their general sins. Moreover, we note that following Jesus' words about church discipline in Matthew 18 is the parable of the unforgiving servant, prompted by Peter's question regarding how often he should forgive his brother. Implied in Peter's question and Jesus' answer in the parable is the idea of personal offenses.

The Proper Sequence

"Church discipline," of course, should rarely involve the whole church. It begins with one person who is devoted to being holy. He must be holy for at least two reasons. First, if he is not personally holy to some degree, he will play the part of the man with a log in his eye who is trying to remove the speck in the eye of another (see Matt. 7:3-5). What right do I have to correct a sinning brother if I am a greater sinner?

Second, if the offense committed is personal, then the offended one must be holy enough to desire reconciliation. Too many of us, when offended, talk about the offense with everyone but the offender, preferring to gossip rather than work for reconciliation. Scripture warns us that, when we do this, we are in danger of judgment (see Matt. 7:1-2; Jas. 4:11; 5:9).

So, let's imagine that a fellow believer sins,[17] and let's say his offense is against you. You should then lovingly, gently, and humbly confront him. Most times you will discover that the offender didn't realize what he'd done, and he will immediately ask your forgiveness. You, of course, will then be obligated to forgive him, and you may want to question at that point if you are a little bit too sensitive. Many "offenses" that people "suffer" ought to be overlooked with the assumption that the offender intended no harm. For example, just because it *seemed* as if your pastor was avoiding you at church doesn't mean he *was* avoiding you. He may have just been busy looking after others.

Another possibility when you confront the offender is that he may enlighten you as to your contribution in the breach. He may tell you that he did what he did because you offended him. Of course, if that is the case, he should have already come to you! Nevertheless, you may now understand that you were the real cause of the problem and need to ask forgiveness. Your brother, then, will be obligated to forgive you, and reconciliation will occur.

---

17 It's a different story when an unbeliever sins against you, because he is not submitted to Christ. Trying to correct him could result in a fulfillment of Proverbs 9:7: "He who corrects a scoffer gets dishonor for himself, And he who reproves a wicked man gets insults for himself."

Steps Two and Three

But let's say that neither of these things happens, and the offender refuses to acknowledge his guilt or ask your forgiveness. Then you should "take one or two more with you, so that by the mouth of two or three witnesses every fact may be confirmed" (Matt. 18:16).

Of course, before you'll be able to convince one or two others to confront the offender, you'll have to convince them of your case. They may want to quiz the offender before they'll take your side. They may even become convinced that the supposed offender is guiltless and correct you! If that is the case, you should then seek the "offender's" forgiveness.

If you are able to convince the one or two others of your case, then together, you should all confront the offender once again. Hopefully, their siding with you should be enough to convince him to admit his wrong and seek your forgiveness, resulting in reconciliation.

Rarely does it happen, but if he still refuses to admit his wrong, then the matter should be taken before the whole church. This will, of course, require that those in church leadership be involved; they will doubtlessly want to investigate everything fully before deciding to join your cause. Again, the possibility exists that they may discover that both sides have valid complaints, and that both parties need to seek each other's forgiveness. However, if they join your side, you can be reasonably sure that you have a justified complaint against your brother.

When he discovers that the entire church has taken your side and is planning to confront him publicly, he will then either repent or leave the church. It is quite unlikely that he will have to be excommunicated. Jesus said that he should be treated as a "Gentile and a tax-gatherer" (18:17). That is, he should be treated as an unregenerate person, because that is what he obviously is. One who is truly born again would not have resisted the collective conviction of the entire church. Thus, he should be treated like an unbeliever—in need of being evangelized and born again.

Keep in mind that Jesus never envisioned the large congregations that often comprise churches today. The early churches were small groups that met in homes. So the third step Jesus envisioned would have involved probably no more than twenty people, all of whom knew and loved both the offender and offended persons. This being so, it would be better to follow this third step in the context of a small group.

If the Offender Repents...

If, at any point before, during, or after the process of church discipline, the offender asks your forgiveness, you must forgive him, or you will experience God's discipline. Within seconds of giving instructions regarding church discipline, Jesus told a story about a slave who was forgiven an enormous debt by his king. Yet that slave then refused to forgive a fellow slave who owed him a much smaller debt, and he had that fellow slave thrown into prison. When the king heard of his slave's unforgiveness, he was "moved with anger" and "handed him over to the torturers until he should repay all that was owed him" (Matt. 18:34). Jesus then promised us, "So shall My heavenly Father also do to you, if each of you does not forgive his brother from your heart" (Matt. 18:35).

Clearly, the unforgiving servant again became responsible for his past debt which he could never repay, and found himself in the same state as he had been previously: unforgiven. Does this not indicate that he "lost his salvation?" Jesus promised that unless we forgive the sins of others, we would not be forgiven (see Matt. 6:14-15).

False Forgiveness

Do we have an obligation to forgive those who wrong us, but who never admit their offenses? Must we treat unrepentant offenders as if nothing has happened? These are important questions that plague the minds of many Christians.

First, we must realize that there can be no true reconciliation apart from communication, repentance and forgiveness. This is easily understood in the context of marriage. When one spouse offends another, there is tension between them. Perhaps they stop talking to one another. One sleeps on the couch.

What is it that can restore their relationship? Only communication, repentance and forgiveness. They may simply try to ignore what has happened. They may force themselves to smile at one another and chat about other subjects. But there is still something between them. Their relationship has been damaged, and it will remain that way until there is communication, repentance and forgiveness.

If one person is the sole offender, the offended one may attempt to "forgive," trying to forget what has happened and go on with life as if nothing happened. But every time he or she sees the offender, the offense comes to mind. "Why can't I forgive?" is the anguished thought.

The reason is because he or she attempts the impossible, doing what God Himself doesn't practice. God only forgives those who repent. He doesn't expect an offended believer to pretend that there has been no offense committed against him, while trying to convince himself that the offender is really a wonderful person with no flaws. That is precisely why Jesus instructed us to confront the offender, and, if he doesn't repent, to take him through the steps of church discipline. At any point in the process, if he repents, then we *must* forgive him. If Jesus expected an offended believer just to "forgive" and go on, He would never have said what He did about church discipline. Again, Jesus said,

> Be on your guard! If your brother sins, rebuke him; and *if he repents, forgive him.* And if he sins against you seven times a day, and returns to you seven times, saying, *"I repent"* forgive him" (Luke 17:3-4, emphasis added).

It is possible, and expected, that believers will love everyone, even unrepentant offenders, just as God does. But loving them doesn't necessarily require unconditional forgiveness. God loves everyone, but not everyone is forgiven by Him.

Impossible Cases

But what if it is impossible, because of circumstances beyond your control, to follow the three-step process Jesus outlined? For example, you've been seriously offended by an influential believer, such as a pastor, and he won't let you make an appointment with him. Or, you confront an offender who refuses to repent, and you can't find anyone willing to go back with you for the second step.

In such cases, Paul's words apply: "If possible, so far as it depends on you, be at peace with all men" (Rom. 12:18). Do what you can do; that is all God expects.

Regardless of the situation, the Lord always wants us to "turn the other cheek" and "go the extra mile." As I've previously said, this doesn't mean that we should allow ourselves to be abused, but that we should go beyond what people would normally expect. This is especially true when we deal with unbelievers. They've made no claim to be Christ's followers, so to try to take them through the process that God has given to the church would be foolish.

As I've already said, although God does not forgive anyone unless he repents, He still loves unrepentant people and longingly waits with open arms to receive them at any time. That should be our attitude toward *any* unrepentant offender. We can't forgive him until he repents, but we can love him, pray for him, and wait with open arms of love. The prodigal son's father didn't journey to a distant land to offer his son a low-interest loan, but neither did he turn his back when he saw his son coming home in shame. He ran and embraced him. Joseph didn't reveal himself to his brothers when they first visited him in Egypt, but once they demonstrated their repentance some time later, he received them with tears.

The Other Side of the Coin

What if *you* are the object of church discipline? A brother comes to you with word that you've offended him. What should you do? You should swallow any pride that might try to surface, listen carefully, and consider what he's saying. If you think his gripe is justified, you should apologize and ask forgiveness. If you think otherwise, you should gently discuss your feelings and work for understanding and reconciliation. Hopefully you'll succeed.

If he returns with one or two others, and they side with the offended one even after listening to your version of the story, you should very seriously consider what they tell you and admit your wrong, asking forgiveness.

If you are convinced that all three are wrong and they take the matter to the church, you should willingly meet with any of the leadership who requests a meeting, carefully explaining your version of the story. If the entire church sides with the offended brother, you should realize that you are wrong, admit it, and ask forgiveness.

Reverse Church Discipline

Church discipline is a form of God's discipline since it is done at His command. It is another way He motivates us to be holy and a means whereby He keeps His true church pure.

In churches full of phony Christians, however, it is an entirely different story. I know a godly pastor who refused to sing a duet with a man who attended his church and who was living in a fornicating relationship. The fornicator was the member of a family of long-standing "pillars" in the church, and when they learned of this pastor's "offense," they worked to get him removed from his pastorate. He was too judgmental and intolerant, they said, and most of the congregation sided with them. Consequently, they were able to remove him. That is church discipline in reverse, and is another way that God keeps *His* church pure!

We should consider all three of the motivations—love of God, hope of reward, and fear of discipline—as further evidence of God's amazing grace toward us. Each is a gift He didn't have to give, but He has, by His grace. All glory be to Him for our holiness!

NINE

Striving Against Sin

"Sin is crouching at the door; and its desire is for you, but you must master it" (Gen. 4:7, emphasis added).

As was pointed out in the previous chapter, our sanctification is a joint effort on the part of God and ourselves. We grow to be progressively more like Jesus as we cooperate with the Father. He provides our ability and motivation to be holy. His "divine power has granted to us everything pertaining to life *and godliness*" (2 Pet. 1:3, emphasis added). He gives us a new nature and leads us by His indwelling Spirit. *But He still leaves something for us to do.* We still have a free will. We must follow the Spirit who indwells us, and this every true Christian does to some degree. Otherwise, he shows himself to be a counterfeit believer (see Rom. 8:5-14).

It is also our responsibility to renew our minds with God's Word, for we must know His will before we can do it. Even in that, God helps us through the teaching ministry of the Holy Spirit and through divinely-anointed human teachers. As our minds are renewed with His truth, we are transformed (see John 8:31-36; Rom. 12:2). And, of course, we also have the responsibility of being not just hearers of the word, but doers (see Jas. 1:22).

This balance we must maintain. Although Scripture speaks of both human and divine responsibility, too many emphasize one at the other's neglect. Historically, to the one side are the pietists, who strive to be holy in their own strength. To the other side are the quietists, who are abhorred with the idea of human striving, and who leave everything in God's lap. Both sides are armed with long lists of scriptures, and if they'd each only take a look at the other side's list, they'd realize they're both right and both wrong. The truth lies in the middle, where both lists are given equal honor. Perhaps no single scripture expresses this balance better than Philippians 2:12-13:

> So then, my beloved, just as *you* have always *obeyed,* not as in my presence only, but now much more in my absence, *work out your salvation* with fear and trembling; *for it is God who is at work in you,* both to will and to work for His good pleasure (emphasis added).

The fruit that the Spirit produces within us is love, joy, peace, patience, kindness, goodness, faithfulness, gentleness and self-control, but only with our cooperation will these fruit be manifest in our lives. We must do something, because, according to Scripture, there are at least three forces that oppose the fruit:

(1) God has allowed us to remain "in the world," a world that tempts us to be unloving, downcast, anxious, impatient, unkind, evil, unfaithful, harsh and self-indulgent.

(2) Although God has filled us with His Spirit, given us a new nature and broken sin's power over us, He has also allowed a residue of the old sinful nature to remain in us, what Paul called "the flesh."

(3) Although we have been delivered from Satan's kingdom and are no longer his spiritual offspring, we find ourselves, like the Christians of old, in an arena filled with roaring lions who desire to devour us (see 1 Peter 5:8). Satan and his demons harass and tempt us to do what God forbids.

These three are our enemies: the world, the flesh, and the devil.

Why Has God Left Us in Enemy Territory?

If God desires our holiness, why has He allowed these enemies to live among us? What divine purpose do they serve?

Like the wicked nations God permitted to remain in Israel's land after Joshua's death, our enemies are also allowed to remain that God might test us (see Judges 2:20-3:1). By them our love and obedience, and thus our faith, are tested. Faith can only be tested where unbelief is possible. Love can be tested only when hatred is an alternative. Obedience can only be tested where disobedience is possible.

To the ancient Israelites God said:

> If a prophet or a dreamer of dreams arises among you and
> gives you a sign or a wonder, and the sign or the wonder
> comes true, concerning which he spoke to you, saying, 'Let
> us go after other gods (whom you have not known) and
> let us serve them,' you shall not listen to the words of that
> prophet or that dreamer of dreams; for the Lord your God
> is testing you to find out if you love the Lord your God with
> all your heart and with all your soul. You shall follow the
> Lord your God and fear Him; and you shall keep His com-
> mandments, listen to His voice, serve Him, and cling to
> Him (Deut. 13:1-4).

Incredibly, God tested His people by means of a false prophet!
But does He not possess all knowledge as well as perfect foreknowl-
edge? Why then is there need of a test?

The reason is this: in order for God to foreknow the outcome of a
free moral agent's test, that free moral agent must be tested at some
point in time. Only what can be known in time can be foreknown
before time. Consequently, our temptations, tests and trials, limited
by time and space, serve a purpose in the plan of the One who lives
outside time and space. They provide the means whereby our faith
is proved genuine. Peter wrote to Christians under fire:

> In this you greatly rejoice, even though now for a little while,
> if necessary, you have been distressed by various trials, that
> *the proof of your faith*, being more precious than gold which
> is perishable, even though tested by fire, may be found to
> result in praise and glory and honor at the revelation of Je-
> sus Christ....Beloved, do not be surprised at the fiery ordeal
> among you, *which comes upon you for your testing*, as though
> some strange thing were happening to you; but to the degree
> that you share the sufferings of Christ, keep on rejoicing; so
> that also at the revelation of His glory, you may rejoice with
> exultation (1 Pet. 1:6-7; 4:12-13, emphasis added).

If for no other reason, we should rejoice under persecution because it allows us the opportunity to show our enduring faith. Saving faith perseveres, but faith can persevere only if there is opposition and temptation not to persevere.

What is Our Responsibility?

Because modern evangelical theology has become so contaminated with antinomian ideas that distort God's grace and nullify human responsibility, today too many professing Christians piously pass off their biblical responsibilities to God. Beguiled by false teaching about grace, to them any mention of human effort is considered anathema, and under the subtle guise of defending God's glory, they label any teaching about holiness as legalism. *Works* is a dirty word that doesn't belong in a Christian's vocabulary. And certainly we don't want to entertain any thought that we must do anything now that Christ's work is finished. That would be adding works (God forbid!) to our salvation!

In hopes to remedy this unscriptural reasoning, I've compiled a list of what a significant portion of the New Testament says that believers should *do*. The essential component of human responsibility in the sanctification process is easily understood from the many scriptures that contain commandments and instructions. When we read them, we can no longer doubt that Christians are free moral agents who can will to be holy. Likewise, exposed is the folly of those who want us to believe that God is robbed of glory when we add our efforts toward sanctification. Clearly, God expects those who possess His Holy Spirit to *do* certain things by the power of the Spirit. Stated succinctly, *we* must strive against sin in all its forms (see Heb. 12:4). *We* must pursue the sanctification "without which no one will see the Lord" (Heb. 12:14).

The following list reveals, from the four Gospels and the book of Romans, God's expectations for our behavior. If the New Testament states that a certain behavior is wrong or sinful, then God obviously holds people accountable for such behavior, indicating that human responsibility is a factor in that wrong behavior.

Although you might be tempted to skip over the following list, for your own benefit I ask that you read it slowly. It can impact you in a way that could be life changing.

What does God expect us to do? Here is a list. Clearly, *none* of these things will happen in our lives unless *we do* what God says.

God expects us to:

> Not tempt Him (Matt. 4:7).
> Worship the Lord our God and serve Him only (Matt. 4:10).
> Repent in order to be saved (Matt. 4:17).
> Rejoice and be glad when we are persecuted (Matt. 5:12).
> Let our lights shine before men so they may see our good
>   works (Matt. 5:16).
> Keep and teach God's commandments, even the least of

them (Matt. 5:19).

Not murder, hate, or harm another person in any way
(Matt. 5:21-22).

Work toward reconciliation with those we've offended
(Matt. 5:24-25).

Not commit adultery or be lustful (Matt. 5:27-28).

Remove anything that causes us to stumble into sin
(Matt. 5:29-30).

Not divorce except for cases of unrepentant unchastity
(Matt. 5:32).

Make no swearing oaths and never lie, but always keep
our word (Matt. 5:33-37).

Not take our own revenge, but be extremely tolerant of
others, even doing good to those who mistreat us
(Matt. 5:38-42).

Love our enemies and pray for our persecutors
(Matt. 5:44-47).

Strive to be perfect (Matt. 5:48).

Do no good deed for the purpose of receiving the praise of
others (Matt. 6:1).

Give alms (Matt. 6:2-4).

Pray (Matt. 6:5-6).

Not use meaningless repetition when we pray (Matt. 6:7).

Pray after the pattern of "the Lord's prayer" (Matt. 6:9-13).

Forgive others (Matt. 6:14).

Fast (Matt. 6:16).

Not lay up treasures upon earth, but lay them up in
heaven (Matt. 6:19-21).

Serve God and not money (Matt. 6:24).

Not worry about our material needs (Matt. 6:25-32).

Seek first God's kingdom and righteousness (Matt. 6:33).

Not judge others (Matt. 7:1-5).

Not give what is holy to dogs (Matt. 7:6).

Ask, seek and knock (Matt. 7:7-11).

Do for others what we want them to do for us (Matt. 7:12).

Enter by the narrow gate (Matt. 7:13).

Beware of false prophets (Matt. 7:15-20).

Do what Jesus said or face destruction (Matt. 7:24-27).

Beseech the Lord to send out workers into His harvest
(Matt. 9:38).

Confess Jesus before others and not deny Him
(Matt. 10:32-33).

Love Jesus more than our closest relatives (Matt. 10:37).

Take up our cross and follow Jesus (Matt. 10:38).

Lose our life for Jesus' sake (Matt. 10:39).

Take Jesus' yoke upon us (Matt. 11:28-30).

Be "for" Jesus and gather with Him (Matt. 12:30).

Not blaspheme the Holy Spirit (Matt. 12:31).

Do the will of the Father (Matt. 12:50).

Honor our parents (Matt. 15:4-6).

Not be defiled by evil thoughts, murder, adultery, fornication, theft, lying and slandering (Matt. 15:19-20).

Deny ourselves (Matt. 16:24).

Be converted and become like children, humbling ourselves (Matt. 18:3-4).

Not cause any child who believes in Jesus to stumble (Matt. 18:6).

Cause no one to stumble (Matt. 18:7).

Not despise any children (Matt. 18:10).

Rebuke in private any brother who sins against us (Matt. 18:15).

Obey Jesus' instructions regarding church discipline (Matt. 18:16-17).

Forgive our brothers from our hearts (Matt. 18:35).

Love our neighbor as ourselves (Matt. 19:19).

Be the servant of others (Matt. 20:26-28).

Pay our government's rightful taxes and give to God what is His (Matt. 22:21).

Love the Lord our God with all our hearts, souls and minds (Matt. 22:37).

Allow no one to call us "teacher," or "leader," and call no one our father but our heavenly Father (Matt. 23:8-10).

Not exalt but humble ourselves (Matt. 23:12).

Hinder no one from entering God's kingdom (Matt. 23:13).

Never take advantage of widows (Matt. 23:14).

Never influence others to act hypocritically (Matt. 23:15).

Not neglect the weightier provisions of the law, such as justice, mercy and faithfulness (Matt. 23:23).

Not be hypocritical in any way (Matt. 23:25-28).

Not be frightened about wars and rumors of wars prior to Jesus' return (Matt. 24:6).

Not fall away, or betray or hate a brother (Matt. 24:10).

Not allow ourselves to be misled by false prophets (Matt. 24:11).

Not allow our love to grow cold because of the increase of
lawlessness (Matt. 24:12).

Endure to the end (Matt. 24:13).

Not believe false reports about the return of Christ
(Matt. 24:23-26).

Recognize the true signs of Christ's return (Matt. 24:32-33).

Be on the alert for Christ's return (Matt. 24:42).

Always be a faithful and sensible slave, anticipating our
Lord's imminent return, never backsliding but always
obeying Him (Matt. 24:45-51).

Utilize the time, talents and treasures that God has
entrusted to us for His service (Matt. 25:14-30).

Provide food, drink, shelter and clothing for impoverished
Christians; visit sick and imprisoned Christians
(Matt. 25:34-40).

Partake of the Lord's Supper (Matt. 26:26-27).

Make disciples of all nations, baptizing them in the name
of the Father, Son, and Holy Spirit, teaching them to
observe all that Jesus commanded (Matt. 28:19-20).

Take care what we listen to (Mark 4:24).

Not neglect the commandments of God in order to keep
traditions (Mark 7:9).

Not be ashamed of Jesus or His words (Mark 8:38).

Be at peace with one another (Mark 9:50).

Not hinder children from coming to Him (Mark 10:14).

Have faith in God (Mark 11:22).

Believe that we have received all things for which we
pray and ask (Mark 11:24).

Beware of religious teachers who wear clothing that makes
them stand out, who like respectful greetings, chief
seats and places of honor, who take advantage of
widows and pray long prayers for appearance's
sake (Mark 12:38-40).

Not be anxious about what we are to say when put on trial
for our faith, but say what the Holy Spirit tells us in
that hour (Mark 13:11).

Be baptized (Mark 16:16).

Bless those who curse us (Luke 6:28).

Give to everyone who asks of us, and not demand back
what others have taken from us (Luke 6:30).

Lend to others, expecting nothing in return (Luke 6:35).

Be merciful (Luke 6:36).

Not condemn others (Luke 6:37).

Give (Luke 6:38).

Not point out the speck in a brother's eye when we have a
    log in our own (Luke 6:41-42).

Not call Him "Lord" unless we do what He says
    (Luke 6:46-49).

Receive God's word in our hearts and hold it fast so that
    we bear fruit with perseverance (Luke 8:12-15).

Hear God's word and do it (Luke 8:21).

Receive children in Christ's name (Luke 9:48).

Not look back after putting our hands to the plow
    (Luke 9:62).

Ask for the Holy Spirit (Luke 11:13).

Watch out that the light in us may not be darkness
    (Luke 11:35).

Not love seats of honor and respectful greetings
    (Luke 11:43).

Not weigh down other people with hard burdens that we
    are unwilling to personally bear (Luke 11:46).

Not persecute His prophets (Luke 11:49).

Not take away the key of knowledge or hinder people
    from entering into true knowledge of God (Luke 11:52).

Beware of hypocritical religious leaders (Luke 12:1).

Not be afraid of those who can only kill us physically
    (Luke 12:4).

Fear Him who after He has killed has authority to cast into
    hell (Luke 12:5).

Not speak against or blaspheme Jesus or the Holy Spirit
    (Luke 12:10).

Beware and be on guard against every form of greed
    (Luke 12:15).

Not lay up treasure for ourselves but be rich toward God
    (Luke 12:21).

Sell our possessions and give to charity (Luke 12:33).

Bear fruit (Luke 13:6-9).

Strive to enter by the narrow door (Luke 13:24).

Never take a place of honor, exalting ourselves. Rather,
    we should humble ourselves, taking the last seat
    (Luke 14:8-10).

Love Him much more than our loved ones (Luke 14:26).

First count the cost of becoming His disciple
    (Luke 14:28-32).

Put all our material possessions under His control
(Luke 14:33).

Rejoice when God shows mercy to sinners in saving them
(Luke 15:1-32).

Be faithful in small things and with money (Luke 16:9-11).

Have compassion on the poor (Luke 16:19-31).

Rebuke a brother if he sins and forgive him if he repents
(Luke 17:3-4).

Consider ourselves unworthy slaves even when we've
done everything we've been commanded
(Luke 17:7-10).

Pray at all times and not lose heart (Luke 18:1).

Not trust in ourselves that we are righteous, nor view
others with contempt (Luke 18:9).

Receive the kingdom like a child (Luke 18:17).

Keep on the alert at all times, praying in order that we may
have strength to escape the trials preceding Christ's
return and stand before Jesus (Luke 21:36).

Proclaim repentance for the forgiveness of sins in Christ's
name to all nations (Luke 24:47).

Be born again (John 3:3).

Believe in Jesus (John 3:16).

Worship Him in spirit and truth (John 4:23-24).

Honor Jesus (John 5:23).

Seek glory from God (John 5:44).

Believe Moses' writings (John 5:46-47).

Not to work for the food that perishes, but for the food
which endures to eternal life which is given by Jesus
(John 6:27).

Eat the flesh and drink the blood of Christ (John 6:53-54).

Not judge according to appearance, but with righteous
judgment (John 7:24).

Abide in Jesus' word (John 8:31).

Keep Jesus' word (John 8:51).

Serve Jesus (John 12:26).

Love one another, even as Jesus loves us (John 13:34).

Believe that He is in the Father and the Father is in Him
(John 14:11).

Do the works that Jesus did and greater works
(John 14:12).

Love Jesus and keep His commandments (John 14:15).

Abide in Jesus' love (John 15:9).

> Ask Him for anything in Jesus' name (John 16:24).
> Take courage in tribulation (John 16:33).

This ends Jesus' commands found in the Gospels. *These are the things that we're supposed to be teaching Christ's disciples to obey* (see Matt. 28:20).

The commands and instructions given to believers in the epistles are essentially no different than what is found in the Gospels. We next consider human responsibility from just the book of Romans.

God expects us to:

> Not suppress the truth (Rom. 1:18).
> Not be guilty of idolatry (Rom. 1:23).
> Not exchange God's truth for a lie (Rom. 1:25).
> Not be involved in homosexual behavior (Rom. 1:26-27).
> Not be greedy, envious, deceitful, malicious, insolent, arrogant, boastful, disobedient to our parents, untrustworthy, unloving or unmerciful (Rom. 1:29-31).
> Not gossip or slander (Rom. 1:29-30).
> Not give our approval to those who practice sin (Rom. 1:32).
> Not think lightly of the riches of His kindness, forbearance and patience (Rom. 2:4).
> Persevere in doing good (Rom. 2:7).
> Seek for glory, honor and immortality (Rom. 2:7).
> Not be selfishly ambitious (Rom. 2:8).
> Not to curse or speak bitter words (Rom. 3:14).
> Consider ourselves dead to sin, but alive to God in Christ (Rom. 6:11).
> Not let sin reign in our bodies, obeying its desires (Rom. 6:12).
> Not go on presenting the members of our bodies to sin as instruments of unrighteousness (Rom. 6:13).
> Present ourselves to God as those alive from the dead, and our members as instruments of righteousness to God (Rom 6:13).
> Not covet (Rom. 7:7).
> Not live according to the flesh, but put to death the deeds of the body by the Spirit (Rom. 8:12-13).
> Present our bodies a living and holy sacrifice (Rom. 12:1).
> Not be conformed to this world, but be transformed by the

renewing of our minds (Rom. 12:2).

Not think more highly of ourselves than we ought (Rom. 12:3).

Exercise our gifts according to the grace given to us (Rom. 12:6).

Love others without hypocrisy (Rom. 12:9).

Abhor what is evil and cling to what is good (Rom. 12:9).

Be devoted to one another in brotherly love, giving preference to one another in honor (Rom. 12:10).

Not lag behind in diligence (Rom. 12:11).

Be fervent in spirit as we serve the Lord (Rom. 12:11).

Rejoice in hope (Rom. 12:12).

Persevere in tribulation (Rom. 12:12).

Be devoted to prayer (Rom. 12:12).

Contribute to the needs of the saints (Rom. 12:13).

Practice hospitality (Rom. 12:13).

Bless those who persecute us and not curse them (Rom. 12:14).

Rejoice with those who rejoice and weep with those who weep (Rom. 12:15).

Not be haughty of mind but associate with the lowly (Rom. 12:16).

Not be wise in our own estimation (Rom. 12:16).

Never pay back evil for evil to anyone (Rom. 12:17).

Respect what is right in the sight of all men (Rom. 12:17).

Be at peace with all men as far as possible (Rom. 12:18).

Never take our own revenge (Rom. 12:19).

Feed our enemy if he is hungry and give him a drink if he is thirsty (Rom. 12:20).

Not be overcome with evil, but overcome evil with good (Rom. 12:21).

Be subject to the governing authorities (Rom. 13:1).

Owe nothing to anyone except to love one another (Rom. 13:8).

Lay aside the deeds of darkness and put on the armor of light (Rom. 13:12).

Behave properly as in the day, not in carousing and drunkenness, sexual promiscuity and sensuality, strife or jealousy, but put on the Lord Jesus Christ, and make no provision for the flesh in regard to its lusts (Rom. 13:13-14).

Accept those who are weak in faith (Rom. 14:1).

Not judge our brother or regard him with contempt
   (Rom. 14:10).
Not put an obstacle or stumbling block in a brother's way
   (Rom. 14:13).
Pursue the things which make for peace and the building
   up of one another (Rom. 14:19).
Bear the weakness of those without strength if we are
   strong, not just pleasing ourselves (Rom. 15:1).
Accept one another, just as Christ accepted us (Rom. 15:7).
Keep our eyes on those who cause dissensions and
   hindrances contrary to biblical truth, and turn away from
   them (Rom. 16:17).

Now, may I ask, is there such a thing as human responsibility for Christians? What should we say to the person who says he's leaving his sanctification completely in the hands of God, lest he rob God of glory and be guilty of adding his own works to his salvation?

Spiritual War

Every one of the commandments and instructions listed above not only prove the concept of human responsibility but also imply that all of us are faced with alternate choices. We can choose to do or not do what Jesus said. From within our regenerated spirits, the Holy Spirit leads us to obey, while other forces, namely the world, the flesh, and the devil, tempt us to disobey. Thus we find that we're caught in a war.

Two points about this war need to be made. First, false Christians sometimes mistakenly suppose they are experiencing this spiritual war. In reality, however, they are experiencing a somewhat similar war between their conscience and their sinful nature. As Paul wrote, even unsaved people possess a conscience that alternately accuses or defends them (see Rom. 2:15). Because they have violated it so many times, however, their conscience is defiled (see Tit. 1:15), and its voice grows more dim as they continue to ignore its nagging. The true Christian, on the other hand, has a conscience that has been fully awakened, that speaks to him constantly and is not easy to ignore. The Spirit of God is leading all the true children of God (see Rom. 8:14).

The second point is that professing Christians often use the fact of the spiritual war as an excuse to sin. "We're in a war," they quip, "and so it's inevitable that we're going to lose a lot of battles." This excuse is in the same category as, "No one is perfect, you know! (So I'll be pathetic.)"

God is the one who has sovereignly permitted this spiritual war to exist, and His purpose in allowing it is *not* that His children would yield to sin. Rather, His purpose is that we would prove ourselves to be overcomers to His glory. Consider what Paul said about the war between the flesh and the Spirit in Galatians 5:

> But I say, walk by the Spirit, and you will not carry out the desire of the flesh. For the flesh sets its desire against the Spirit, and the Spirit against the flesh; for these are in opposition to one another, so that you may not do the things that you please. But if you are led by the Spirit, you are not under the Law. Now the deeds of the flesh are evident, which are: immorality, impurity, sensuality, idolatry, sorcery, enmities, strife, jealousy, outbursts of anger, disputes, dissensions, factions, envying, drunkenness, carousing, and things like these, of which I forewarn you just as I have forewarned you that those who practice such things shall not inherit the kingdom of God. But the fruit of the Spirit is love, joy, peace, patience, kindness, goodness, faithfulness, gentleness, self-control; against such things there is no law. Now those who belong to Christ Jesus have crucified the flesh with its passions and desires (Gal. 5:16-24).

Christians are obviously two-natured, possessing a sinful nature that opposes the indwelling Holy Spirit. But is this an excuse to yield to sin? Absolutely not. Paul warns that those who practice the sins of the flesh will not inherit God's kingdom. In fact, no true Christian habitually yields to the flesh, because, as Paul said, "Those who belong to Christ Jesus have crucified the flesh with its passions and desires" (5:24). This occurred at the initial point of salvation, when heart faith was manifested in repentance and submission to Christ's lordship. At that point, metaphorically speaking, we nailed the old sinful man to a cross. And there he must stay. He is still very much alive and may cry out to have his way, but by the power of the Spirit, his calls go unheeded.

In the Flesh or in the Spirit?

In the eighth chapter of Romans, Paul contrasts the unsaved person, whom he describes as being "in the flesh," with the regenerate person, whom he describes as being "in the Spirit." This is very important for us to understand. Read Paul's words carefully as we consider this passage of Scripture:

> For what the Law could not do, weak as it was through the
> flesh, God did: sending His own Son in the likeness of sinful
> flesh and as an offering for sin, He condemned sin in the flesh,
> in order that the requirement of the Law might be fulfilled in
> us, who do not walk according to the flesh, but according to
> the Spirit (Rom. 8:3-4).

Notice that already Paul has described believers as those who "do not walk [live their lives] according to the flesh, but according to the Spirit."

> For those who are according to the flesh [the unsaved] set
> their minds on the things of the flesh, but those who are ac-
> cording to the Spirit [the saved], the things of the Spirit. For
> the mind set on the flesh [what the unsaved do] is death,
> but the mind set on the Spirit [what the saved do] is life and
> peace, because the mind set on the flesh [what the unsaved
> do] is hostile toward God; for it does not subject itself to the
> law of God, for it is not even able to do so; and those who are
> in the flesh cannot please God. However, you [the believers]
> are not in the flesh but in the Spirit, *if indeed the Spirit of God
> dwells in you. But if anyone does not have the Spirit of Christ, he
> does not belong to Him* (Rom. 8:5-9, emphasis added).

Clearly, Paul is not contrasting two kinds of Christians, those who set their minds on the flesh and those who set their minds on the Spirit. He is contrasting those who are indwelt by the Spirit and who thus set their minds on the Spirit, with those who are not indwelt by the Spirit and whose minds are set on the flesh—Christians and non-Christians.

Christians can be said to have Christ in them, by the indwelling Spirit, even though they still possess the sinful nature of the flesh:

> And if Christ is in you, though the body is dead because of
> sin, yet the spirit is alive because of righteousness. But if the
> Spirit of Him who raised Jesus from the dead dwells in you,
> He who raised Christ Jesus from the dead will also give life
> to your mortal bodies through His Spirit who indwells you
> (Rom. 8:10-11).

Our body, what Paul calls the "outer man" in 2 Corinthians 4:16, is "dead" or "decaying" (2 Cor. 4:16) because of sin. But our spirit, the "inner man" (2 Cor. 4:16) is now alive because we've been made righteous. It is being renewed every day (see 2 Cor. 4:16). Yet we can look forward to the day when the Spirit within us will give life to our "mortal bodies," and our bodies will also be made new. Obviously, God intends that the indwelling Spirit dominate the flesh. It is destined to dominate to the point of changing our bodies and eradicating the sinful nature completely.

Finally, Paul warns the believers to whom he was writing about yielding to the flesh. By the power of the Spirit within them, they can put "to death the deeds of the body." This they must do:

> So then, brethren, we are under obligation, not to the flesh, to live according to the flesh—for if you are living according to the flesh, you must die; but if by the Spirit you are putting to death the deeds of the body, you will live. For all who are being led by the Spirit of God, these are sons of God (Rom. 8:12-14).

Do you fit the description of the one Paul said will not die, but live—the one who is "by the Spirit...putting to death the deeds of the body"? Then you are an authentic Christian. Clearly Paul believed that true Christians act differently than non-Christians. As he said, it is those who are being led by the Spirit who are God's true sons (see Rom. 8:14).

The Answer to an Objection

Some may object: "But didn't Paul confess that he himself practiced the very evil he hated, referring to himself as a 'wretched man'?"

Yes, he did. In fact, Paul said those words in the seventh chapter of Romans, just prior to what we've just been considering in the eighth chapter of Romans. Christians have debated if Paul was speaking of his experience before or after his conversion. Antinomians, in particular, love to set Paul's word in Romans 7 as the standard for normal Christian experience.

However, once we read Romans 7 in context with the two adjacent chapters, all of Paul's other writings, and the rest of the New Testament, there can be only one reasonable interpretation. Paul could only have been speaking of his experience before being indwelt by the Spirit. Otherwise, in chapter 7 he contradicted what he himself wrote about normal Christian experience in chapters 6 and 8. As has been appropriately asked, "If the man in chapter 7 is a born-again believer, who is the man in chapters 6 and 8?" They are obviously two vastly different people.

First, we note that the main theme of chapter 6 is the incompatibility of sin with the new creation. Paul began with the rhetorical question, "Are we to continue in sin that grace might increase?" (6:1). His reply? "May it never be!" He then wrote of the impossibility of a believer being in such a condition: "How shall we who died to sin still live in it?" (6:2).

In the verses that follow, Paul made it ever so clear that all believers have been united with Jesus in His death and resurrection that they might "walk in newness of life" (6:4) now that they are no longer "slaves of sin" (6:6, 17, 20). Rather, they are now "freed from sin" (6:7, 18, 22), are "slaves of righteousness" (6:18), and "enslaved to God" (6:22), having become "obedient from the heart to that form of teaching to which [they] were committed" (6:17). Sin is no longer "master" over them, and so they should not let it "reign" in their bodies, obeying its desires (6:12). Rather, they should present their members as "slaves to righteousness, resulting in sanctification" (6:19).

How does this chapter 6 Christian compare to the man in chapter 7, whom Paul describes as "of flesh, sold into bondage to sin" (7:14), who practices the very evil he does not want to do, doing what he hates (7:15, 19), a virtual "prisoner of the law of sin" (7:23), and a "wretched man" (7:24)? Is the man of chapter 6, set free from sin, the same wretched man of chapter 7 who is a prisoner of sin? Is the man of chapter 6, whose old self was crucified with Christ that his "body of sin might be done away with" (6:6) the same man of chapter 7 who longs for someone to set him "free from the body of this death" (7:24)? This certainly doesn't seem likely, does it?

Moreover, the first 14 verses of chapter 8, which we've already considered, raise even more questions if the chapter 7 man is a Christian. In chapter 8, Paul described the true Christian as one who does "not walk according to the flesh, but according to the Spirit" (8:4), whose mind is set on the Spirit, and not the flesh, unlike non-Christian minds (8:5-6). The true Christian is one who is not "in the flesh" but "in the Spirit" because the Spirit dwells in him (8:9). Paul even warned those who are living according to the flesh that they must die, and promises that those who, "by the Spirit...are putting to death the deeds of the body" (8:13) that they will live. If Paul was speaking of his own present experience in chapter 7, we'd be tempted to tell him to read his own letter so he could find out how to be saved and set free from sin! And in light of all his many other exhortations to holiness directed to others, we'd have to classify him as a hypocrite who preached "Do as I say, not as I do."

Paul in Context

If Paul was presently *practicing* the very evil that he hated, then by his own description of unbelievers in this and other letters, he was not saved (see Rom. 2:8-9; 1 Cor. 6:9-11; Gal. 5:19-21; Eph. 5:5-6). According to what John also wrote, Paul would not be saved: "The one who practices sin is of the devil....No one who is born of God practices sin....anyone who does not practice righteousness is not of God..." (1 Jn. 3:8-10).

If Paul was speaking in chapter 7 of his present condition as a wretched prisoner of sin, practicing evil, it greatly surprises those of us who have read what he said about himself in other places. Although he admitted that he had not reached perfection (see Phil. 3:12), he wrote to the Corinthians that he was "conscious of nothing against [himself]" (1 Cor. 4:4), and further stated,

> For our proud confidence is this, the testimony of our conscience, that in holiness and godly sincerity, not in fleshly wisdom but in the grace of God, we have conducted ourselves in the world, and especially toward you (2 Cor. 1:12).

To the Thessalonian Christians, he wrote:

> You are witnesses, and so is God, how devoutly and uprightly and blamelessly we behaved toward you believers (1 Thes. 2:10).

He testified to Timothy that he served God with a clear conscience (see 2 Tim. 1:3). One gets the impression as he reads Paul's story and his letters that Paul was a very, very Christ-like man.[1] His devotion is unparalleled to anyone else in the New Testament other than Jesus. How then can we imagine him practicing evil?

The only reasonable conclusion we can draw from all this evidence is that Paul was speaking in Romans 7 of his experience prior to his salvation.

"But didn't Paul write chapter 7 in the present tense? Does that not prove he was writing about his present condition?" some ask.

No, the tense Paul used does not prove anything. We often use the present tense when telling of a past experience. I might tell a fishing story that happened ten years ago by saying, "So, here I am in my boat, at my favorite spot on the lake. Suddenly I feel a little

---

1 See, for example, Acts 20:24; 23:1; 1 Cor. 4:11-13, 17; 10:32-33; 2 Cor. 5:9; 6:3, 6-7; Phil. 4:9; 1 Thes. 2:3-7.

tug on my line—I'm not sure if it's a fish or a snag. Then it strikes! I start reeling in the biggest fish I've ever caught! Right as I bring it up to the boat, the line snaps, and off swims a monster-sized bass. Oh, wretched man that I am! Who will deliver me from this crazy sport?"

"But didn't Paul say in Romans 7 that he didn't want to do wrong, but wanted to do right? Didn't he even say, "I joyfully concur with the law of God in the inner man" (7:22)? How could he say those things as an unsaved man? Aren't unsaved people wicked to the core and totally depraved?"

You must remember that Paul was a very zealous Jewish Pharisee before his salvation. He, unlike the average unsaved person, was doing everything he could to obey God's laws, to the point of even persecuting the church! But he found that no matter how hard he tried, he couldn't measure up to God's standards. He was a slave to sin. He eventually realized that he couldn't be holy without the Holy Spirit's supernatural help. Truly, there is no more wretched person than the one who is trying to live by God's standards but who is not born again!

Romans 7 "Christians"

It is to be greatly regretted, in spite of all that Jesus, John, James, Peter, Jude and Paul said that contradicts the idea that the Romans 7 man is born again, that so many today think he is. The reason is not because of the scriptural evidence for such a view, but because of the multitudes of professing Christians who identify with the Romans 7 man, practicing what they hate, in bondage to sin. They interpret the Scripture from their experience with a logic that says, "I identify with the Romans 7 man, and I'm a Christian, so the Romans 7 man must be a Christian."

This wrong interpretation of Romans 7 bolsters the shaky and spurious faith of many, who have not yet experienced the freedom from sin's power that Paul promised in Romans 6 and 8 and personally enjoyed throughout his Christian life. This is a great tragedy in light of the wonderful grace of God that is freely available to all through Jesus Christ, if people will only come to Him on His terms, with a living, submissive faith.

TEN

Beware of False Teachers

Accustomization to the New Testament, the outstanding characteristic of a false teacher is his underrating the necessity of holiness, which is reflected by his teaching and personal life. Numerous scriptures bear this out. For example, consider what Jesus taught about false prophets in His Sermon on the Mount:

> Beware of the false prophets [or anyone claiming to speak God's word], who come to you in sheep's clothing, but inwardly are ravenous wolves. You will know them by their fruits. Grapes are not gathered from thorn bushes, nor figs from thistles, are they? Even so, every good tree bears good fruit; but the bad tree bears bad fruit. A good tree cannot produce bad fruit, nor can a bad tree produce good fruit. Every tree that does not bear good fruit is cut down and thrown into the fire. So then, you will know them by their fruits. Not everyone who says to Me, "Lord, Lord," will enter the kingdom of heaven; but he who does the will of My Father who is in heaven. Many will say to Me on that day, "Lord, Lord, did we not prophesy in Your name, and in Your name cast out demons, and in Your name perform many miracles?" And then I will declare to them, "I never knew you; depart from Me, you who practice lawlessness" (Matt. 7:15-23).

Jesus said that false prophets can be known by their fruits, which, within the context of the Sermon on the Mount, are obviously fruits of holiness and obedience. Jesus said that only those who do the will of His Father "will enter the kingdom of heaven" (7:21). They may have prophesied, cast out demons and worked miracles, but if they practiced lawlessness, He will declare that He never knew them (7:23).

A Foreign Grace

It is not only the fruit of people's deeds that mark them as false teachers, but also the fruit of their words. If they teach what is contrary to essential New Testament doctrine, they are false teachers.

Of course, no teacher in the church is going to stand up and declare that he is teaching what is contrary to the New Testament. Rather, he will neglect certain important scriptures and twist others to persuade his constituency that he is teaching the truth. This is being done today by many very popular and influential teachers who teach about a grace that is foreign to the Bible. The grace they proclaim is not the true grace that leads to holiness, of which Paul, a true grace teacher, wrote:

> For the *grace of God* has appeared, bringing salvation to all men, *instructing us to deny ungodliness and worldly desires* and to live sensibly, *righteously and godly* in the present age (Titus 2:11-12, emphasis added).

Rather, it is the false grace that Jude warned about, a grace that has been radically modified into a license to sin:

> Beloved, while I was making every effort to write you about our common salvation, I felt the necessity to write to you appealing that you contend earnestly for the faith which was once for all delivered to the saints. For certain persons have crept in unnoticed, those who were long beforehand marked out for this condemnation, *ungodly persons who turn the grace of our God into licentiousness and deny our only Master and Lord, Jesus Christ* (Jude 3-4, emphasis added).

How is it possible that people who denied the only Master and Lord, Jesus Christ, could have "crept in unnoticed"? The answer is that they were not standing in front of congregations declaring, "I deny Jesus Christ." Rather, they were denying Jesus Christ through their false teaching about grace, turning it into licentiousness.

Their message could be summarized as follows: "Isn't God's grace wonderful? Because our salvation stems from His grace and not from our meritorious works, holiness is not essential for salvation. Because of God's wonderful grace, adulterers and fornicators who believe in Jesus are saved."

Forget the scripture that says without holiness, no one will see the Lord (see Heb. 12:14). Never mind that Jesus taught that we will not enter the kingdom of heaven unless our righteousness surpasses that of the scribes and Pharisees, and that it is only those who do the will of God who will enter the kingdom of heaven (see Matt. 5:20; 7:21). Don't be concerned that He told us to strive to enter by the narrow gate, the only gate to life, and that His true brothers are those who "hear the word of God and do it" (see Matt. 7:13-14; Luke 8:21). Ignore the fact that James taught that faith without works is dead and cannot save us (see Jas. 2:14, 17). Pay no attention to Paul's warnings that those who practice the works of the flesh will not inherit God's kingdom (see Gal. 5:20-21). Close your eyes to John's first epistle, all about the identifying marks of true Christians. And ignore the scores of other scriptures in the New Testament that emphasize these same truths.

"No, we are not like the legalists who emphasize works so much. We have discovered the truth about God's grace."

Denying the Master

These false teachers literally *deny* (notice the titles Jude used) the "only *Master* and *Lord*" (Jude 4; emphasis added). Because obedience is, in their minds, optional for those on the way to heaven, Jesus need not be one's Master and Lord. Thus they deny that He is who He is by their teaching and lifestyles.

To the undiscerning, the slogans of the false grace teachers sound scriptural, taken from Paul's own writings (and ripped from their biblical context): "We're not under law, but grace!" "Praise God for the liberty we have in Christ!" And, "Even if we are faithless, He remains faithful!" Their twisting of Paul's words is as old as Paul's letters. To them and their predecessors, Peter warns:

> And regard the patience of our Lord to be salvation; just as also our beloved brother Paul, according to the wisdom given him, wrote to you, as also in all his letters, speaking in them of these things, in which are some things hard to understand, *which the untaught and unstable distort, as they do also the rest of the Scriptures, to their own destruction* (2 Pet. 3:15-16, emphasis added).

Peter had more to say about those who distort Scripture to their own destruction. The entire second chapter of his second epistle warns about the "destructive heresies" that false teachers will "secretly introduce...even denying the Master who bought them" (2 Pet. 2:1).

Again, how could any doctrine that denies the Master be *secretly* introduced? Obviously, these false teachers were not publicly proclaiming, "We deny the Master!" No, they were denying the Master by denying the Master's role. They were downplaying the necessity of obedience. Peter wrote that they led people to "follow their sensuality, and because of them the way of the truth will be maligned" (2:2). These false teachers maintained that one could practice sensuality and be saved. Indulging in the desires of the flesh was perfectly acceptable, even encouraged; thus "the way of the truth" was maligned.

Refuting such grievous error, Peter cited historical examples of God's dealings with the godly and the ungodly. His point is unmistakable: The holy are saved, the unholy are condemned. Holiness is essential:

> For if God did not spare angels when they sinned [unholy], but cast them into hell and committed them to pits of darkness, reserved for judgment; and did not spare the ancient world [unholy], but preserved Noah, a preacher of righteousness [holy], with seven others, when He brought a flood upon the world of the ungodly; and if He condemned the cities of Sodom and Gomorrah [unholy] to destruction by reducing them to ashes, *having made them an example to those who would live ungodly thereafter*; and if He rescued righteous Lot [holy], oppressed by the *sensual conduct* of unprincipled men [unholy] (for by what he saw and heard that righteous man, while living among them, felt his righteous soul tormented day after day with their lawless deeds), then the Lord knows how to rescue the godly [holy] from temptation, and to keep the unrighteous [unholy] under punishment for the day of judgment, and especially those who indulge the flesh in its corrupt desires and despise authority... (2 Pet. 2:4-10, emphasis added).

Agreeing wholeheartedly with Paul, in no uncertain terms, Peter labels those who "indulge the flesh in its corrupt desires" as "unrighteous." They are heading for hell, whether they claim to be Christians or not.

These false teachers have even lured true believers from the path of holiness; thus they are defiled once again, returning to a spiritual condition that is even worse than before they were first saved:

> For speaking out arrogant words of vanity they entice by fleshly desires, by sensuality, those who barely escape from the ones who live in error, promising them freedom while they themselves are slaves of corruption; for by what a man is overcome, by this he is enslaved. For if after they have escaped the defilements of the world by the knowledge of the Lord and Savior Jesus Christ, they are again entangled in them and are overcome, the last state has become worse for them than the first. For it would be better for them not to have known the way of righteousness, than having known it, to turn away from the holy commandment delivered to them. It has happened to them according to the true proverb, "A dog returns to its own vomit," and, "A sow, after washing, returns to wallowing in the mire" (2 Pet. 2:18-22).

We gain a better idea of the message of the false teachers from this passage. Peter wrote that they enticed "by fleshly desires, by sensuality," and promised a freedom that actually resulted in slavery to sin. Their message sounded so much like the messages of the modern false grace teachers who have redefined holiness as being legalism and obedience as "trusting in works." "Enjoy the freedom you have in Christ" they proclaim. "Don't listen to these grace-killers with their lists of dos and don'ts."

The result is that even true believers are deceived, turn from the narrow path, and begin heading down the broad road to destruction. Thinking that they've discovered the grace that Jesus offers and Paul preached, they ignore Jesus' list of dos and don'ts in the Sermon on the Mount and Paul's lists of exclusionary sins throughout his epistles.

Note that the believers Peter wrote about had "escaped," although just barely, from those who "live in error" (2:18) that is, the unsaved. He said the same thing again in the next sentence, declaring that they had "escaped the defilements of the world by the knowledge of the Lord and Savior Jesus Christ" (2:20). Make no mistake about this. These were not people who were considering becoming Christians. Neither were they false believers. They were people who had been born again and had been living differently than prior to their salvation.

But they were deceived by false teaching that downplayed the importance of holiness and emphasized a false grace. Consequently, they were once again, "entangled" in the "defilements of the world" and "overcome" (2:20). Now their "last state" had "become worse for them than the first" (2:20). Previously they had "known the way of *righteousness*," but now they had turned away from "the holy commandment" (2:21, emphasis added).

Sadly, so many professing Christians today have *never* "known the way of righteousness," because they heard a false gospel from the start. They've been enjoying their slavery to sin all of their "Christian" lives, thinking they've been enjoying the liberty of God's wonderful grace. In this respect they are different from those about whom Peter wrote. They are not pigs who have returned to the mire after washing; they are pigs who have never left the mire.

"Tickle Our Ears, Please!"

As in Paul's day, many today flock to listen to false grace teachers who will tell them what they want to hear, just as Paul predicted:

> For the time will come when they will not endure sound doctrine; but wanting to have their ears tickled, they will accumulate for themselves teachers in accordance to their own desires; and will turn away their ears from the truth, and will turn aside to myths (2 Tim. 4:3-4).

Clearly, the time which Paul said will come has arrived. People naturally love to hear the message of God's wonderful love and grace, how their sin has been dealt with by Jesus, how salvation is a free gift, and how it is received by faith and not earned by works, all of which are true. But this is where God's grace begins to be modified.

Today we are told that repentance is only a change of mind that may result in no change of actions. People can believe in Jesus and continue practicing sin. They can be born again and never give any outward indication of the Holy Spirit's indwelling. Christians can be adulterers and fornicators, and we certainly don't want to judge them because we don't know their hearts. Those who maintain that heaven is only for the holy are legalists. Faith without works can save. Those who *don't* do God's will are still heaven-bound as long as they've made a verbal profession of faith in Christ. If a person has faith for one minute of his life, he is eternally secure, regardless of whether he abandons his faith, becomes an atheist, and returns to a life of immorality. Many true Christians are indistinguishable from non-Christians, placed in a special category of believers called "carnal Christians."

These and many lies like them are being propagated to millions of unsuspecting people. Consider the following quotations from some of the most popular teachers in the church today, people whose names are household words in modern Christian circles:

> Shortly after that campaign was held, the evangelist that led him to Christ defected from the faith. His family was broken apart. He wandered across the United States like an animal, finally died a drunkard in the gutter of South Chicago....If you have trusted the Lord Jesus Christ as your Savior, you are still a child of God. You may deny Him, but He will never deny you.

Is this true? Jesus said, "But whoever shall deny Me before men, I will also deny him before My Father who is in heaven" (Matt. 10:33). Additionally, Paul wrote that no drunkard will inherit God's kingdom (see 1 Cor. 6:9-10).

> We are saved because at a moment in time we expressed faith in our enduring Lord....Even if a believer for all practical purposes becomes an unbeliever, his salvation is not in jeopardy.

Are we eternally secure in our salvation if we believe for just "a moment in time"? Is that what Jesus meant for us to believe when He said, "He who has believed...shall be saved" (Mark 16:16)? If so, then we must also conclude that if we disbelieve for a moment in time, then our damnation is eternally sealed, because Jesus went on to say, "He who has disbelieved shall be condemned" (Mark 16:16).

This same popular grace teacher, desperate to mold Scripture to accommodate his theology, has actually turned hell into heaven:

> Where is this place represented by the "outer darkness" in Jesus' parables? To be in the "outer darkness" *is to be in the kingdom of God but outside the circle of men and women whose faithfulness on this earth earned them a special rank or position of authority.*

> The "outer darkness" represents not so much an actual place as it does a sphere of influence and privilege. It is not a geographical area in the kingdom where certain men and women are consigned to stay. It is simply a figure of speech describing their low rank or status in God's kingdom (emphasis his).

Amazingly, this teacher also wants us to believe that "gnashing of teeth....does not symbolize pain as many have thought." Rather, it is symbolic for the frustration unfaithful believers will feel in heaven when they realize the rewards they could have earned by earthly obedience:

> Just as those who are found faithful will rejoice, so those who suffer loss will weep. As some are celebrated for their faithfulness, others will gnash their teeth in frustration over their own short-sightedness and greed.

> We do not know how long this time of rejoicing and sorrow will last. Those whose works are burned will not weep and gnash their teeth for eternity.

Is this all true? When Jesus spoke of the "outer darkness," was He speaking of a place in heaven where unfaithful and *greedy* Christians will temporarily weep and gnash their teeth out of regret for the rewards they could have earned for themselves? For the obvious answer, see Matt. 8:10-12; 13:24-30, 36-43; 24:42-51; 25:14-30; Luke 13:22-28. And will there be any greedy people in heaven? See 1 Cor. 6:9-10; Eph. 5:3-6.

It is amazing how far some teachers will go to make allowance for Christians to practice grievous sins and still make it into heaven. In reference to Paul's warning that those who practice the works of the flesh will not inherit the kingdom of God, one popular radio preacher says:

> Inheriting the kingdom has to deal with the bonuses that you get in the kingdom. It's not the same as entering the kingdom. So unless you distinguish between inheriting and entering, you'll think you're not gonna get in the kingdom because of these problems [notice he doesn't even call them *sins*]. But you can lose benefits from the kingdom because of them.

Is this true? Compare 1 Cor. 6:9-10 with 1 Cor. 15:50-54 and Jesus' words in Matt. 25:34-41.

While Jesus and Paul both stated that adulterers and fornicators will not gain heaven, one very influential television minister says:

> But Christians may still lose rewards in heaven. Indeed, we can only wonder what some Christians will feel like and experience on that day when they lose those heavenly rewards

because of the spiritually numbing and other consequences of *fornication* or *adultery* while on earth. It will certainly be an infinitely poor exchange—losing eternal rewards in heaven for a few fleeting moments of sexual pleasure on earth (emphasis added).

Another long-standing radio minister is asked by a listener:

Q. I thought that I was born again when I was fifteen years old. I felt happy and secure in Christ. But over time, sin surely crept in, and I went the downward path. Three marriages, adultery, drinking. Was I born again?

A. The very fact that you were disturbed indicates to me that when you say you were born again at fifteen, you are accurate.

Is the test of authentic salvation a person's guilt? See Romans 2:14-15 for the answer. Are adulterers and drunkards saved? I think you know the answer to that by now.

Why Doesn't God Stop False Prophets and Teachers?

Under the old covenant, there were also false prophets who arose to mislead God's people. They, too, could be known by their fruits. Their lives and lips gave testimony of their inward impurity, and as they downplayed the necessity of holiness, they led people away from whole-hearted obedience to the Lord.

We might ask why God doesn't just stop every false prophet and teacher, or at least somehow silence them when they make unbiblical assertions that turn God's grace into licentiousness. Perhaps the answer is found in the word of God through one of His true prophets, Moses:

If a prophet or a dreamer of dreams arises among you and gives you a sign or a wonder, and the sign or the wonder comes true, concerning which he spoke to you, saying, 'Let us go after other gods (whom you have not known) and let us serve them,' you shall not listen to the words of that prophet or that dreamer of dreams; *for the Lord your God is testing you to find out if you love the Lord your God with all your heart and with all your soul. You shall follow the Lord your God and fear Him; and you shall keep His commandments, listen to His voice, serve Him, and cling to Him.* But that prophet or that dreamer

> of dreams shall be put to death, because he has counseled rebellion against the Lord your God who brought you from the land of Egypt and redeemed you from the house of slavery, to seduce you from the way in which the Lord your God commanded you to walk. So you shall purge the evil from among you (Deut. 13:1-5, emphasis added).

Could it be that God actually allows false teachers to propagate their false teachings as a means of testing us? What does it say about us when we are attracted to teaching that makes us feel good about our sin and even leads us away from the paths of righteousness? A sobering thought indeed.

What shall the discerning do? Under the old covenant, the discerning were commanded to purge from their midst those who attempted to seduce them "from the way in which the Lord [their] God commanded [them] to walk." Death was the penalty.

The church, of course, does not have the right of capital punishment, but this does not mean that false teachers should be tolerated by us in the least. They should, at minimum, be lovingly confronted and corrected, in case they might be guilty of error only because of biblical ignorance. Many only parrot what they've learned from reading someone's book. Those who will not cease propagating their heresies should be exposed and not supported in any way so that their "ministries" die (see 3 John 1:9-10). Few would survive long if people stopped giving them money and buying their books and tapes.

You can be certain, however, that no matter what we do, there will be false teachers right up until the end, because the Bible predicts it (see 1 Tim. 4:1-3; 2 Tim. 3:13; 4:3-4). Paul succinctly describes them in a warning to the Roman Christians as being men who *are not slaves* of "our Lord Jesus Christ," which marks them as being unsaved. Let us beware.

> Now I urge you, brethren, keep your eye on those who cause dissensions and hindrances *contrary to the teaching which you learned,* and turn away from them. For *such men are slaves, not of our Lord Christ* but of their own appetites; and by their *smooth and flattering speech* they deceive the hearts of the unsuspecting (Rom. 16:17-18, emphasis added).

ELEVEN

The Assurance of Salvation

Is it possible to have assurance of salvation? Can a person know for certain that, if he died at this moment, he would be saved? Absolutely yes. The apostle John wrote:

> These things I have written to you who believe in the name of the Son of God, in order that you may know that you have eternal life (1 John 5:13).

False grace teachers frequently quote this single verse to prop up the confidence of all who profess to believe in Jesus. But they often completely miss John's meaning.

First, John said he wrote to those who believe in the name of the *Son of God*, not those who believe they are saved by believing in a doctrine about salvation. It is not believing that salvation is by grace through faith that saves us—we are saved *by believing in a divine person*. And if we believe that Jesus is a divine person, we will act, talk and live like we do.

Additionally, notice that John said he had written "these things" in order that his readers might know they have eternal life. Of what *things* was he speaking? John made this statement at the close of his letter in reference to everything he had written. He had written his entire letter so that his readers might know they had eternal life. By evaluating their lives in light of what he said marks all true believers, they could determine if they were genuinely saved.

By comparing ourselves with what John said marks true believers, we, too, can determine if God's grace has really changed us. If it has, we are assured that we are saved. This is not trusting in our works to save us. Rather, it is receiving assurance of salvation through the evidence of God's grace through His works in and through us. Many antinomians cling to the memory of a prayer once prayed for the false assurance of their salvation, whereas true believers can look at their lives and see the work of God's transforming grace. We can know[1] that we are saved.

What did John write that helps us make our evaluation? What are the distinguishing traits of true believers? John repeatedly mentions three tests. One is moral (see 2:3-6; 2:28-3:10); one is social (see 2:7-11; 3:11-18; 4:7-21) and one is doctrinal (see 2:18-27;.4:1-6). Let's consider all three.

The Moral Test: Obedience to Jesus' Commands

> *And by this we know that we have come to know Him, if we keep His commandments.* The one who says, "I have come to know Him," and does not keep His commandments, is a liar, and the truth is not in him; but whoever keeps His word, in him the love of God has truly been perfected. *By this we know that we are in Him:* the one who says he abides in Him ought himself to walk in the same manner as He walked (1 John 2:3-6, emphasis added).

If we keep Jesus' commandments, we (1) know that we have come to know Him and (2) know that we are in Him.

Some would like us to believe that "knowing Jesus" is an expression that refers to Christians who are more mature in Christ. Young, immature Christians don't really "know" Jesus as well as older Christians do. Therefore, some conclude that John was saying that we can tell if we are mature or immature Christians by our obedience or disobedience. But is that what John meant?

Clearly not, for several reasons. In the passage we've just read, John also used the expression, "in Him," stating that we can also

---

1 Indeed, John's first epistle could be labeled "the letter about knowing." The word know (or knows) is found forty times in its five chapters.

know if we are *in Christ* if we keep His commandments. Anyone who has read the New Testament knows that all true believers are *in Christ*, not just the more mature believers. Since those who are *in Him* and those who *know Him* are both distinguished by keeping His commandments, *knowing Him* must be equivalent to being *in Him*.

Second, Jesus Himself used the same expression, *knowing Him*, as equivalent to being saved:

> And so [the Pharisees] were saying to Him, "Where is Your Father?" Jesus answered, "*You know neither Me, nor My Father; if you knew Me, you would know My Father also*" (John 8:19, emphasis added).

> "I am the good shepherd; and I know My own [all those who are saved], *and My own know Me*" (John 10:14, emphasis added).

> "If you had *known Me*, you would have known My Father also; from now on you know Him, and have seen Him" (John 14:7, emphasis added, cf. 1 John 3:6).

> "And this is *eternal life, that they may know Thee, the only true God, and Jesus Christ* whom Thou hast sent" (John 17:3, emphasis added).

Third, John also used the expression, *know Him*, in another place in his first epistle that clearly equates knowing Jesus with being saved:

> See how great a love the Father has bestowed upon us, that we should be called *children of God;* and such we are. For this reason the world does not know us, because *it did not know Him* (1 John 3:1, emphasis added).

Fourth, the context of the expression, *knowing Him,* within John's first epistle, which is all about the tests of authentic faith, lends further support that the expression is applicable to all true believers. For example, in John's second discussion of the moral test, he unmistakably states that "practicing righteousness" is the evidence of being born again:

> And now, little children, abide in Him, so that when He appears, we may have confidence and not shrink away from Him in shame at His coming. If you know that He is righteous, you know that *everyone also who practices righteousness*

is born of Him (1 John 2:28-29, emphasis added).

For these reasons, we can conclude that when John writes of "knowing Jesus," he is not referring to being intimately acquainted with Jesus as more mature Christians are, but is referring to being saved. Those who know Him, obey Him.

John restates the moral test again in later paragraphs:

> Beloved, now we are children of God, and it has not appeared as yet what we shall be. We know that, when He appears, we shall be like Him, because we shall see Him just as He is. And *everyone who has this hope fixed on Him purifies himself, just as He is pure.* Everyone who practices sin also practices lawlessness; and sin is lawlessness. And you know that He appeared in order to take away sins; and in Him there is no sin. *No one who abides in Him sins; no one who sins has seen Him or knows Him. Little children, let no one deceive you; the one who practices righteousness is righteous, just as He is righteous; the one who practices sin is of the devil;* for the devil has sinned from the beginning. The Son of God appeared for this purpose, that He might destroy the works of the devil. *No one who is born of God practices sin,* because His seed abides in him; and he cannot sin, *because he is born of God. By this the children of God and the children of the devil are obvious: anyone who does not practice righteousness is not of God* (1 John 3:2-10a, emphasis added).

How much clearer could it be? By His grace, God transforms those who truly believe in Jesus into obedient children. John wrote "these things" so that we "may know that [we] have eternal life" (1 John 5:13).

Are you obeying Jesus' commandments? You may want to review the list of Jesus' commandments in chapter nine. No Christian is obeying them perfectly, but all true Christians are certainly characterized much more by obedience than disobedience.

The Social Test: Loving the Brethren

> For this is the message which you have heard from the beginning, that we should love one another; not as Cain, who was of the evil one, and slew his brother. And for what reason did he slay him? Because his deeds were evil, and his brother's were righteous. Do not marvel, brethren, if the

world hates you. [What is John's implication here about the behavior of believers compared to unbelievers?] *We know that we have passed out of death into life, because we love the brethren.* He who does not love abides in death. Everyone who hates his brother is a murderer; and you know that no murderer has eternal life abiding in him (1 John 3:11-15, emphasis added).

When we are born again, God, by His Holy Spirit comes to live inside of us. Naturally, He does not leave His nature behind. God is love, John says (1 John 4:8), and so when God moves in, love moves in. Paul wrote, "The love of God has been poured out within our hearts through the Holy Spirit who was given to us" (Rom. 5:5).

Those who are spiritually reborn find that, in particular, they possess a supernatural love for fellow believers, their spiritual brothers and sisters. In fact, if their natural relatives are unsaved, they find that they actually prefer to spend time with their spiritual relatives. Or, when a car on the Interstate highway passes theirs with an "I love Jesus" bumper sticker, they feel a warmth within for the unknown occupants of that car. Had they lived during the time of the second-century Greek Philosopher, Celsus, they also would have been the target of his criticism: "These Christians love each other even before they get acquainted!"

This divinely-given love goes much deeper than just passing out hugs and handshakes after church. It is the same love God has for His children, caring and compassionate:

> We know love by this, that He laid down His life for us; and we ought to lay down our lives for the brethren. But whoever has the world's goods, and beholds his brother in need and closes his heart against him, how does the love of God abide in him? Little children, let us not love with word or with tongue, but in deed and truth (1 John 3:16-18)

The love true Christians have for each other is so real that it identifies them as Christ's disciples in the sight of unbelievers (see John 13:35) and distinguishes them from unbelievers in the sight of God (see Matt. 25:31-46). Those who do not love their brothers do not love God (see 1 John 4:20).

Of course, this love can grow, and those who truly possess it don't always display it perfectly. Nevertheless, every true believer is conscious of the inward reservoir that tends to seep through his eyes, hands, thoughts and words. He loves other disciples of Jesus.

Do you? John wrote "these things" so that we "may know that [we] have eternal life" (1 John 5:13).

The Doctrinal Test

> Who is the liar but the one who denies that Jesus is the Christ? This is the antichrist, the one who denies the Father and the Son. Whoever denies the Son does not have the Father; the one who confesses the Son has the Father also.... Whoever confesses that Jesus is the Son of God, God abides in him, and he in God....Whoever believes that Jesus is the Christ is born of God (1 John 2:22-23; 4:15; 5:1).

This doctrinal test is often the only test considered valid by antinomians. If someone confesses that Jesus is the Christ, the Son of God, he is considered saved, even if he fails John's other two tests. Keep in mind that it is possible to verbally confess one's faith that Jesus is the Christ and Son of God, while denying the same facts by one's actions. At least four times in his first epistle, John writes of those whose actions nullify their words:

> The one who *says*, "I have come to know Him," and does not keep His commandments, *is a liar, and the truth is not in him* (1 John 2:4, emphasis added).

> The one who *says* he abides in Him ought himself to walk in the same manner as He walked (1 John 2:6, emphasis added).

> The one who *says* he is in the light and yet hates his brother is *in the darkness* until now (1 John 2:9, emphasis added).

> If someone *says*, "I love God," and hates his brother, *he is a liar;* for the one who does not love his brother whom he has seen, cannot love God whom he has not seen (1 John 4:20, emphasis added).

In light of this, we would be foolish to think we are truly passing John's doctrinal test if we are failing his moral and social tests. All three are equally important. Notice how John unites all three in a summarizing statement near the close of his letter:

> Whoever believes that Jesus is the Christ [the doctrinal test] is born of God; and whoever loves the Father loves the child born of Him [the social test]. By this we know that we love

the children of God, when we love God and observe His commandments [the moral test] (1 John 5:1-2).

John wrote these things "in order that you may know that you have eternal life" (1 John 5:13). John's letter fills with assurance those who are truly born again, while it warns those whose faith is false. As I wrote in the introduction to this book, if I were self-deceived concerning my salvation, I'd rather find out now than after my death. Now there is time to repent and trust in Jesus—then it will be too late.

Those with Overly-Sensitive Consciences

There is, I've discovered, a small percentage of true believers in Christ who are likely to be unduly alarmed about their spiritual state after reading a book like this one, primarily because of their own personality. They are already very devoted to Christ and have very high standards for themselves. Often they are perfectionists in their personal lives. In some cases, they were raised under the influence of a very demanding parent, in whose eyes they never felt as if they quite "measured up." In other cases, they have spent time imprisoned in legalistic churches, where sin was always the sermon topic and never grace, or where external standards such as hair style or dress length were the litmus tests of one's salvation. Perhaps they were indoctrinated to believe that they lost their salvation every time they sinned.

These are Christians who, for lack of a better way to say it, have overly-sensitive consciences. They are quick to condemn themselves. If they tithe *and* financially support three impoverished children, they feel guilty that they don't support four, and consequently wonder if they are saved. They serve others unselfishly in their church, but because they struggle getting along with one cranky old deacon, question if they are truly born again. They share the gospel with co-workers, but feel guilty because they haven't quit their jobs to be a missionary in Haiti. They're thirty-fold Christians but not one-hundred fold Christians (see Mark 4:8). They're not adulterers, fornicators, homosexuals, idolaters, drunkards, liars or thieves, but because they aren't perfect, fear they might go to hell, even though their lives are characterized by righteousness.

Such believers can only be balanced by God's Word. If you are such a Christian, I encourage you to read through the New Testament and note the imperfections of the many who were redeemed. We all still stumble in many ways, particularly in what we say (see

Jas. 3:2). The fruit of the Spirit still has room to grow and mature in all our lives. God's work in us isn't completed yet. So don't let the devil twist what God has said and condemn yourself. God loves you, and, so far, His only perfect child is Jesus.

TWELVE

Revival When?

Today I received a letter in the mail. It was from a man who heard me refuting antinomian errors on our daily radio broadcast. He said it was the first letter he'd written to anyone in twelve years.

He confessed that he had been a practicing homosexual. For a long time he had rationalized that as long as he did some good deeds and believed *about* Jesus, he was safe. But he heard me sharing what the Bible says about God's transforming grace available to sinners, including homosexuals. He heard me quote from scriptures that declare, *no homosexual will inherit God's kingdom*. Realizing that his dead faith was taking him to hell, he repented. He wrote to tell me that he is no longer a homosexual, quoting his paraphrase of the first few words of 1 Corinthians 6:11 in capital letters: "AND SOME OF US WERE." He has been saved by God's grace and transformed.

If antinomians had their way, this man would have remained a practicing homosexual, destined to spend eternity in hell. But, to the praise of God's grace, he heard the truth and believed it. As Jesus promised in John 8:32, the truth had set him free.

Set Free from Obedience?

Perhaps no verse in scripture is more misused by antinomians than John 8:32. They speak of how the truth sets us free from what they term "legalistic bondage," but what the Bible calls obedience to

God's clear commands. When Jesus spoke of the truth setting us free, however, He was clearly speaking about freedom from sin:

> Jesus therefore was saying to those Jews who had believed Him, "If you abide in My word, then you are truly disciples of Mine; and you shall know the truth, and the truth shall make you free." They answered Him, "We are Abraham's offspring, and have never yet been enslaved to anyone; how is it that You say, 'You shall become free'?" Jesus answered them, "Truly, truly, I say to you, *everyone who commits sin is the slave of sin.* And the slave does not remain in the house forever; the son does remain forever. *If therefore the Son shall make you free, you shall be free indeed* (John 8:31-36, emphasis added).

This is the message of God's transforming grace. This is the gospel. Jesus forgives and sets people who believe in Him free from sin. Those who truly believe in Him will abide, or live, in His word, proving themselves to be His disciples.

The Satanic Revival

It is indeed a dark hour. Our society is like a freight train that has lost its brakes and is picking up speed. How much longer before it is derailed? Yet, how can we decry the deteriorating spiritual state of our nation while at the same time we are offering a gospel that is void of any transforming power, a gospel that is nothing more than a thin veneer for sin? How can we hope for revival when God's grace is turned into licentiousness?

As long as filling pews, which is often called "church growth," rather than making disciples is our goal, there will be no true revival. As long as we look at people as "unchurched" rather than *unsaved*, there will be no true revival. As long as pastors and evangelists care more about pleasing people than God, there will be no true revival. Until the church recovers the biblical gospel, until the church is characterized by holiness so that it stands out from the world, there will not be true revival. Until then, the only revival will be the continuation of Satan's present revival, fueled by false grace, false faith, and false salvation. Under the banner of freedom, his evangelists will continue to pour forth his original lie in print, on Christian radio and television, and from church pulpits: "Go ahead and sin. You won't die."

It is indeed a very dark hour. Scores of popular teachers proclaim that if a person has faith in Jesus for only ten seconds at some point in his life, but then abandons his faith and returns to a life of practicing sin, he is saved and eternally secure. Mind you, this imaginary person could be a practicing prostitute or serial rapist right up until the time of his death and still go to heaven. All he will forfeit are some heavenly rewards that he could have earned had he been a better Christian! Is this not turning God's grace into licentiousness? Does this kind of preaching precede revivals? Yet the Bible still declares:

> It is a trustworthy statement:
> For if we died with Him, we shall also live with Him;
> *If we endure,* we shall also reign with Him;
> *If we deny Him, He also will deny us;*
> *If we are faithless,* He remains faithful; for He cannot deny Himself
> (2 Timothy 2:11-13, emphasis added).

How is this verse interpreted by modern false grace teachers? Ignoring or twisting the first three lines, they maintain that the fourth line proves their view. "Even if we are faithless, abandoning our faith" they say, "He will remain faithful to save us."

But is that the intended meaning? Absolutely not.

What Does 2 Timothy 2:11-13 Teach?

First, Paul says, "if we died with Him, we shall also live with Him." Our living with Him is contingent upon our dying with Him. Scripture teaches that all who truly believe in Jesus have died and have been made alive in Christ. This is the new birth, regeneration by the Holy Spirit. It is a radical change.

Second, Paul declares, "if we endure, we shall also reign with Him." Paul is not promising a *special* reward of future reigning for the *special* group of Christians who endure. Rather, he is promising that which awaits every true believer whose faith endures. Scripture teaches that it is not just a select group of Christians who will reign with Jesus. *All* who have been purchased by His blood will reign with Him:

> And they sang a new song, saying, "Worthy art Thou to take the book, and to break its seals; for Thou wast slain, and *didst purchase for God with Thy blood men from every tribe and tongue and people and nation.* And Thou hast made them to be a kingdom and priests to our God; and *they will reign* upon the earth" (Rev. 5:9-10, emphasis added, see also. Rev. 20:6; 22:3-5).

Those believers who endure in true faith have the promise of reigning with Jesus. We must continue in faith to be saved in the end, and if we do, we will reign with Jesus.

Third, Paul warns against *not* enduring: "If we deny Him, He also will deny us." This is a direct quotation from the Lord Jesus Christ who said:

> Everyone therefore who shall confess Me before men, I will also confess him before My Father who is in heaven. But *whoever shall deny Me before men, I will also deny him before My Father who is in heaven* (Matt. 10:32-33, emphasis added).

Jesus unmistakably promised that if we deny Him, He will deny us. It's a warning to anyone who is considering abandoning his faith, not enduring under threat of what others might think or do. Will people whom Jesus denies before the Father be permitted into heaven? If we deny Jesus, saying "I don't know Him" before others, and Jesus denies us before the Father, saying "I don't know him," will we be saved? The answer is obvious.

Finally, Paul says, "If we are faithless, He remains faithful; for He cannot deny Himself." This is a continuation of what he just said about denying Jesus. Even though we may not keep our promise to follow Him, Jesus will always keep His promises. He promised to deny us if we deny Him, and He will. (Of course, if we return in repentance and faith, He will keep His promise to accept us back.)

Notice that Paul did not say in the fourth declaration, "If we are faithless and deny Him, He will remain faithful and not deny us." That would be a direct contradiction of what he just said in the third declaration!

No, God is always faithful even though people are often not. He always keeps His promises *and* His threats. Consider what Moses and Joshua said about the *faithfulness* of God:

> Know therefore that the Lord your God, He is God, *the faithful God*, who keeps His covenant and His lovingkindness to a thousandth generation with those who love Him and keep His commandments; *but repays those who hate Him to their faces, to destroy them; He will not delay with him who hates Him, He will repay him to his face* (Deut. 7:9-10, emphasis added).

> And it shall come about that *just as all the good words which the Lord your God spoke to you have come upon you, so the Lord*

will bring upon you all the threats, until He has destroyed you from off this good land which the Lord your God has given you (Josh. 23:15, emphasis added).

With this is mind, consider how one very popular antinomian teacher, whose name is a household word in Christian circles, interprets 2 Timothy 2:11-13:

Just as the faithful will receive the Father's recognition and approval, so the unfaithful will lose His special recognition and approval....The unfaithful believer will not receive a special place in the kingdom of Christ like those who are fortunate enough to be allowed to reign with Him....*The apostle's meaning is evident. Even if a believer for all practical purposes becomes an unbeliever, his salvation is not in jeopardy. Christ will remain faithful* (emphasis added).

When the church gladly swallows a teaching that reverses the clear meaning of Scripture, need we ask why there is no revival? God's sacred message has been edited, stripped of every reason for anyone to repent of sin and follow Jesus Christ. People who don't believe in Jesus can now get into heaven, guaranteed. One can be an atheist, a Buddhist, a follower of Islam or a Satan worshipper and still go to heaven, as long as he verbalizes faith in Jesus for a few seconds during his life. And this lie is being proclaimed by some of the foremost evangelical teachers in America.

What Now?

If you didn't understand the true gospel before you began reading, surely you do now. Perhaps revival has begun in your own life. And what is a major revival but many individuals being revived? You can and should share what you know. Like me, you also have a sacred obligation to spread the truth, regardless of the cost. Our message is the one proclaimed by Jesus, Jude, Peter, Paul, James and John, as well as millions of true and faithful believers before us. Let us not be "ashamed of the gospel, for it is the power of God for salvation to everyone who believes" (Rom. 1:16).

Will there be true revival? Yes—in everyone's life who hears and heeds the true gospel. Those truly revived ones will pray and labor that others might share their joy. With that thought in mind, I close with a parable the Lord gave to me, one that fills me with hope:

A Parable of Revival...

As I was praying and fasting about the need for revival and the work of the Holy Spirit, I received a revelation that helped me understand what is and what will be happening in the church. It was not a vision that I saw with my eyes, but a revelation that I "saw" in my heart. May I say that I am not one who is "given to visions," and this was the first time anything like this ever happened to me. I will describe what I saw in the revelation.

First, I saw many crowds of people. Some crowds were very large, some were medium-sized, and some were quite small. The largest groups contained thousands of people. The smallest groups contained only a handful. The members of each group huddled close together for warmth, because it was very cold. All were shivering, and when one spoke, you could see his breath. Additionally, most within the crowd were dirty. Some were filthier than others, as if they had been workers in a coal mine, covered with soot from head to toe. These ones also stunk, like the stench of garbage. Others were not as filthy, but most were in desperate need of cleansing.

These masses of people all stood at the base on an immense dam with held back a huge reservoir. The dam was hundreds and hundreds of feet high, and it stretched as far as I could see in either direction. The body of water it held back was of equal proportion.

Looking more closely at the dam, I noticed that it was built of bricks. Words were written on each brick, and as I began to read what was written on some of the bricks, I noticed that all were similar in this respect: Each one had written upon it a single sin. For example, written on one brick it said, "Gossip," and on another was written the word. "Lustful." Also written under each sin was someone's name. For example, a brick might have written on it, "Liar," and under that, "John Doe." There were many bricks that had the same sin written on them, and many people's names were written on more than one brick.

I looked back at the crowds of filthy, shivering people. Most all of them were standing, but occasionally one in the crowds would kneel, or fall on his face and begin to weep, confessing his sins and asking God to cleanse him. When he did, a brick from the dam would burst out of its place by the force of the water behind it, and once ejected, the brick would shatter into fine dust and disappear. The water that would then gush through the hole would stream through the air, pouring itself on the kneeling one, washing him of his filth. Sometimes several (or even many) bricks would burst from the dam, either all at the same time or over a period of time, as long as the person continued to kneel and pray. In those cases, the streams that would pour forth from the holes in the dam would converge to fall together with great force upon the one kneeling, and the change in the person's appearance would be quite dramatic. Some of the dirtiest became the most clean in a short period of time.

I also discovered that the water that poured forth from the holes in the dam was quite warm. When it fell upon those who knelt, it not only cleansed them, but it also warmed them to the core. They would laugh and delight and sing with joy as they were washed.

The reaction of those in the groups who stood and watched the kneeling ones was mixed. Often, many of those nearby would move away from the kneeling one, not wanting to get wet. On occasion, the entire group would draw back so far that the kneeling one was left alone under his warm waterfall.

However, just as often, some of those near one who knelt would also kneel, confessing their sins. Again, bricks would burst from the dam and water would gush out, cleansing and warming them.

On occasion, the *large majority* of people standing in one group would, one after the other, kneel or bow and begin to weep for their sins. The force of the many streams of water that consequently converged and fell over them would be very great, bringing enormous blessing, powerful anointing and many gifts. *However, in no case did I see a group in which everyone knelt.* Often, those who stood among groups in which many people were kneeling would leave to join another group in which many people were standing. Also, I sometimes saw a person kneel only because so many others were kneeling. When he did, however, no bricks burst forth from the dam, no water was poured forth, and that person remained filthy and cold.

Two other things I witnessed as I watched the crowds of people: Occasionally one of those who were standing would look up at the dam and see a brick with his name on it. Out of embarrassment, he would climb up the dam's face to that brick and try to pull it from its place with his own hands. None who attempted this ever succeeded, however, because it was impossible. Also, I occasionally saw one who had been kneeling stand up again. When he did, he immediately became somewhat dirty, and force of the waterfall upon him lessened. And if he began pointing his finger at those who never knelt, proudly criticizing them with his mouth, his waterfall stopped, and became very dirty again. Most of those who were kneeling, however, would speak lovingly to those standing around them, saying, "Oh it's wonderful under this warm, cleansing stream! You can be washed of your filth! Please, won't you join me?"

Let me tell you some of the sins that were written on the bricks. One which had my name written on it said, "Fearful of Man." When I saw it, I immediately admitted my guilt before God and asked for His forgiveness and grace to fear no one but Him.

As a pastor, I was shown numerous bricks that belonged to people in my own congregation. There were many of the same sins written on the bricks. Some said, "Friend of the World." Many said, "Lukewarm." Others said, "Judgmental." Others: "Idolater," which means you make other things in your life more important than God. Many people in the church are more excited about their hobbies and pleasures than God.

Some said, "Immorality," which includes not only adultery, but dwelling on immoral thoughts. Some said, "Entertains Herself by Watching People do Immoral Things on Television." One said, "Views Internet Pornography." One said, "Meditates on Acts of Homosexuality." Another said, "Sexually Active Teenager."

On some bricks were written, "Bitterness Against Another," "Mistreats His Wife," and "Speaks Against Brothers." There was "Lover of Money," "Lover of Pleasure," and "Cares Only About Himself." There was "Receives Payment for Work Under the Table to Avoid Taxes," "Wasteful Steward," "Uses God's Money to Support What God Hates," and "Does Not Care About the Poor." Many said, "Does Not Even Tithe," and around those bricks were many other bricks that had justifications for this sin.

There was "Immodest," "Always Convinced She's Right," and "Not Submissive to Her Husband." I also saw many which said, "Does Not Care About Those Who Have Never Heard the Gospel."

Some said, "Gossip," "Slandered," "Fault-Finder," "Uses Offensive Speech," and "Worthless Religion—Does Not Bridle Tongue." One said, "Does Not Financially Support Young Children From A Former Marriage." Others said, "Does Not Honor Parents," "Rarely Keeps Promises," and "Listens to Music that Exalts What God Hates."

There was "Full of Unbelief," "Unclean Habits and Addictions," and "Self-Indulgent." There was "Prayerlessness," "Forsakes the Assembling of the Church," and "Does Not Desire to Read God's Word." Many bricks said, "Is not Training Children in the Nurture and Admonition of the Lord."

There are many others which I have not mentioned but which are all found in the Bible—the Bible which we all profess to believe is the Word of God. On some bricks were even written, "Twists Scripture to Make it Mean What it Does Not," and "Redefines the Commandments to Fit His Lifestyle."

The mortar that held the bricks in place also had words written on it, symbolizing four sins that held all the other sins in place. They were "Pride," "Hypocrisy," "Little or No Love for God," and "Sins of Shepherds." Before other sins can be dislodged, these must first be weakened. Pride keeps us from admitting our sins. Hypocrisy, acting one way at church and another way at other times, must be confessed. All sins are symptom of one bigger sin, "Little or No Love for God" —If we loved Him with all our heart, mind, soul and strength, we would serve and obey Him passionately. Jesus said, "If you love Me, keep My commandments" (John 14:15). Finally and fourth, if leaders in the church set the wrong example, their followers have an excuse to hold on to their sins.

Let's go back to the people in the crowds. As I watched, occasionally a person who was standing would point his finger at a nearby group that was laughing and singing as they knelt under a waterfall, and say, "That waterfall can't be from God, because their doctrine is wrong in some ways." But the Lord reminded me that He didn't say that it is those who have pure doctrine who will see God, but those who have pure hearts (Matt. 5:8). Jesus didn't say that we would know them by their doctrine, but by their fruits (Matt. 7:20). He said the mark of His true disciples was not perfect doctrine, but love for one another (John 13:35). Just because a group's doctrine is partially wrong in certain non-essentials does not mean that God will not pour His Spirit on them when they humble themselves and begin to "hunger and thirst for righteousness" (Matt. 5:6). Some of the bricks in the dam said, "Puffed Up With Knowledge," "Doctrinal Pride," and "Denominational Loyalty that Transcends Love for the Entire Body."

As time passed, more and more of those standing began to kneel, weeping as they confessed their sins and repented. Bricks exploded from the great dam like kernels of popcorn, and more water poured forth with a mighty roar, until the scene compared to Niagara Falls (only on a much larger scale). The kneeling ones lifted their hands, laughed, sang and prayed in what became a great river that flowed to many dry places in the earth. Eventually, it became such a torrent that those kneeling in it were swept away, as they rejoice and sang songs to their God.

Finally the water ceased flowing, as the reservoir had run dry. Those who were still standing looked at one another with smug approval. The bricks on which their names were written were still in place, suspended in the air only by human pride. Then suddenly, without the slightest warning, every remaining brick in the dam began to fall, converging with other bricks on which were written the same names. In terror, the standing ones watched as the piles of bricks fell with deadly accuracy, first knocking them to the ground, then killing and crushing them, until all that could be seen were heaps of bricks. I was reminded that Jesus said, "Everyone who exalts himself shall be humbled, but he who humbles himself shall be exalted" (Luke 18:14). Which are you?

Subject Index

Scripture Index

(including references in footnotes, but excluding the
list of scriptures found on pages 190-198)

Also by David Servant...

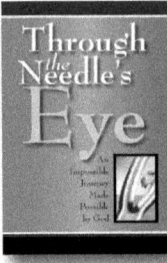

Through the Needle's Eye
An Impossible Journey Made Possible by God

In this book, David Servant considers everything that Jesus, as well as every author of the Old and New Testaments, taught in regard to stewardship. His conclusions are not easy to disregard. Although impossible by pure human effort, the journey through the needle's eye is possible with God! (ISBN 096-296-2592) 269 pages, Paperback, $17.95)

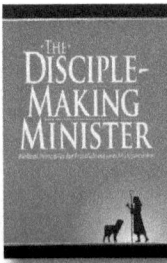

The Disciple-Making Minister
Biblical Principles for Fruitfulness and Multiplication

David Servant has been ministering to Christian leaders in conferences around the world for over two decades. From his experience of speaking to tens of thousands of pastors in over forty countries, he has compiled biblical teaching in this book that addresses the most important issues that Christian leaders are facing today. (ISBN 096-296-2585) 489 pages, Paperback, $19.95)

Forgive Me for Waiting So Long to Tell You This

Searching for a respectful way to share the gospel with a friend or loved one? Give them a copy of this book. In an easy-to-understand style, David Servant presents a convincing and biblical viewpoint that provokes readers to look at themselves, Jesus Christ, and their eternal destiny. (ISBN 096-296-2503, 132 pages, Paperback, $6.95)

www.ingramcontent.com/pod-product-compliance
Lightning Source LLC
Chambersburg PA
CBHW052036090426
42739CB00010B/1925